I0900991

LEGENDARY LOCALS

OF

BEREA

OHIO

PATRICIA M. MOTE

LEGENDARY LOCALS

ISBN 978-1-4671-0015-1

Published by Legendary Locals, an imprint of Arcadia Publishing
Charleston, South Carolina

Printed in the United States of America

Library of Congress Control Number: 2011944555

For all general information, please contact Arcadia Publishing:
Telephone 843-853-2070
Fax 843-853-0044
E-mail sales@arcadiapublishing.com
For customer service and orders:
Toll-Free 1-888-313-2665

Visit us on the Internet at www.arcadiapublishing.com

Dedication

To the committed staff at the Berea Historical Society—David Burnett, Nancy Gillahan, and Karen White. Without their willingness to help and their dedication and persistence, this book could never have happened. Working with each of them was a delight, and I cannot thank them enough for the many days they have spent combing through files, locating photographs, and sharing their wealth of knowledge about our community.

On the Cover: From left to right:
(TOP ROW) Daisy Collins, attorney (Courtesy of Daisy Collins; see page 44), George Pritchard, businessman (Courtesy of Berea Historical Society; see page 55), Dr. William Pierce, pastor (Courtesy of Berea Historical Society; see page 66), Ethel Foster, historian (Courtesy of Berea Historical Society; see page 18), Donald Williams, president of Kiwanis International (Courtesy of Berea Historical Society; see page 73).
(MIDDLE ROW) Edwin Kuekes, artist (Courtesy of Berea Historical Society; see page 84), William and Margaret Nast, prominent Methodists and early settlers (Courtesy of Berea Historical Society; see page 67), Harrison Dillard, Olympic champion (Courtesy of Berea Historical Society; see page 114), Dr. John Knight, Baldwin-Wallace College president (Courtesy of Berea Historical Society; see page 33), Fr. John Garrity, priest (Courtesy of Berea Historical Society; see page 72).
(BOTTOM ROW) Mary Elmore, Berea School Board member (Courtesy of Berea Historical Society; see page 20), Otto Mahler, businessman (Courtesy of Berea Historical Society; see page 13), Lou "The Toe" Groza, Cleveland Browns player and unidentified youth (Courtesy of Berea Historical Society; see page 112), Myron "Bree" Thornburg, sports booster (Courtesy of Berea Historical Society; see page 110), Eloise Tressel, mother of coaches and Berea Historical Society's first lady (Courtesy of Berea Historical Society; see page 117).

LEGENDARY LOCALS

OF

BEREA

OHIO

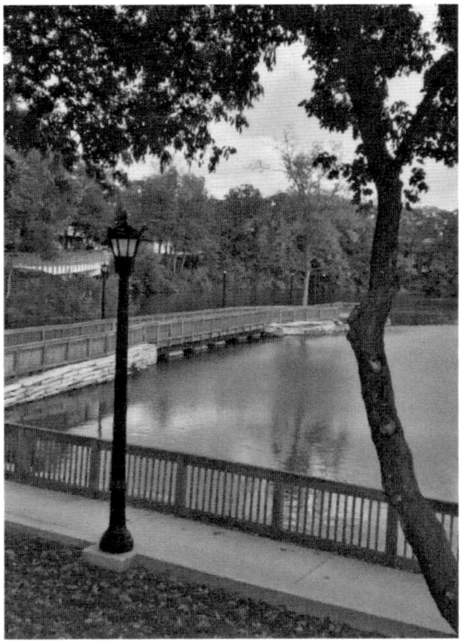

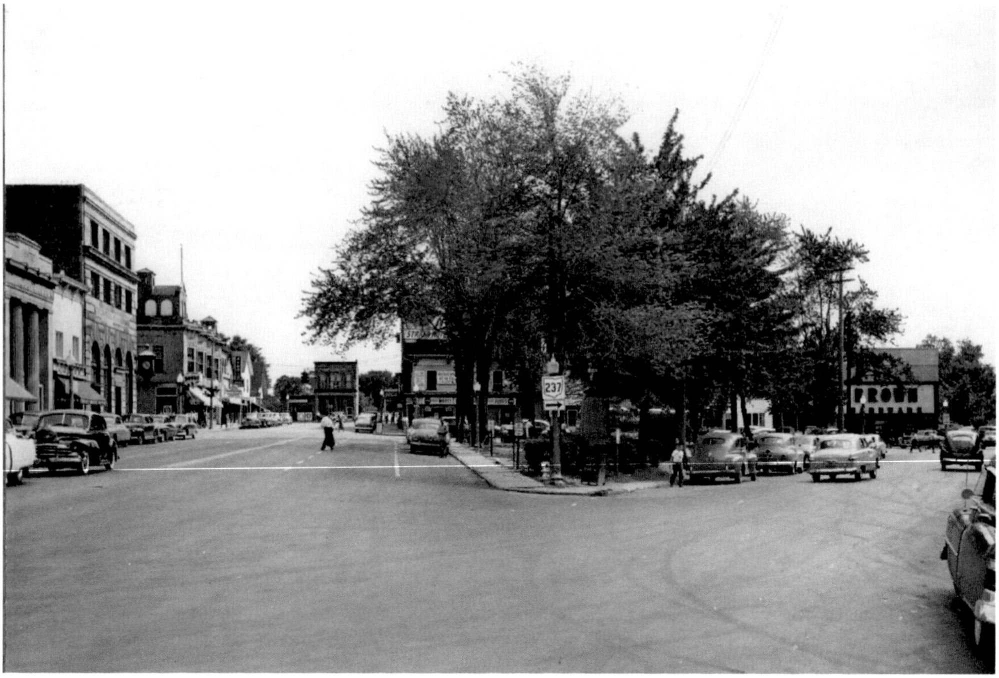

Page 1: Coe Lake and the Henry M. Barr Memorial Bridge
Pictured are Coe Lake and the Henry M. Barr Memorial Bridge near downtown Berea. (Photograph by Patricia Mote.)

Page 2: The Triangle in 1948
Once the centerpiece of Berea's commerce, the Triangle still boasts remnants of earlier times. The Huntington Bank now occupies the bank building at left (with clock). It once housed the local Commercial Bank. The graceful old elm tree is gone, but colorful plantings and hanging flower baskets add charm to this historic area.

CONTENTS

ACKNOWLEDGMENTS

I wish to thank Susan Lee, my daughter and photography editor, whose willingness, skill, and artistic eye made working on this book a pleasure, and the Berea Historical Society staff, David Burnett, Nancy Gillahan, and Karen White.

Unless otherwise noted, all images appear courtesy of the Berea Historical Society. Other contributors include Louise Allen, Betty Bainbridge Vitez, Suzanne Simpson, Diana Emrich, Joan Kamper, Shirley Moon, Joan Kafer, Elaine Myers, Vanessa Prince, Amanda Epperson, Suzanne Simpson, Taylor Hinton, Clint Williams, James Jaworski, Ken McCarthy, Sally King, Pam Simon, the Berea High School Alumni Association, Judy Stull, Judy Drody, the Berea Chamber of Commerce, Lynne Stark, Kelly Peoples, Andrew Schultze, Southwest General Health Center, Linda Dettmer, Tillie Rooney, and the Grindstone Players. I also thank members of the Tuesday A.M. Book Club for their encouragement and suggestions,

INTRODUCTION

An atlas will tell you that Berea, Ohio, is a suburban community of about 18,000 people, southwest of Cleveland, Ohio. But an atlas will not give you a clue to Berea's uniqueness. It is far more than a suburb; it is an uncommon kind of town. Though hemmed in by Cleveland and other "first ring" suburbs, Berea has the ambience and spirit of a small town, not a stereotypical bedroom community.

Throughout this book, you will find frequent references to events happening at "The Triangle," the original business district and heart of Berea. Three times in its history the Triangle was nearly demolished by fire; yet citizens doggedly persisted and rebuilt their businesses each time. Today, shops, restaurants, and condominiums exist at this central spot; some are newer architecture, others operate in century-old buildings. Although large trees no longer create a park-like setting, monuments to the Bereans who served in the nation's wars give citizens pause to reflect on a debt to the past. Bronze tablets bear names of winners of the Grindstone Award, given annually to Berea's Citizen of the Year. This small but historic area blossoms with hanging baskets in summer and boasts the community Christmas tree in December. Like its historic centerpiece, the Triangle, this community has a three-sided base on which it rests: work, culture, and faith. A glance at the clock tower can remind passersby of time gone by as well as an urgent appointment. The Triangle's idyllic setting is only steps away from the Cleveland Metroparks where people fish, jog, or canoe. But those serene lakes were once sandstone quarries; dust and grit filled the air. Drills pounded while little trains called "Dinkies" screeched through the town, carrying sandstone to the railroad at the north side of town.

Against the backdrop of this bustling quarry and grindstone industry lay two colleges, Baldwin University and German Wallace College. In 1913, they would join to become Baldwin-Wallace College. Just as the quarry industry with its burgeoning ethnic work groups emphasized hard work and determination against fierce odds, the academic environment offered an element of culture and refinement and also an emphasis on physical education and competition.

In both cases—the college atmosphere and the industrial setting—Bereans kept a rock-hard faith in God, whether it was the Methodism of John Baldwin who established Baldwin University or the Polish settlers of the North End who founded their own Polish Catholic church, St. Adalbert's.

You will meet on these pages a sampling of legendary persons who shaped—and are still shaping—Berea. Academia and townspeople, often aided by the Cleveland Browns, mingle and work together to preserve and restore what they value, whether it is an 1899 car built by jeweler-inventor Billy Simpson or the ornamental iron arch to the Cuyahoga County Fairgrounds.

One of the most admirable models of joint effort combining old and new is the renovation and expansion of the conservatory at Baldwin-Wallace College. Opened in 2011, the completed Boesel Musical Arts Center seamlessly joins the existing conservatory building to the adjacent 156-year-old First Congregational United Church of Christ. Functional yet appealing use of space couples with preservation of a historic edifice that has been a staunch pillar of Berea's history. The college provided worship space for the congregation of the First Congregational Church in the college chapel until its future plans could be completed. Longtime Baldwin-Wallace College president Dr. Alfred B. Bonds Jr. would be cheering to see this addition to the campus. Bonds set the stage for such cooperative ventures during his tenure by emphasizing the importance of a collegial relationship between "town and gown."

Not all cooperative and creative ventures involve large expenditures. Many small groups and organizations lend willing hands for the benefit of other residents or the town as a whole. Working on a rotating schedule, more than a dozen churches offer a free monthly community meal, held at St. Paul's Lutheran Church, to help folks on fixed incomes stretch their food dollars. Both the city and a private charity operate food pantries for citizens in need. Working with Baldwin-Wallace College and the City of Berea, St. Thomas Episcopal Church gained access to ground adjacent to the church and planted a community garden. Free fresh produce is distributed during the growing season. This effort has been so successful that the City of Berea is demolishing an abandoned house and will turn the site into another community garden. Many groups of all ages pitch in to rake leaves for older or disabled residents. Baldwin-Wallace College and the Berea Children's Home provide vans to transport the workers. The Coe Lake project created nature trails and added wheelchair-accessible walkways, much of the work accomplished by volunteers working with the City of Berea.

Parades still pass by the Triangle just as they did in earlier times. The Grindstone Festival parade on July 4th and the Light Up Berea parade at Christmastime draw enthusiastic crowds with many organizations participating. At the Fourth of July ice cream social, the Berea Historical Society offers trolley rides. Informed members of the society act as tour guides to acquaint riders with sites telling Berea's history. Classic car shows fill the parking lot near Coe Lake in the summer. All of these are events where residents of this friendly community meet and greet their neighbors and where they take pride in their surroundings. And perhaps they may think of the debt they owe to those whose lives helped shape this town, many of whom are pictured in this book.

CHAPTER ONE

A Vision Becomes Reality

This book is a collection of glimpses and images of memorable Berea personalities. It seems fitting to give an opening nod to a few individuals who, from its beginning, played a vital role in Berea's history. So we begin with John and Mary Baldwin. Two happenstances with simple objects—a coin and a pocketknife—propelled these earnest Christians into the forefront of Berea's archives. Then there were the Wallaces, James and Ellen, wealthy quarry owners, who generously gave land to establish German Wallace College. They moved to Michigan, however, when the quarry industry ended. A backward look must include Capt. Edward Kennedy, a Civil War veteran who survived three Confederate prisons and the sinking of the *Sultana*. When he returned to Berea after his months of convalescence, he became an outstanding leader in the community in business and in politics.

Berea is indebted to those whose efforts keep us mindful of our forebears and the debt we owe them. Dorothy Marks McKelvey devoted years of her life as an archivist and preservationist of the history of Berea and Baldwin-Wallace College. Her efforts are reflected on nearly every page of this book. Berea's beautiful Mahler Museum was made possible by the generosity of Otto and Mabel Mahler. The painstaking task of cataloging donations to the museum was led by Ethel Foster.

Nowadays, to learn more about the history of the town and the area, you can take a cemetery tour with historian Betsy Menzel. And if you want to know what it was like to have been a quarryman, spend some time with James Jaworski, whose father, grandfather, and great-grandfather were quarrymen. Have Jaworski show you the historic Billy Simpson automobile that he restored. It's on display at the Berea Historical Society.

Throughout this book you will find occasional Legends in the Making. These are persons who are exploring new areas or undertakings who may very well become legends. One of these individuals is historian Amanda Epperson.

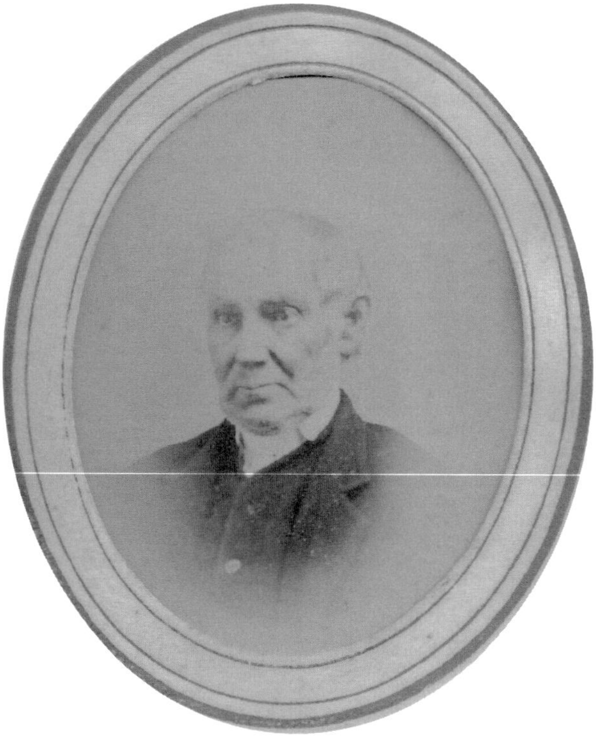

John Baldwin and Mary Baldwin
John Baldwin settled in Berea in 1828. He discovered that a rock on his farm would put a sharp edge on his pocketknife. Thus was born the Berea grindstone industry that flourished from about 1850 to the mid-20th century. Although he suffered financial disappointments in earlier years, Baldwin's grindstone business made him rich. He was a man of brains, farsightedness, and ingenuity but deeply religious and with simple tastes. If an article of his clothing did not suit him, he was known to alter it with his pocketknife or scissors. He and his wife Mary gave generously to worthy causes. Baldwin founded Baldwin Institute, which became Baldwin University, as well as schools in Louisiana and Kansas. He was prominent in the religious, educational, and business life of Berea.

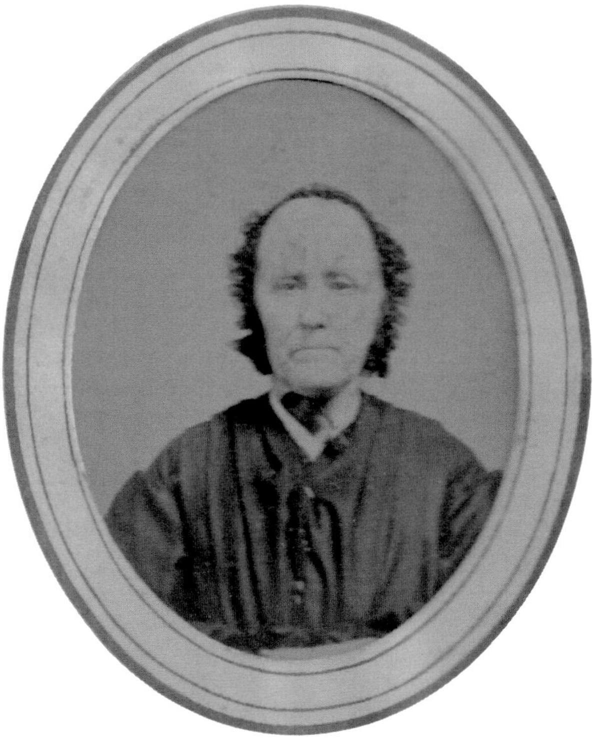

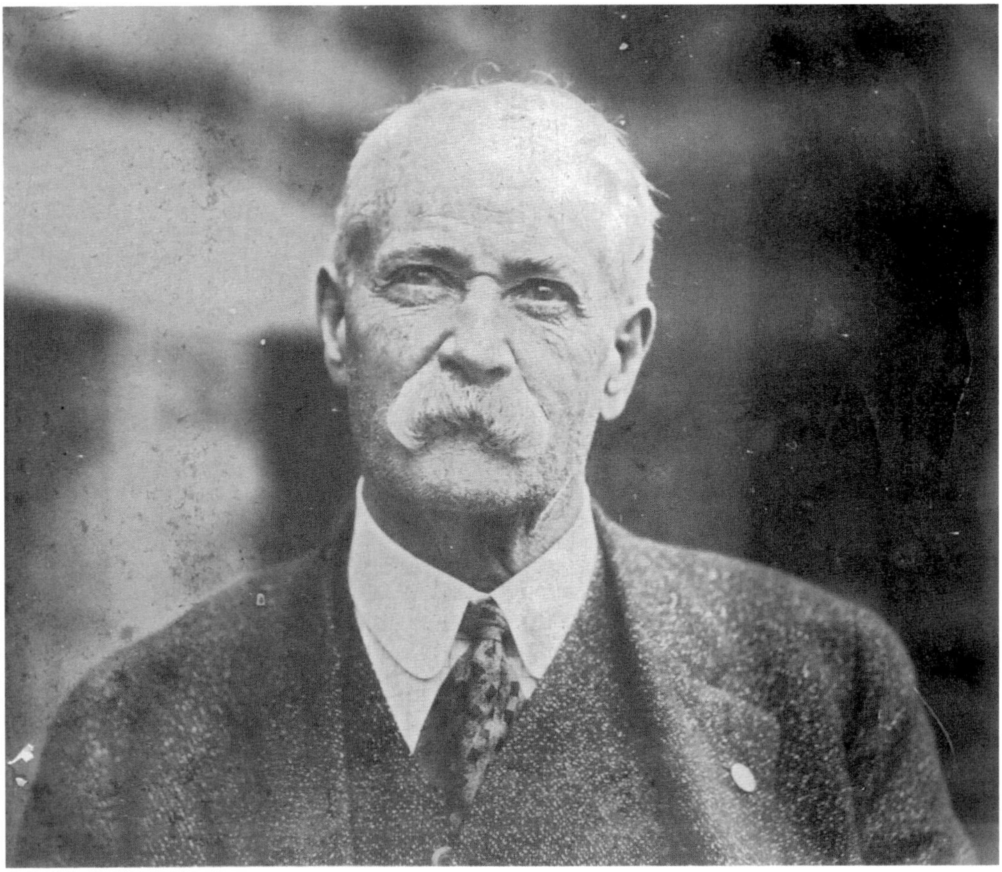

Capt. Edward Kennedy

The explosion of the steamboat *Sultana* on the Mississippi River near Memphis rated only an inside story in the nation's papers in April 1865. Lincoln's assassination gripped the country's attention, although 1,500 souls perished in the muddy waters of that river. Most were Union veterans so weakened from battle and imprisonment that they had little energy to stay afloat. Of the nearly 800 rescued, 200 of these died after the rescue. One who survived five hours by clinging to a piece of wreckage was Berea's Edward Kennedy. A captain in the Union army and a survivor of three Confederate prison camps, including the hellish Andersonville, Kennedy and his fellow soldiers were on their way to Cairo, Illinois, where trains would carry them toward their home states. Carelessness and overloading the steamer caused the explosion into a massive fireball that claimed more lives than the *Titanic*. When he reached his home in Berea after a long convalescence, Kennedy first finished his studies at Baldwin University, which he had postponed when at 19 he had enlisted in the 7th Ohio Volunteer Infantry. He entered business, first with a drugstore, then a dry goods store; he invested in Berea's thriving industry, a sandstone quarry, and in real estate. But his efforts were not all self-centered. He worked for and invested in the Berea Street Railway, and was a founding member of the Berea Board of Trade that brought businesses to Berea. For 50 years, there were few undertakings in Berea in which E.J. Kennedy did not have a hand. He made his way into politics, serving as mayor of Berea, commissioner of Cuyahoga County, and in the state legislature. In the last decade of his public life, he was founder and president of the Commercial & Savings Bank. Upon his passing in 1924 at age 82, the Berea *Enterprise* stated, "it is doubtful if there is any individual in the community who has done more to promote the welfare and prosperity of Berea than Captain Kennedy."

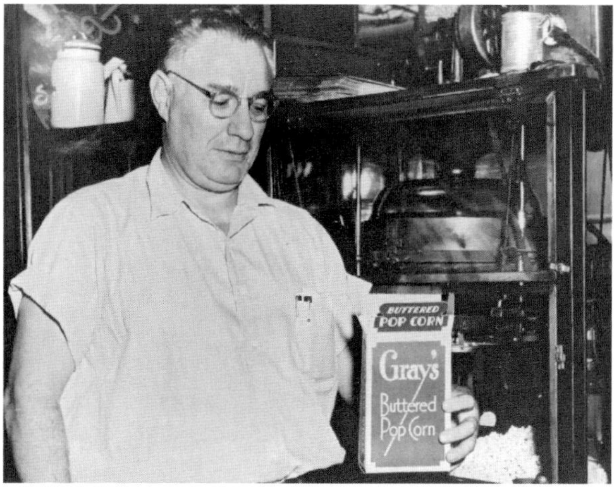

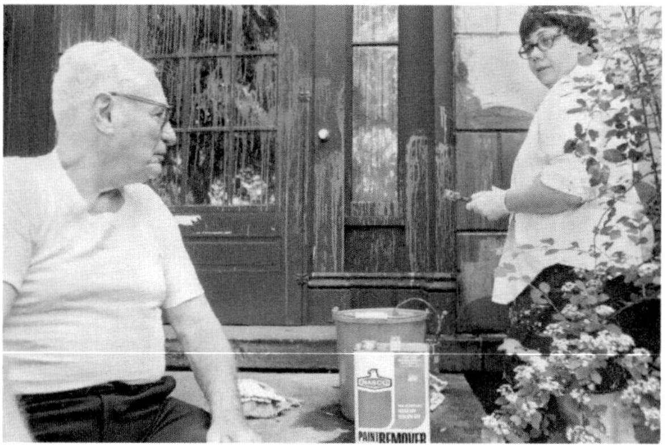

Otto Mahler

After graduating from Berea High School, Mahler washed dishes and did odd jobs for George Gray at the popular Gray's Candy Kitchen on the downtown Triangle. His goal: to earn money to enter Baldwin-Wallace College, but $2 of his weekly wages went to the German Methodist Orphans Home for his room and board. He came to the home at age eight and lived there for 17 years. The home was always near and dear to Mahler's heart. After graduating from Baldwin-Wallace College where he was an outstanding student and athlete in football and basketball, Mahler taught and coached at Bay Village High School. There he met an attractive elementary teacher, Miss Mabel Edward, and they were married on June 12, 1929. Mahler bought Gray's Candy Kitchen from Mr. and Mrs. George Gray. (Above) Mahler operated the popular confectionery for 43 years. He kept the store's original name, and in a peak year sold 12,000 gallons of ice cream, used 13 tons of popcorn, 7,300 pounds of grade A butter, and seven tons of chocolate. Tons of chocolate Easter candy were sold at both retail and wholesale. The popcorn machine from Gray's and a portion of the soda fountain are now displayed in the Mahler Museum. In 1967, the Berea Chamber of Commerce presented Mahler with the first Grindstone Award, now given annually to an outstanding citizen. Mahler served as a trustee of the German Methodist Orphans Home. He had a strong belief that every child has the making of a good citizen if given the proper love, kindness, and direction and treated in a firm, considerate way. The Berea sandstone home that Otto Mahler and his wife Mabel built on East Bridge Street became the Mahler Museum in 1975, home to the Berea Historical Society. Bereans raised $50,000 to match the gift from the Mahlers and one of their heirs, Mary Buehl Adler. (Below) Mahler is assisting Joan Goering, then-Berea Historical Society president, in refurbishing the museum entrance. The home is furnished in the Victorian period and is open to visitors. A reference library and large meeting room have been added to the rear of the building.

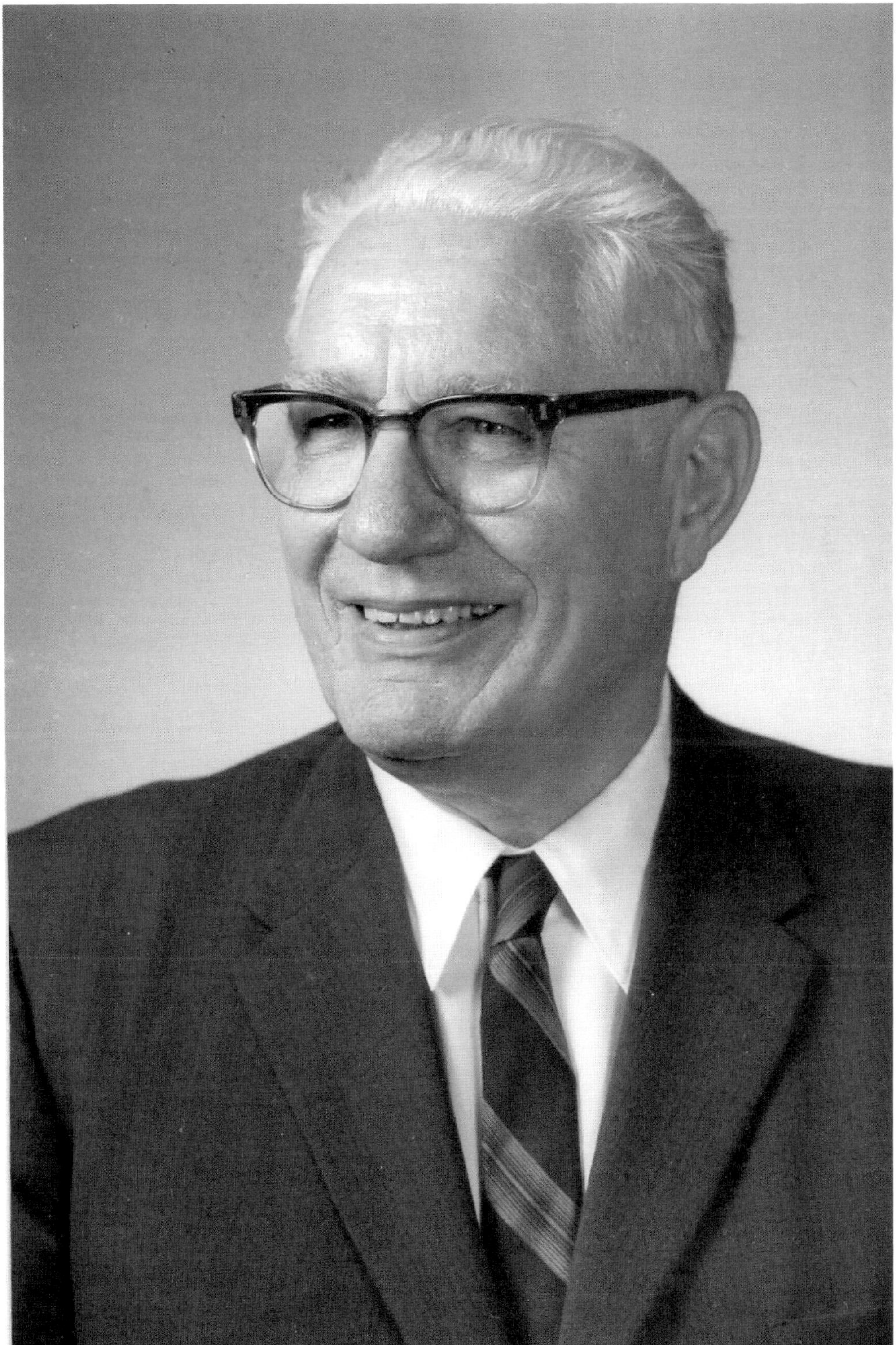

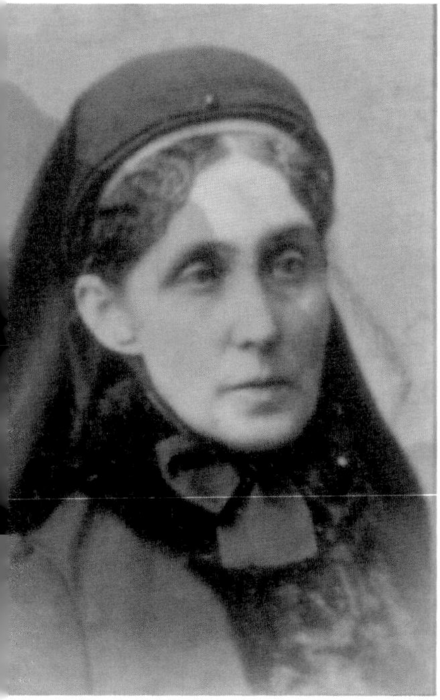

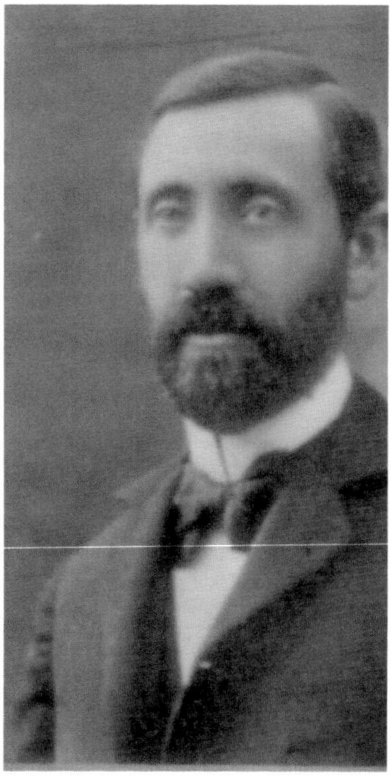

James and Ellen Wallace
Wealthy quarry operator James Wallace and his wife Ellen donated the land, stone, and funds to help establish German Wallace College, an outgrowth of the German department of Baldwin University. The two institutions agreed not to duplicate courses and to grant academic reciprocity to students. The two colleges merged in 1913 to become Baldwin-Wallace College.

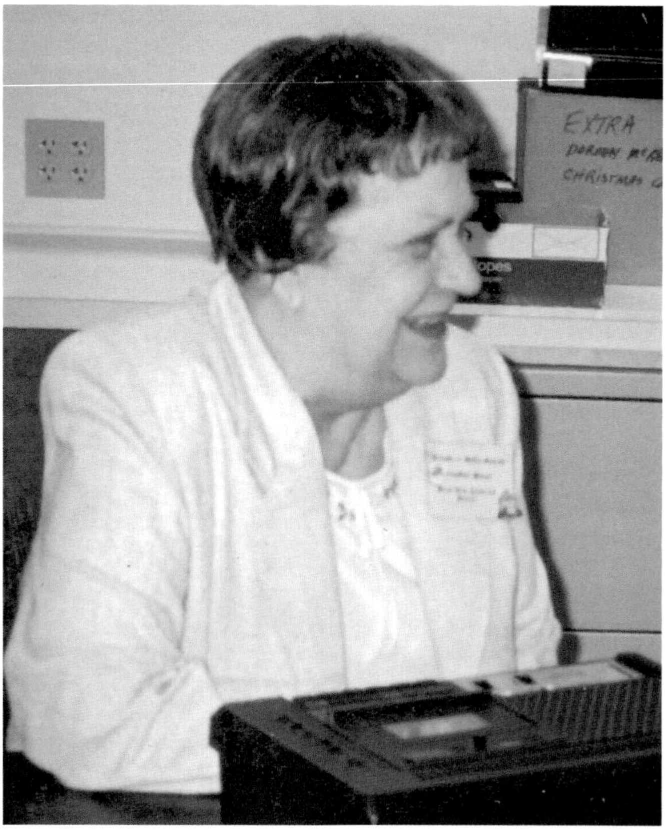

Betsy Menzel
Although legally blind, Betsy Menzel researches Berea's history to share with groups. She knows Woodvale Cemetery, resting place of many well-known Bereans, like the back of her hand. With her white cane pointing the way, she leads anecdote-rich tours of the cemetery. In earlier years, Menzel and her late husband Edward were foster parents to a total of 68 children.

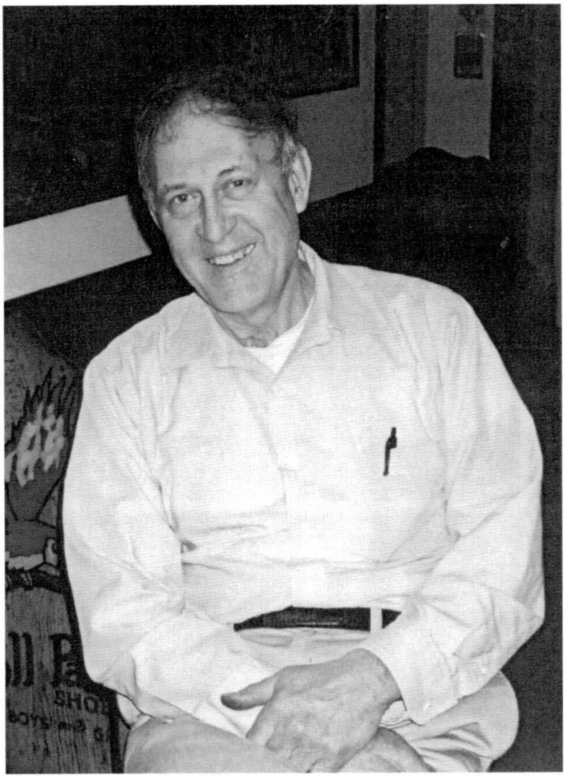

James Jaworski
His great-grandfather, his grandfather, and his father worked in the Berea sandstone quarries, and Jaworski is a veritable encyclopedia on the quarry industry of bygone days. He also keeps Berea history alive in unique ways. A restorer of antique cars at his Berea Motor Works, Jaworski treated the community to a rebirth of an antique two-cylinder car made by part-time inventor Billy Simpson in the 1890s. After working tirelessly to have it ready for the Fourth of July Grindstone Festival in 2008, Jaworski drove it in the parade to the delight of the community (below). The Simpson car now is displayed at the Mahler Museum of the Berea Historical Society. Jaworski's efforts also succeeded in helping raise the town's awareness and funding to restore the ornamental iron gate to the Cuyahoga County Fairgrounds located in Berea.

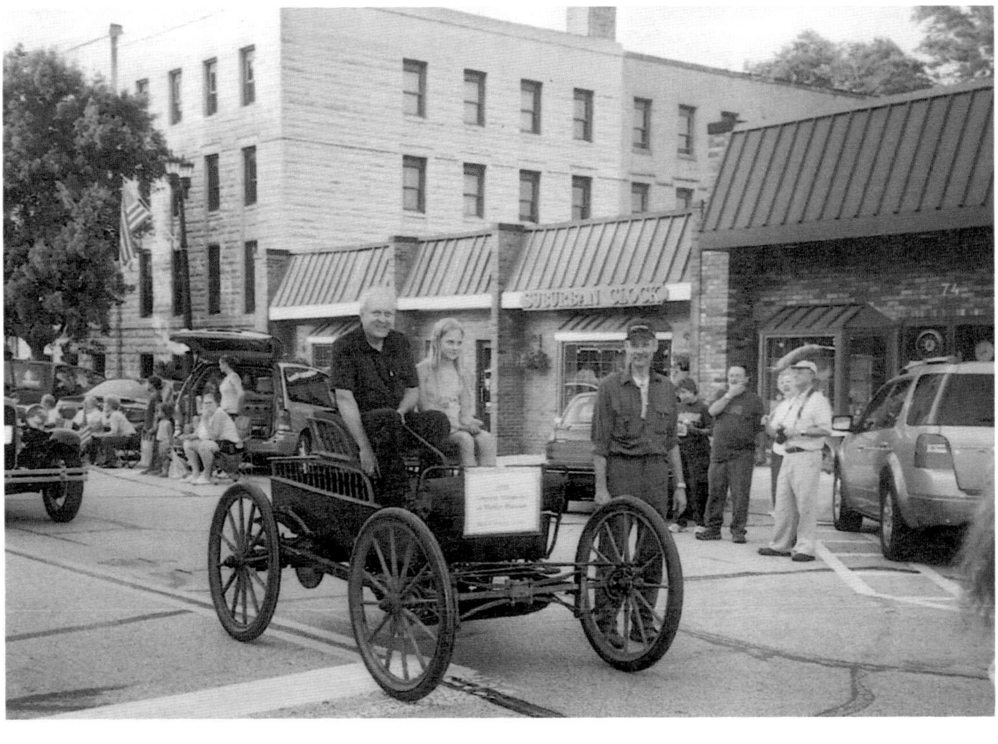

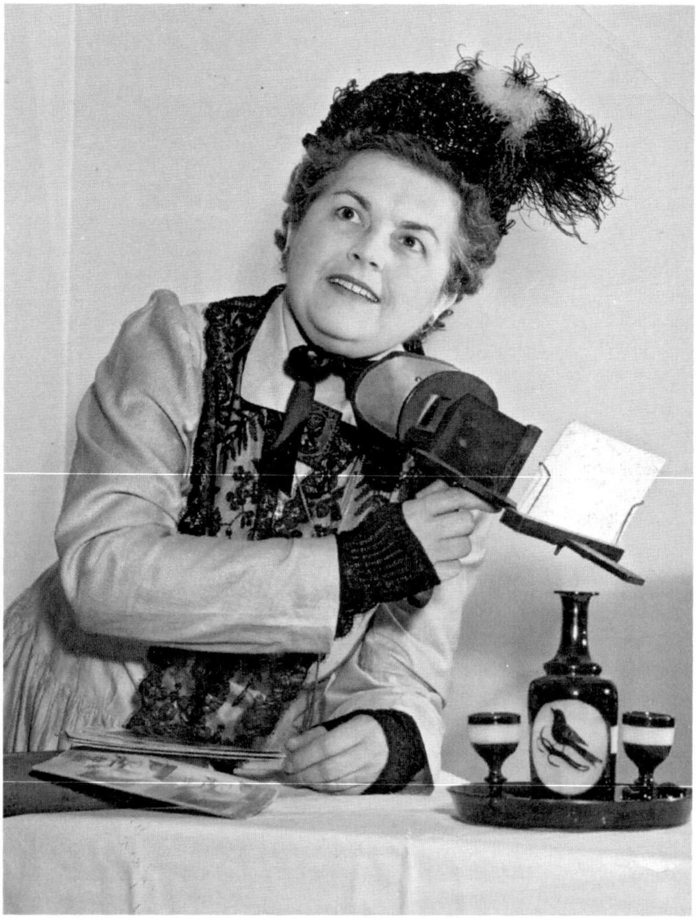

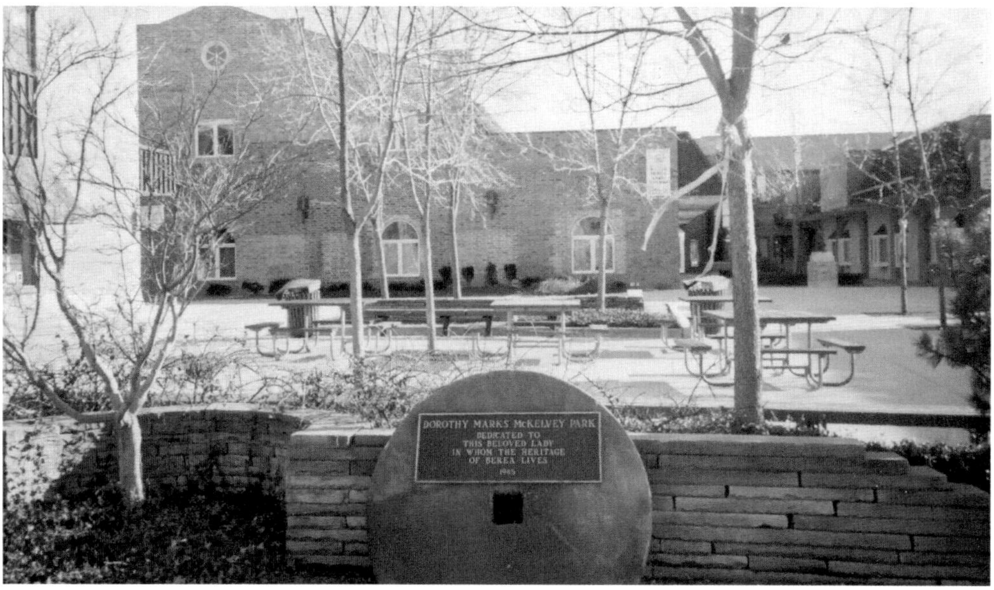
DOROTHY MARKS McKELVEY PARK
DEDICATED TO
THIS BELOVED LADY
IN WHOM THE HERITAGE
OF BEREA LIVES

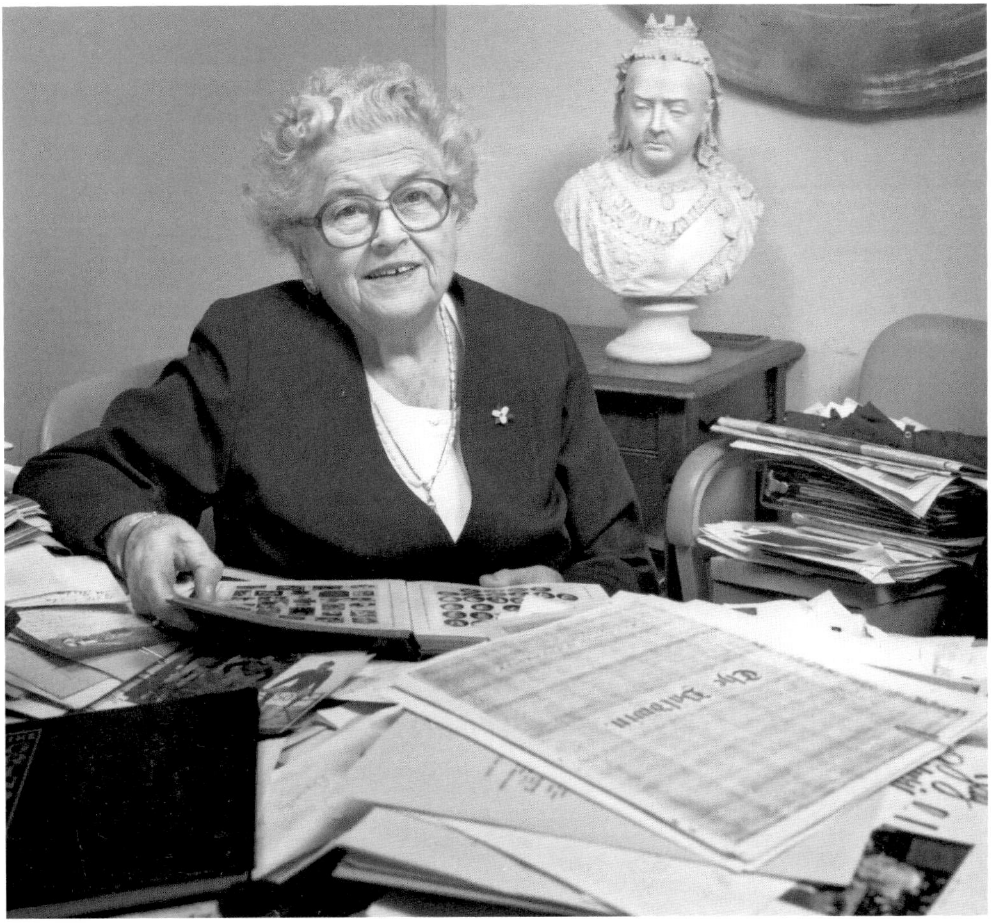

Dorothy Marks McKelvey
She called herself "the keeper of traditions." A fourth-generation descendant of Berea pioneers, McKelvey became the archivist and historian for Baldwin-Wallace College, her alma mater, in 1950. With her knowledge of the community's history, she was a natural to help found the Berea Historical Society in 1959. Serving as its first president and as a director until her death in 1993, McKelvey was the person the newspapers called to verify any facts about Berea's past history. In fact, Mayor Jack Kafer and the city council gave her the non-paying title of official Historian of Berea. She often shared her knowledge and love of the community by speaking to civic groups and school classes. Her collection of Victorian furniture and glassware reflected her passion for the influence of the Victorian period and the life of Queen Victoria. In 1987, the International Women's Writing Guild named McKelvey as one of 26 women to the Artist of Life Honor Roll. Candidates were chosen from a field of 250 nominations for their qualities of wisdom, vision, and special achievements in turning life's stumbling blocks into stepping stones. The Berea Historical Society dedicated an exhibit room to McKelvey in its Mahler Museum, and the City of Berea honored her memory by naming a park for her in the center of the city (left), only a few feet from where the house had stood where she was born. Former Baldwin-Wallace associate dean Stanley Maxwell described McKelvey as "more than the collection of memorabilia and newspaper clippings that cluttered her office, she was a woman with a fantastic memory for not just local history, but for everything." She was fiercely loyal to Baldwin-Wallace. "She never missed a football game," Maxwell said. "She even came to May Day in a wheelchair after breaking her hip. That was a most important tradition to her." She and her husband Wilfred had two sons, Thomas and Wilfred.

Ethel Foster

Aside from her "day" job as an audio-visual professional for Berea schools, Foster helped organize the Berea High School Alumni Association and was registrar for the Berea Historical Society. She supervised cataloging of all donations to the museum such as the license plate (right). Would-be truants easily recognized this plate as truant officer Perle Claflin's.

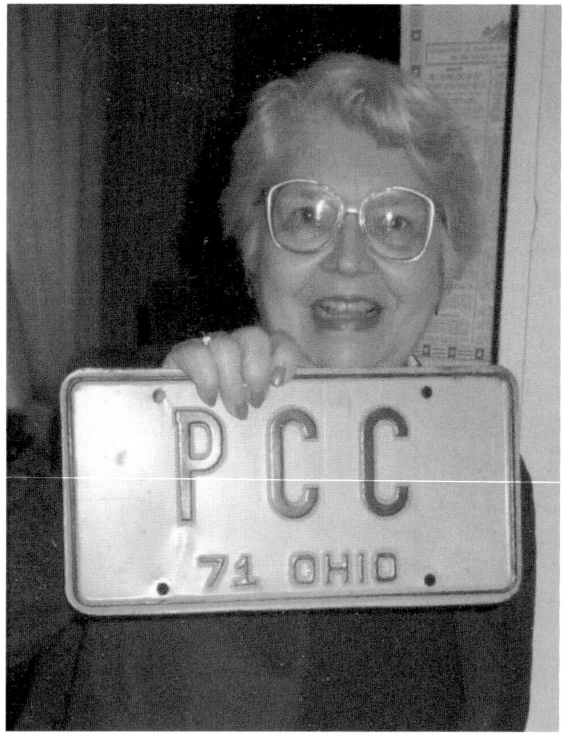

Amanda Epperson, Legend in the Making

Her BA from Baldwin-Wallace College led Amanda Epperson to a master's degree in art history from the Courtauld Institute of Art and a PhD in history from the University of Glasgow. Epperson may have inherited some of her passion for history from her parents, Joseph and Patricia Epperson, active members of the Berea Historical Society. She is a freelance writer, speaker, and researcher.

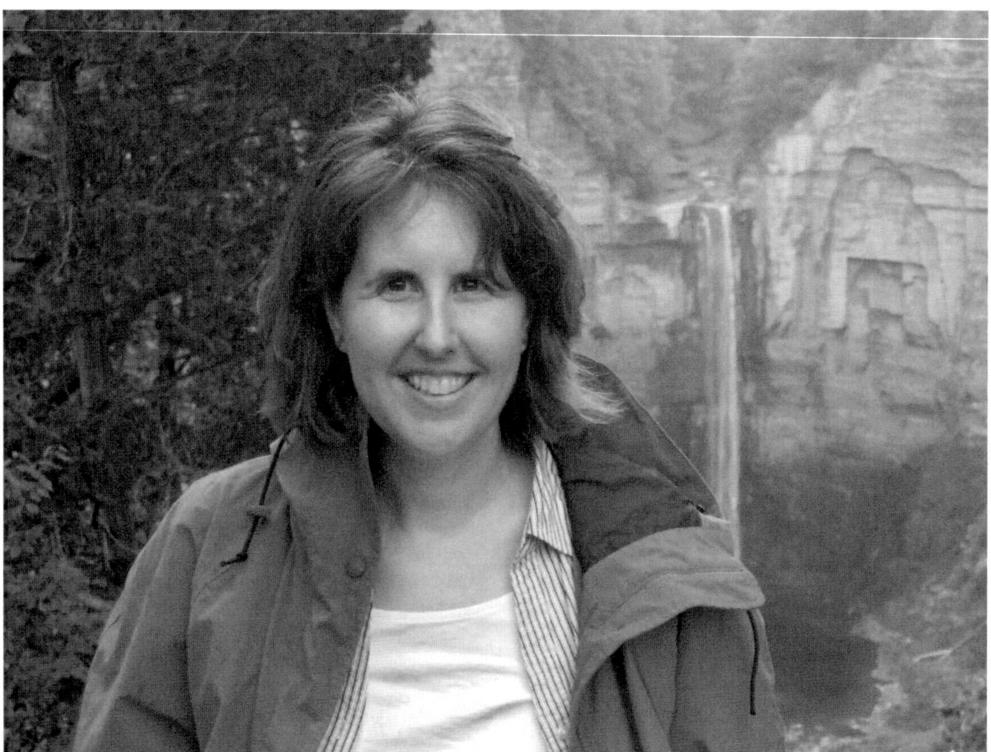

CHAPTER TWO

Government

In early times, when Berea was a village and had not yet adopted a city form of government, the mayor's role was usually a part-time position; as late as 1920, the mayor's salary was only $600 yearly. For example, Mayor Edward Manning was a dairy farmer, while Mayor E. Christian was the village tailor. S.S. Brown, a Civil War veteran who had a half-dozen diverse occupations, was elected for three separate terms as mayor. As the town expanded and offered more services to its citizens, full-time positions attracted candidates with more qualifications. A few of these are profiled here. Also included are a postman, a police chief, a judge, the first chamber of commerce manager, a night watchman, a councilwoman, and the first woman ever elected to the school board, long before women could vote in general elections.

As educators and businesspersons became attracted to public service, the community benefited as these elected officials used their expertise and managerial skills in running the town. The first of these elected mayor was probably businessman Edward Kennedy, whom you met in Chapter One. He even resigned as state representative to return to Berea to serve as mayor. Another educator, Jack Kafer, was twice elected mayor. In the quarter-century following the Civil War, Berea suffered three deadly fires that nearly destroyed the downtown area surrounding the Triangle. Often volunteer firemen battled doggedly with hoses clogged with mud from the Rocky River. Town officials decreed that stone or brick would be used instead of wood in construction of new buildings, reducing the threat of fire. The single most devastating fire, however, occurred in the main building of the German Methodist Orphans Home (now Berea Children's Home) in 1950. The 40 children housed in that building were cared for in the Baldwin-Wallace College field house, assisted by the Red Cross.

The 20th century brought new challenges. Expansion of neighborhoods and attraction of new industry created a need for zoning restrictions. Population growth dictated new schools and, therefore, increased taxes. The Cleveland Metropolitan Park System known as the "Emerald Necklace" came into existence, at very little cost to taxpayers. Berea residents gained parks, trails, and small lakes—all developed from the wasteland of the quarry industry, which had helped the town grow and then threatened to overtake it. An urban renewal effort in the downtown area was a divisive issue, requiring relocation of established businesses. Bereans have developed the Coe Lake area, nearest to downtown, into a charming, versatile setting that serves the community well for many different types of events.

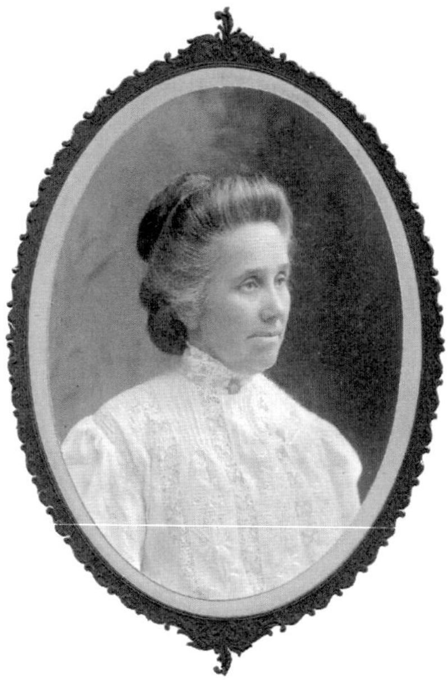

Mrs. Mary Elmore

Nearly 25 years before the 19th Amendment gave American women the right to vote, Elmore was elected to the Berea School Board in 1895. Upon Mrs. Elmore's election, the Berea *Advertiser* stated, ["Woman] suffrage is coming. There is a little hesitation here and there, but we are going to get used to it. . . ."

John J. Baesel

The first mayor elected after Berea changed from village to town government, Baesel (seated) served two terms. His assistant (standing) is unidentified. A veteran of the Mexican expeditionary force of 1916 and a captain in World War I, Baesel became commander of American Legion Post 91, named for his late brother, Albert Baesel. John Baesel died in 1966, one day after his wife, Florence.

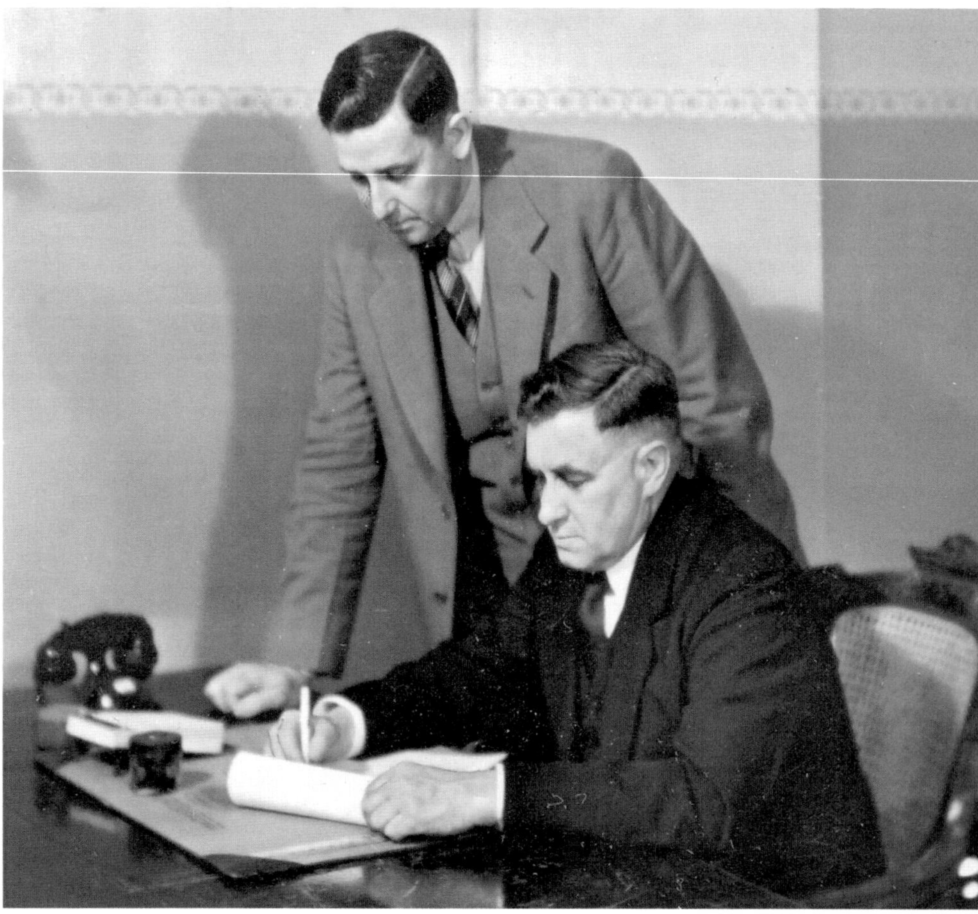

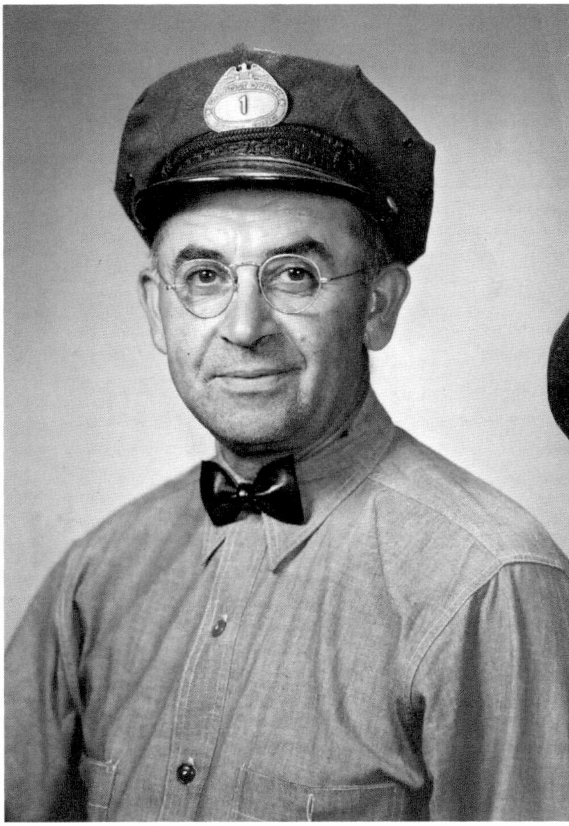

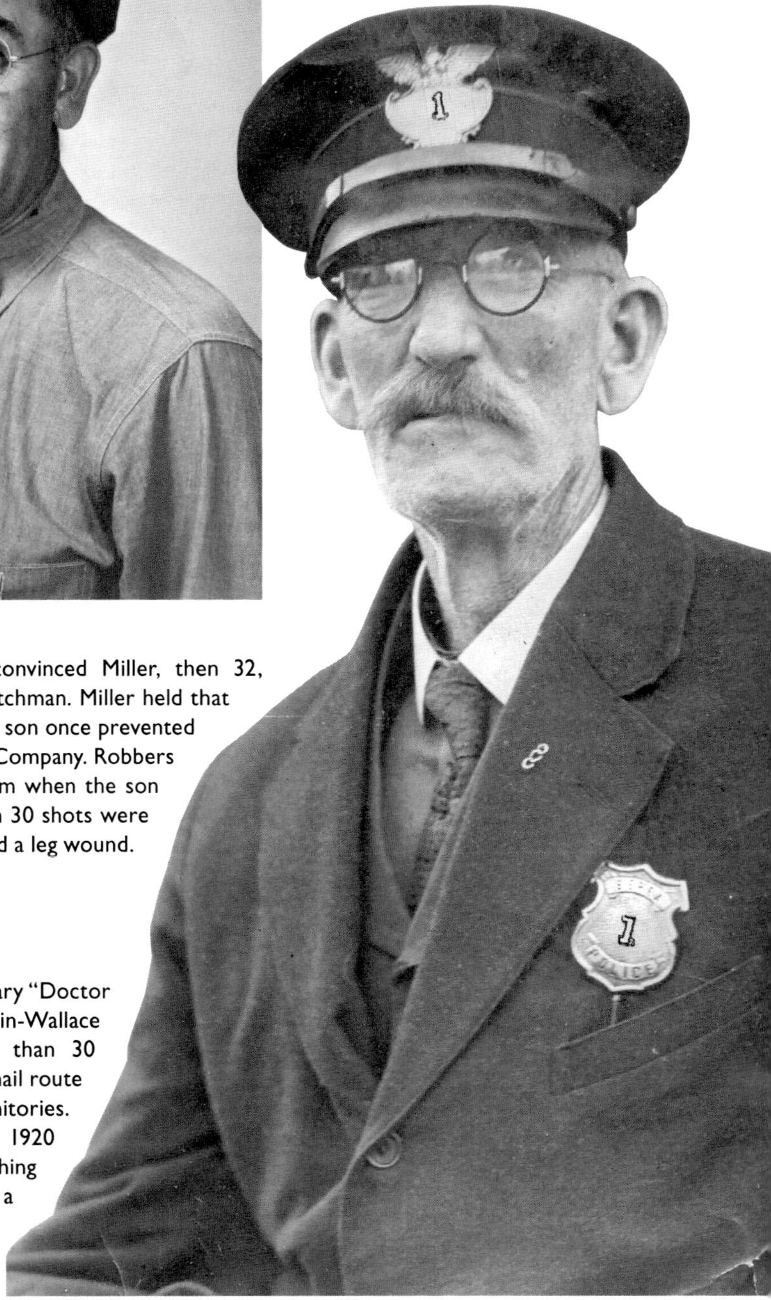

Webster A. Miller

In 1887, Mayor J.C. Nokes convinced Miller, then 32, to become the town's night watchman. Miller held that post for 38 years. Miller and his son once prevented a robbery at the Bank of Berea Company. Robbers captured Miller but released him when the son began firing at them. More than 30 shots were fired, and the Miller boy suffered a leg wound.

G.P. "Doc" Schneider

He was once awarded an honorary "Doctor of Letters" citation by a Baldwin-Wallace College fraternity. For more than 30 years, "Doc" Schneider's U.S. mail route included all of the college dormitories. He became a letter carrier in 1920 when his route covered everything south of Grand Street. "I used a bike in summer and a sled in winter," Schneider recalled in a 1948 interview.

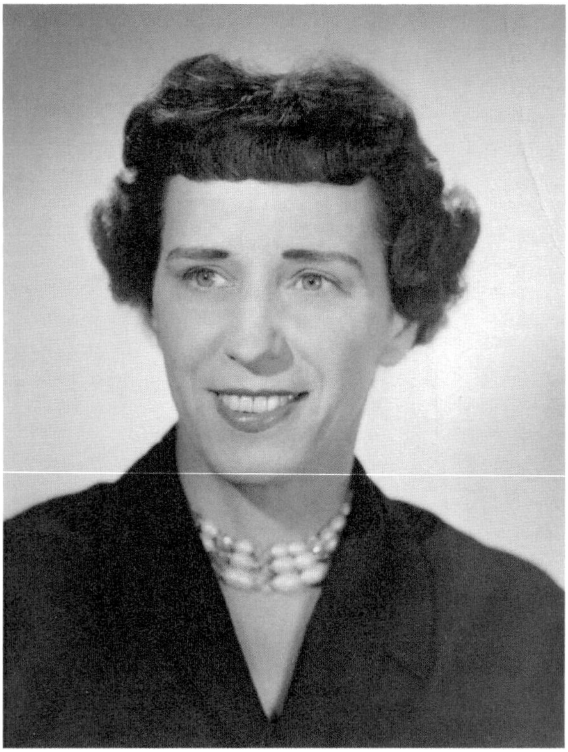

Wilma Sauvey

In 1955, Sauvey arrived from Sandusky to be the first full-time female chamber of commerce manager in Ohio. Hired from a field of seven, six of whom were men, Sauvey fell in love with Berea and led the Berea chamber for 20 years. She implemented a plethora of programs and initiatives for the city and was regarded as a bright, creative, and vivacious individual.

Ceilcote Groundbreaking

Wilma Sauvey and the Berea Chamber of Commerce played a major role in bringing new businesses to town in the mid-20th century.

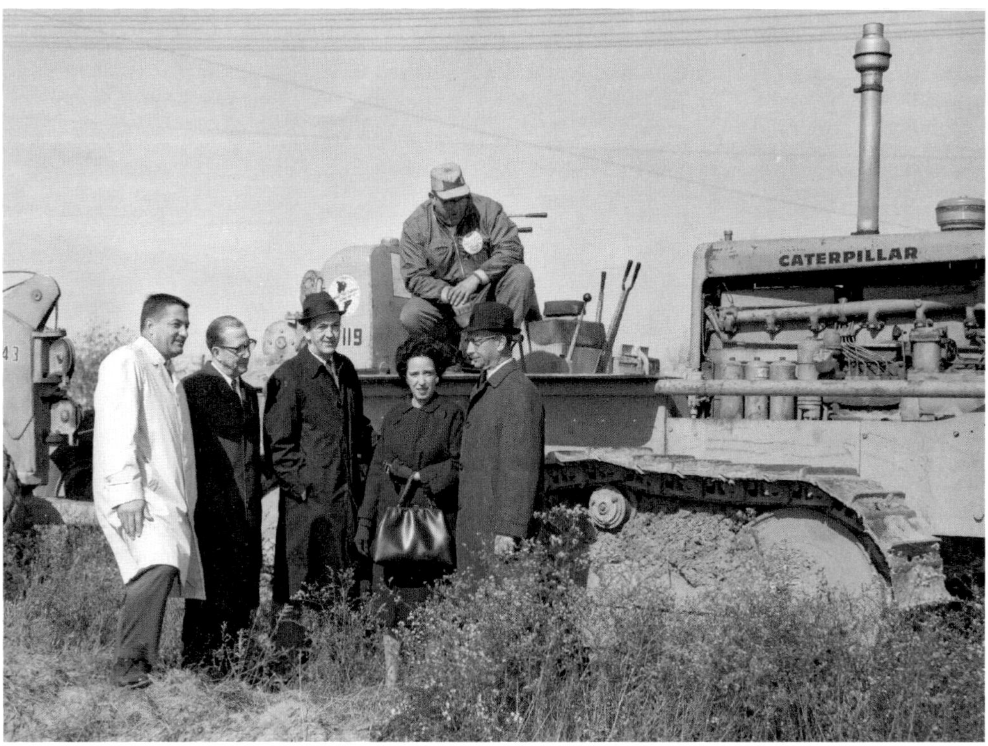

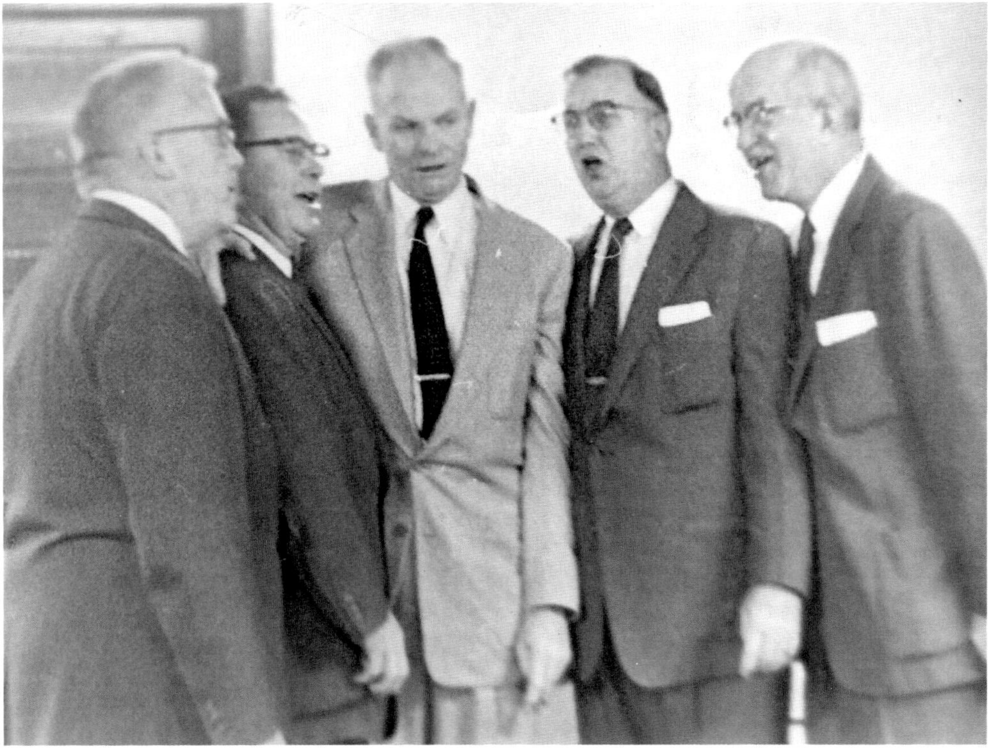

Edward T. Manning
Elected mayor in 1950, Manning (center) was the first Democratic mayor since 1930. He served two terms. A former dairy farmer, Manning developed his property into the residential area of Manning, Ellen, and Karelyn Drives and Miles Lane. One of Manning's favorite pastimes was singing barbershop harmony. After leaving office, he sold real estate until moving to Florida in 1970.

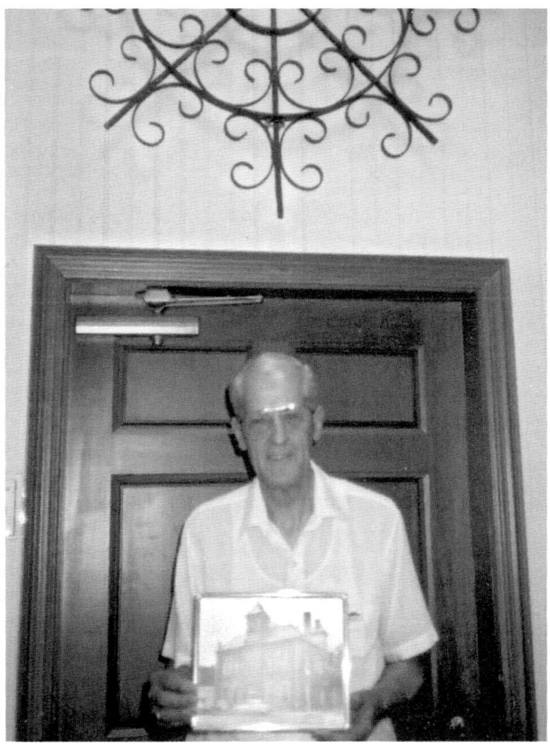

Jerome I. "Doc" Kobie
After serving in the Navy during World War II, Kobie joined the Berea Police Department. He was promoted to captain in 1961. Kobie was credited with landing the conviction of John L. VanNatta for wealthy jeweler Richard Richards' murder in the 1960s. Kobie assisted in questioning more than 300 people before obtaining evidence that convicted VanNatta. Captain Kobie retired in 1976.

Judge Joseph Stangel

Judge Stangel was said to read poetry and crack jokes in his Berea municipal courtroom to ease tension, but he never lost sight of his passion for justice. A bachelor, Stangel was thought by some to be "wedded" to his court. Before every court session, he reviewed the basic tenets of the judicial system for all present.

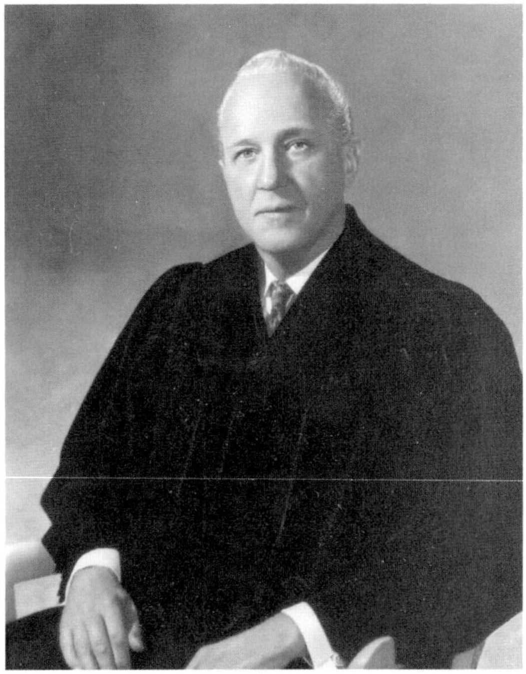

Berea City Hall in 1947

On the right was the fire station. The police station was located on the lower floors along with the jail. Council and the first Berea Municipal Court occupied the chambers at the upper left, and the mayor's office and city hall administration occupied the upper right side. The city hall stood at East Bridge and Seminary Streets where the municipal parking lot is today.

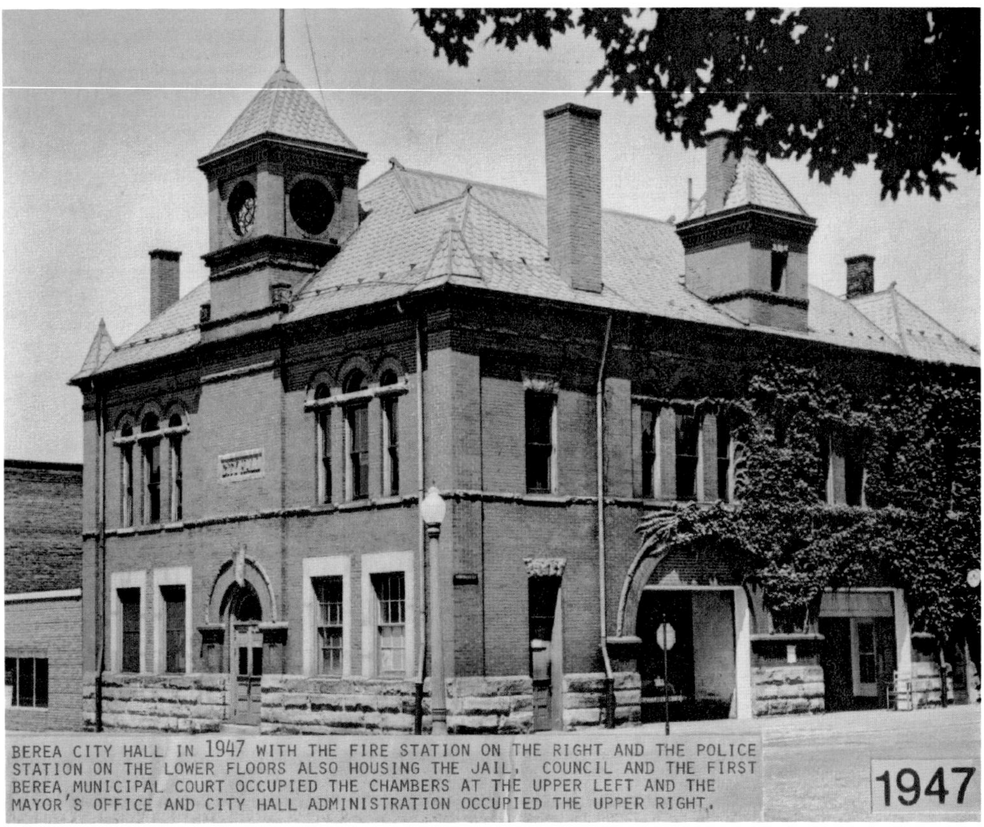

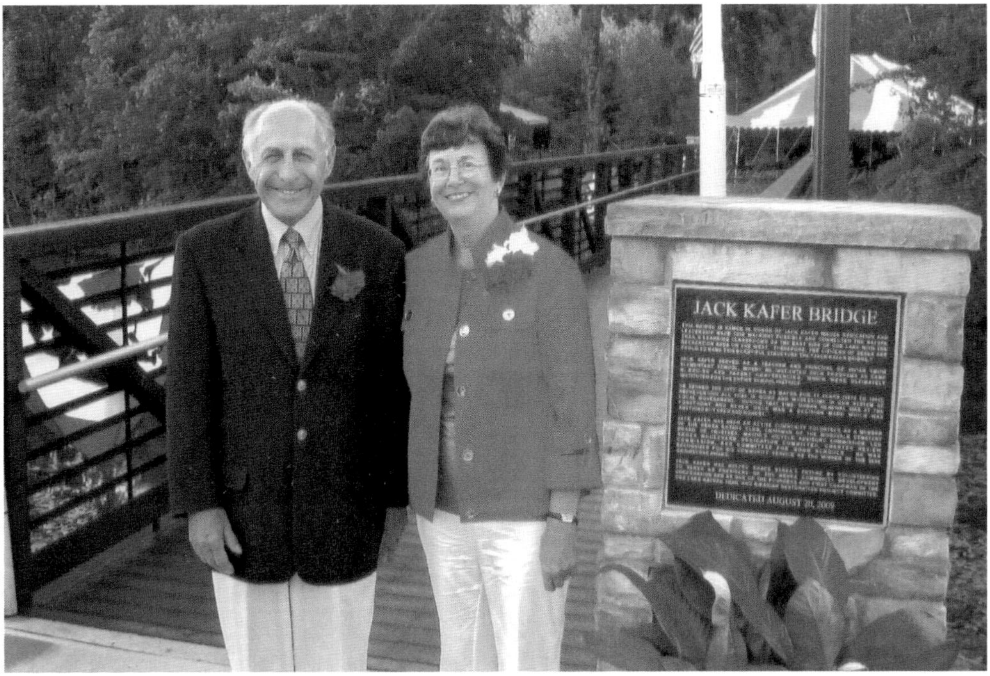

Jack Kafer
As an educator, Kafer stood for responsibility, fair play, and good sense. He brought these qualities to government as Berea's mayor from 1972 until 1984. As an active civic volunteer, Kafer called the city's Coe Lake project "a diamond in the rough," an exciting undertaking for Berea. Kafer and his wife Joan were honored at the dedication of the bridge named in Jack's honor. (Courtesy Kafer family.)

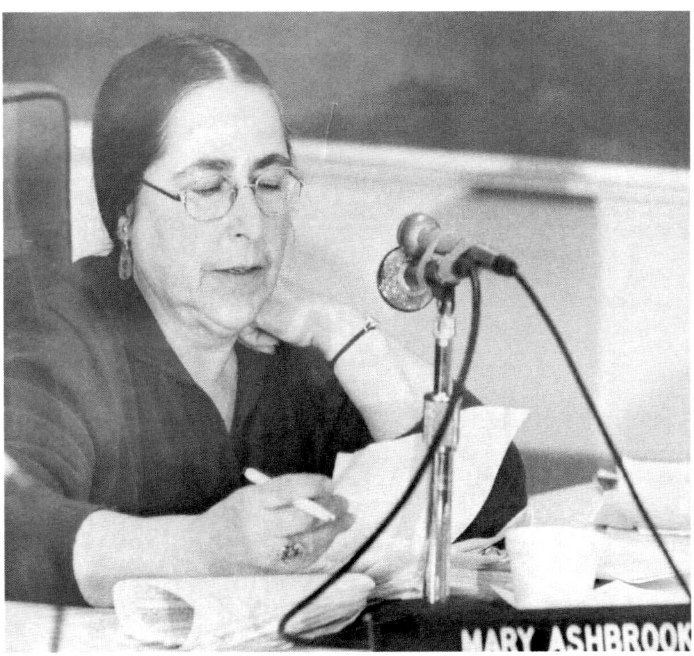

Mary Ashbrook
"Á model to us . . ." "like losing the chief justice of the Supreme Court . . ." These are remarks Ashbrook's colleagues on Berea City Council made upon her retirement from 16 years as a council member, seven as council president. Ashbrook championed openness and public participation in government and believed Berea had made strides in those directions.

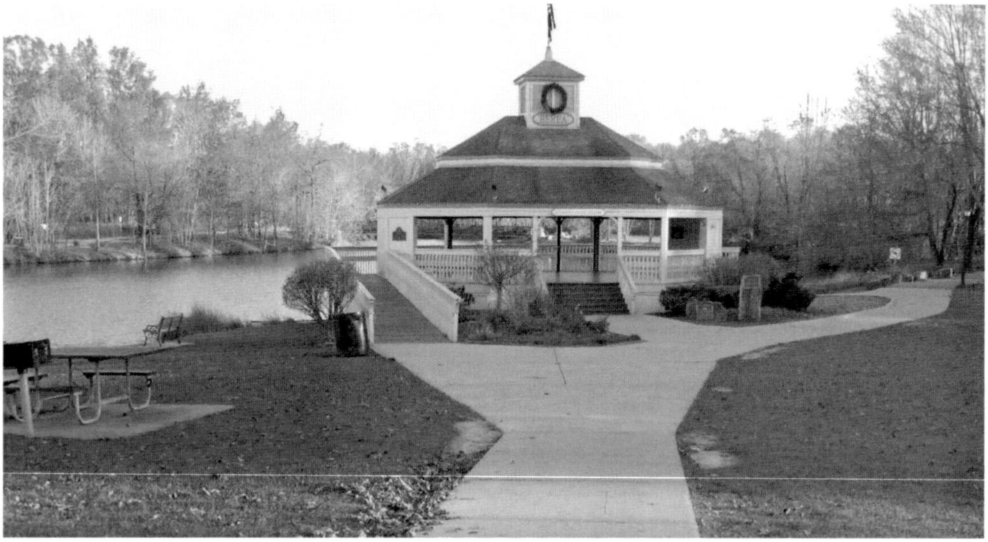

The Gazebo at Coe Lake
The picturesque gazebo is the scene of concerts, art fairs—even weddings. Residents can sit on blocks of sandstone originally drilled from the quarry, a tranquil, pleasant venue. (Photograph by Patricia Mote.)

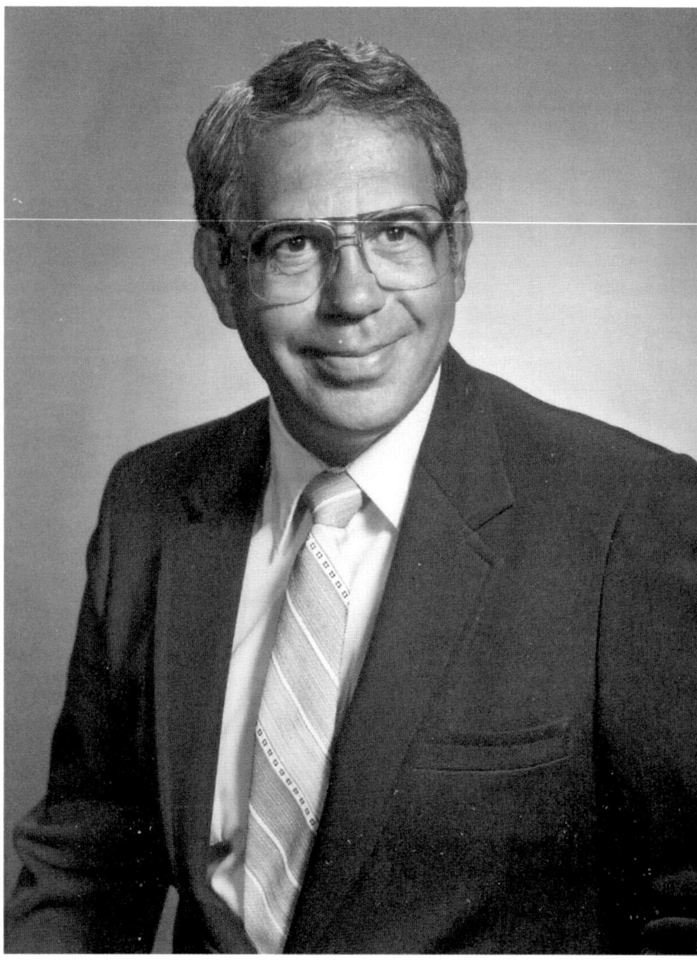

Stanley Trupo
Mayor Trupo served the city for 12 years from 1987 to 1999. He lobbied successfully for the building of the Cleveland Browns' new training facility in Berea in the late 1980s. Later, he was instrumental in the city's agreement with the National Football League (NFL) to require the expansion Browns to return to Berea.

CHAPTER THREE

Education

With an outstanding liberal arts college and a school system pledged to inspire excellence, Berea boasts a veritable hall of fame of distinguished educators. Many who were teachers and administrators in the school system were also coaches or business owners. Some, like Frederick Roehm, became Baldwin-Wallace professors. J.F. Koeppe guided the Berea schools for 23 years. During his tenure, five elementary schools and one junior high were built, and Berea schools pioneered in education for students with special needs. Support personnel are vital to any educational institution. Included here are a school board member, Eleanor Luff, and a colorful personality, Perle Claflin, truant officer and social worker.

At Baldwin-Wallace College, interesting facts about faculty members kept coming to light. Students and alumni paid tribute to beloved music professor James Feldman, honoring him with a tribute and concert before his death. Feldman was a victim of ALS (Lou Gehrig's Disease). A distinguished Baldwin-Wallace College president, Alfred B. Bonds Jr., was the subject of a sculpture by acclaimed artist Felix De Weldon. The two men were close friends from their days in the US Navy. Bonds' wife, Georgianna, undertook finishing a mystery novel her father had begun 75 years earlier.

At the German Methodist Orphans Home (now Berea Children's Home), "Pappa" George Kaletsch was superintendent in the early part of the 20th century. He and his wife, "Mamma" Kaletsch, supervised the children's studies and emphasized music and physical education. The children participated in parades and pageants, making them feel a part of the community. Reverend and Mrs. Kaletsch served the home for 12 years.

You will meet another Legend in the Making, Taylor Hinton, 2010 graduate of Berea High School. Now studying at Allegheny College, she is majoring in environmental studies with emphasis on Third World countries. You will find other educators, such as William Allman and Lee Tressel, included in other sections of this book in their particular areas of excellence.

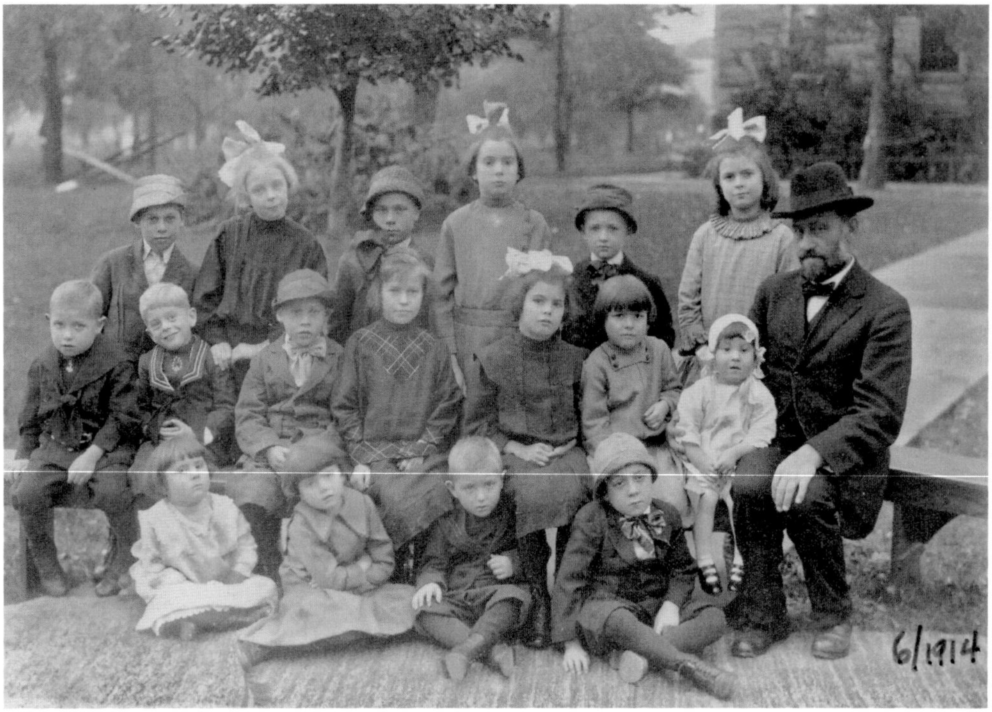

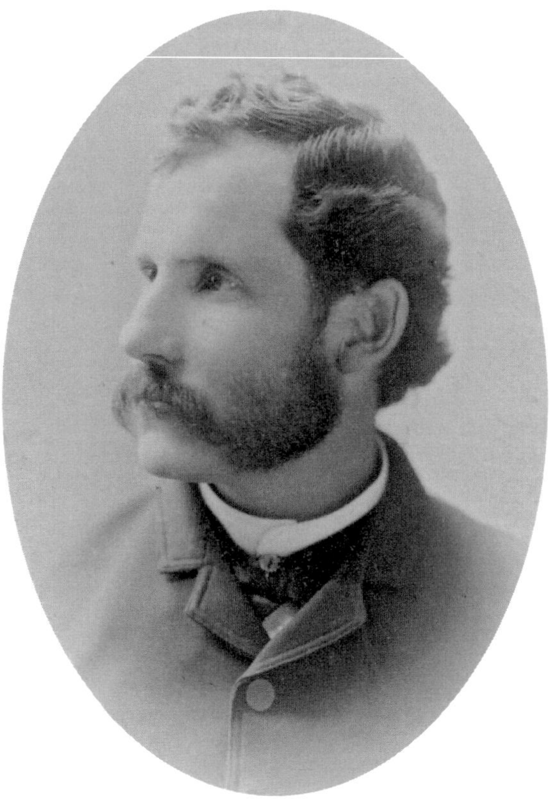

Rev. George "Pappa" Kaletsch
Kaletsch became superintendent of the German Methodist Orphans Home (now known as the Berea Children's Home) in 1907. His wife, known as "Mamma" Kaletsch, served as teacher, secretary, and housemother. The couple served the home until 1919. They encouraged the children in musical, dramatic, and physical fitness activities, which involved the community and helped to give the children a sense of belonging.

Elisha Scott Loomis
Loomis's academic career began with a daunting struggle against poverty. Eventually, he was a professor of mathematics at Baldwin University for 10 years and taught at West High School for 30 years. Loomis owned the first car in Berea, a White steam-car. To get up a hill, one had to wait at the bottom and get up a head of steam.

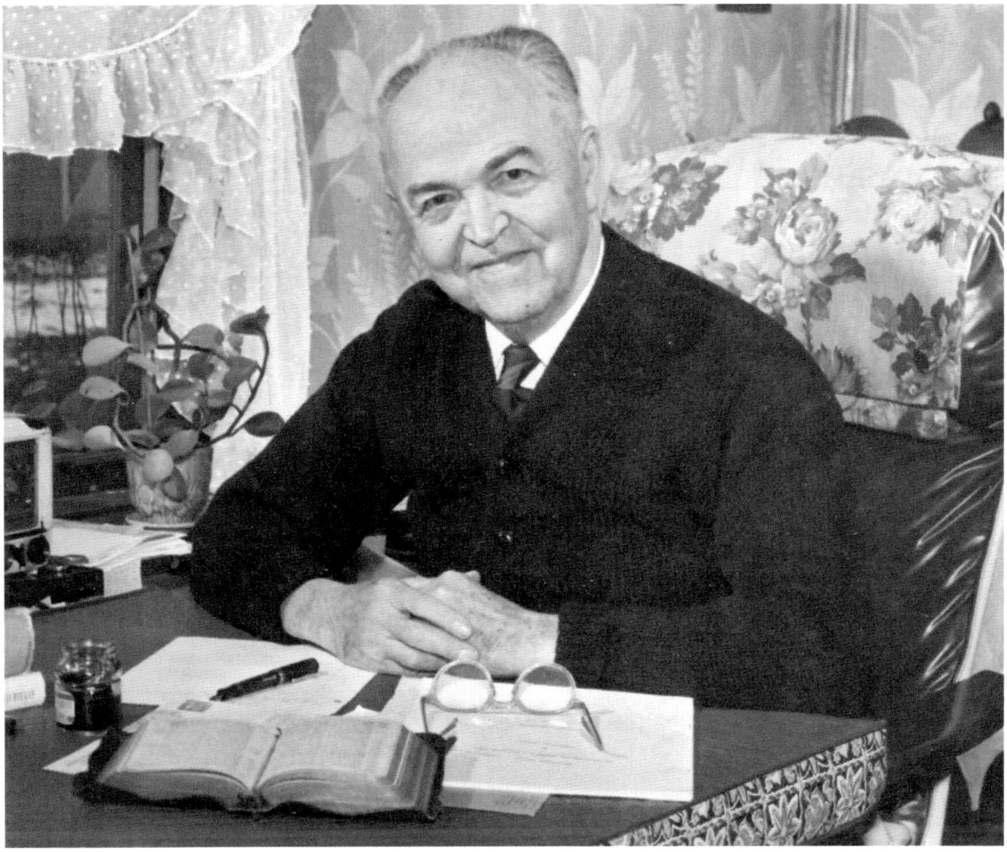

Frederick Roehm

Born in Germany, young Frederick Roehm sold pretzels for his father, a baker. At 15, he came to America, unable to speak English, and lived with an uncle. He earned a BA degree from German Wallace College in 1902 and a master's degree from Columbia University. Roehm became a professor and dean at Baldwin-Wallace College, serving there 26 years.

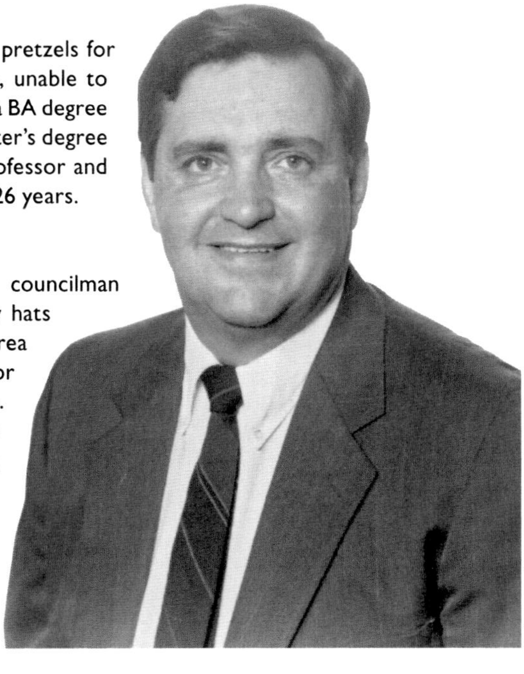

Jeffrey King

Respected teacher, coach, businessman, city councilman and council president—Jeffrey King wore many hats extremely well. He taught in the Parma and Berea schools and for 10 years was an associate professor of government at Baldwin-Wallace College. His 1989 Berea High basketball team won the Pioneer Conference with an 18-2 record. King was named conference coach of the year. He helped create the Berea Recreation Center and the Rocco J. Colonna Industrial Parkway. King was also co-owner of the Bank of Berea Antiques. There were lots of empty shoes to fill when King died at age 62.

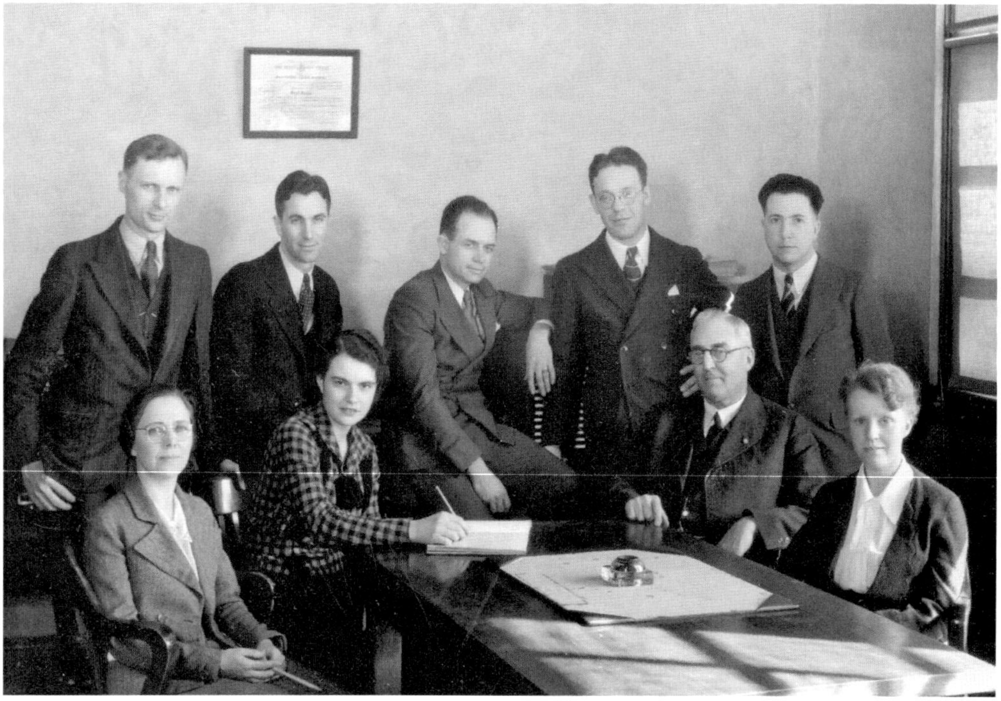

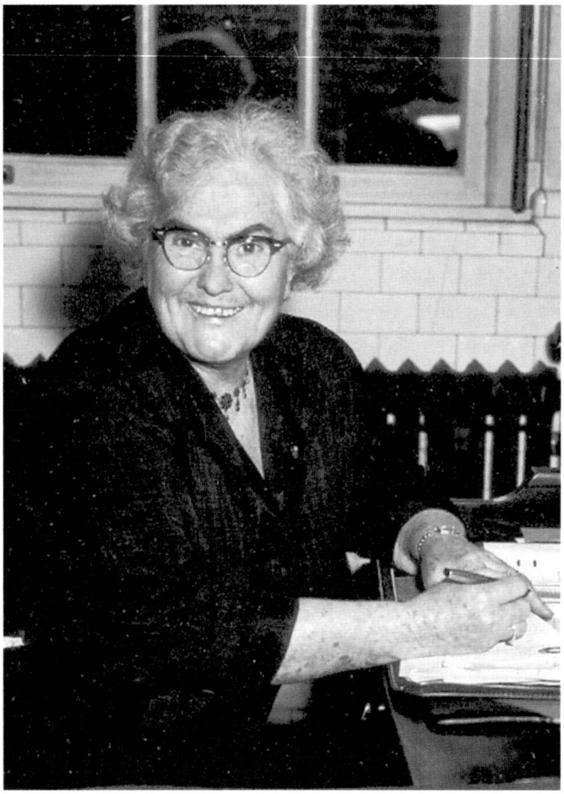

Dr. Donald Dean

Dean (seated, third from left) began teaching biology at Baldwin-Wallace College in 1947 and became head of the department in 1970, a post he held until 1982. Dean also served as a trustee of Southwest Community Hospital (now Southwest General Health Center). He helped the hospital develop policies on using life support systems. His many interests made Dean a frequent writer of letters to the editor of the Cleveland *Plain Dealer.*

Perle Claflin

Social worker, policewoman, police matron, truant officer—Claflin wore many hats. For 46 years, this tireless lady visited homes of students who had academic, health, and other problems and collected clothing and food to give to those less fortunate. When she retired at age 85, the city observed Perle Claflin Day in honor of her service to the city.

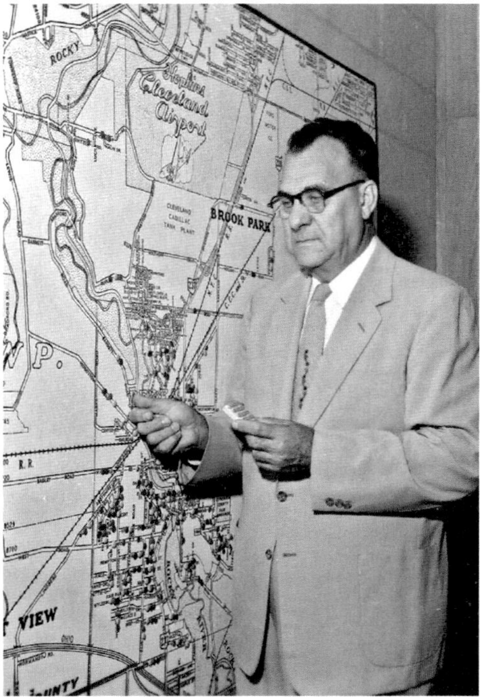

J.F. Koeppe

Koeppe's tenure as superintendent of the Berea School District spanned 23 years. The population growth then, 1935–1958, compelled the district to enlarge school facilities and adapt many educational innovations. After retiring, Koeppe became head of the education department at Baldwin-Wallace College. Koeppe's career began in a one-room schoolhouse in Defiance County, Ohio, while he continued his senior high school studies at night and on Saturdays.

Central School Group

In spring 1973, PTA co-presidents Sue Kechele Simpson and her husband Chuck planned an open house for staff and former students of the Central School. This was just before the school was demolished for the Collins tennis courts. First row, from left, Walter Holzworth, Olive Simpson, Carolyn Donahoe, and Otto Mahler; second row, Hilda Goelbe Grenell, John Koeppe, superintendent, Ruth Kuekes Smith, and Orman Smith; third row, Laura Erf and Art Grinnell.

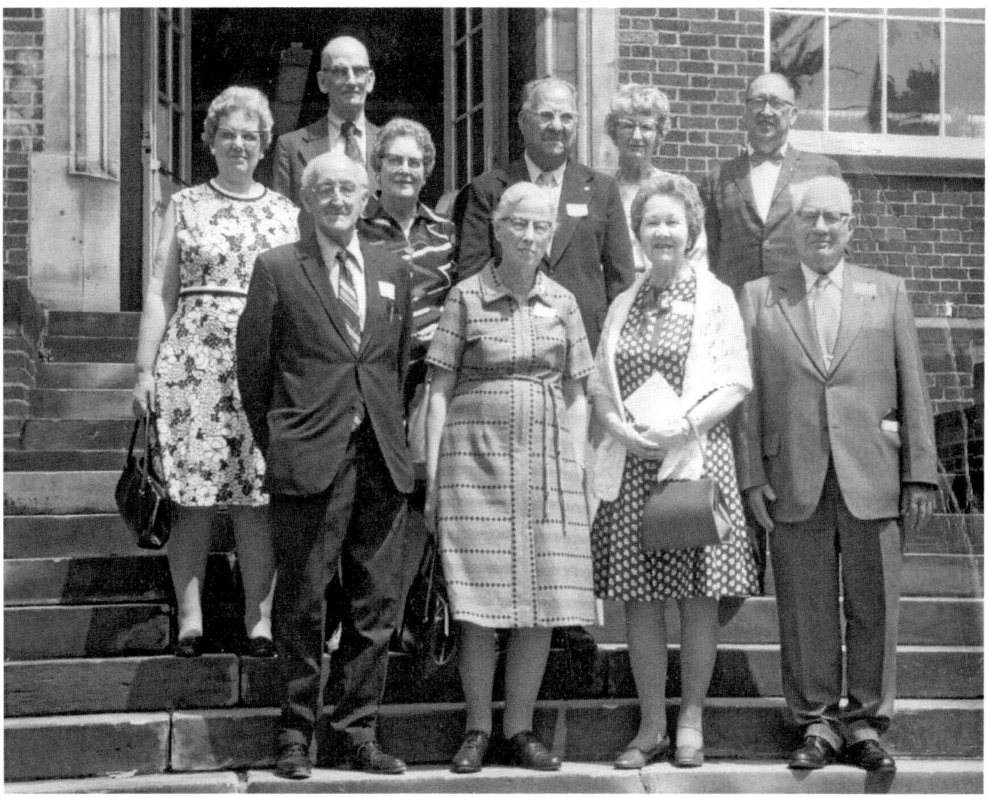

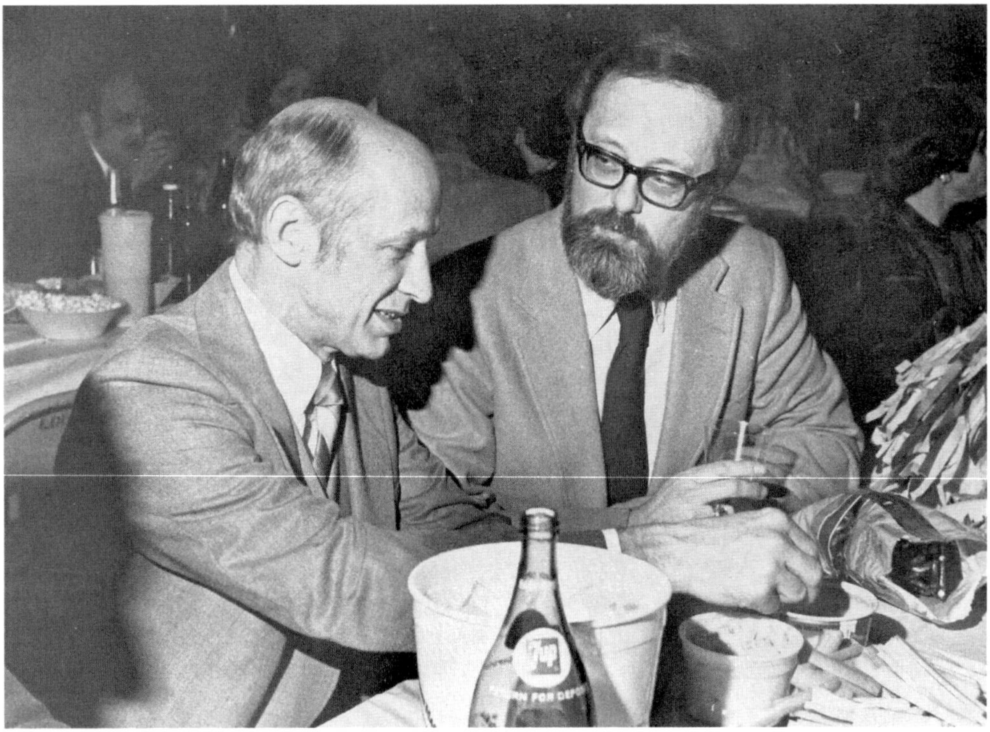

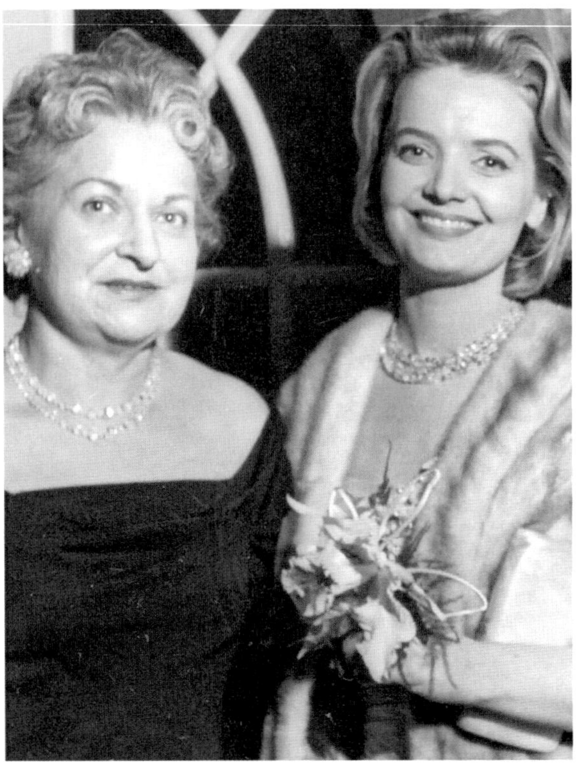

Ronald Schuff

As one of his colleagues said, "If you didn't know Ron Schuff, you sure missed out." As a Berea High counselor, Schuff (right) always put students first. Here he confers with Dr. Edward White. He also volunteered for the Berea Historical Society and organized the "Cruisin'-in-the-Triangle" classic car displays. The entire community felt the loss of Schuff when he died of a heart ailment at age 56.

Eleanor Luff

Luff served the Berea Board of Education for 15 years, two of those as president. The Ohio Association of Elementary School Principals named Mrs. Luff 1967 Outstanding Layman of the Year for her work in improving library service to elementary schools. Here she is hosting actress Florence Henderson at a post-prom party for Berea High School. The actress was appearing at Cleveland's Hanna Theatre in *The Sound of Music*.

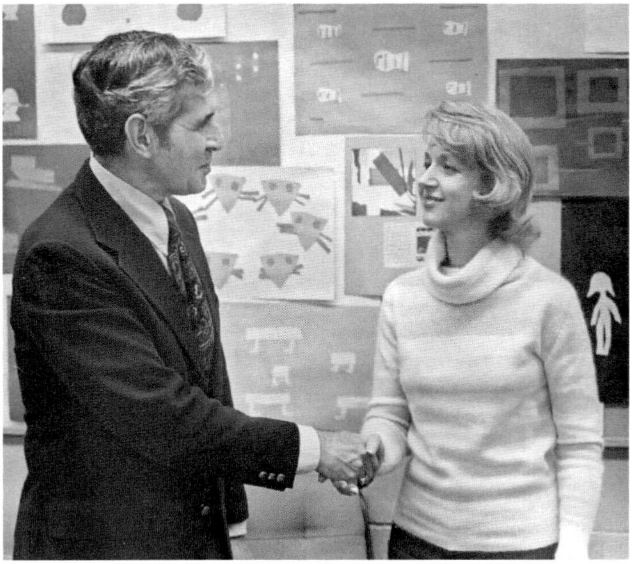

Dr. Richard Andrisek
As superintendent of Berea's schools from 1973 until 1987, Andrisek was proud of involving the community in decision-making processes. He organized citizen review committees to examine school problems and implemented many of their recommendations. Colleagues described Andrisek as a "visionary educator," one with "an insatiable curiosity, boundless energy, and a passion for excellence." He is shown here congratulating Evelyn Wilder.

Dr. John Knight and Commencement Speaker Believed to be William Pearson Tolley, Syracuse University Chancellor
In 1949, Dr. Knight (left), at age 34, became the fourth president of Baldwin-Wallace College. After four years, he returned to the ministry, serving United Methodist churches in Columbus, Ohio, and later Syracuse, New York. He declined two separate invitations to the Methodist episcopacy. In 1967, he accepted the presidency of Wesley Theological Seminary in Washington DC. Knight served there until retirement, living both his passions—ministry and administration.

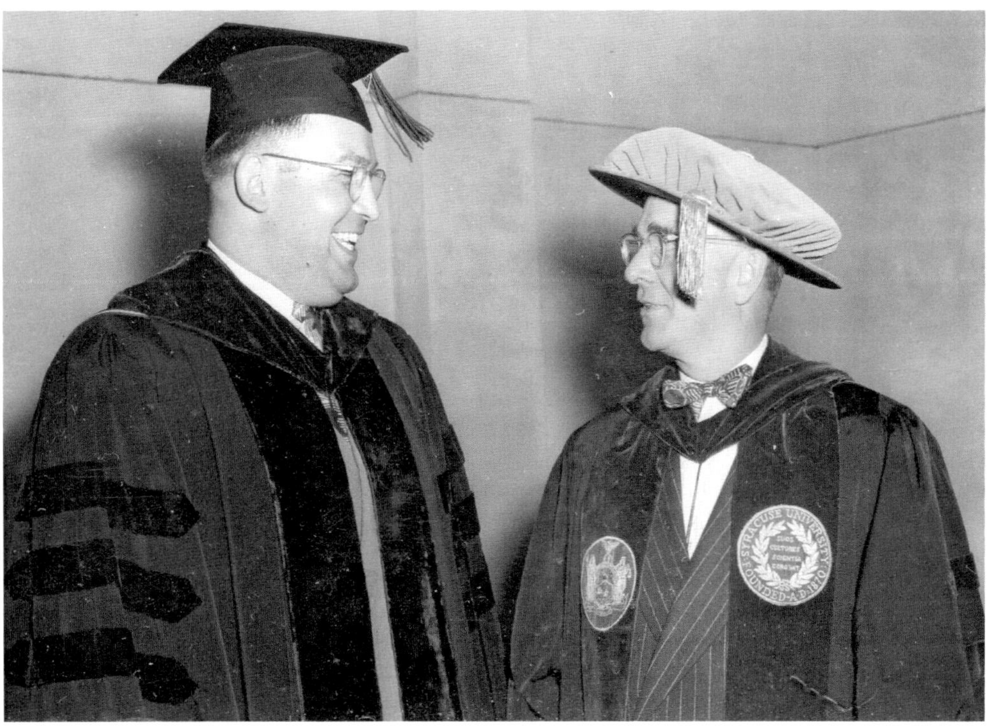

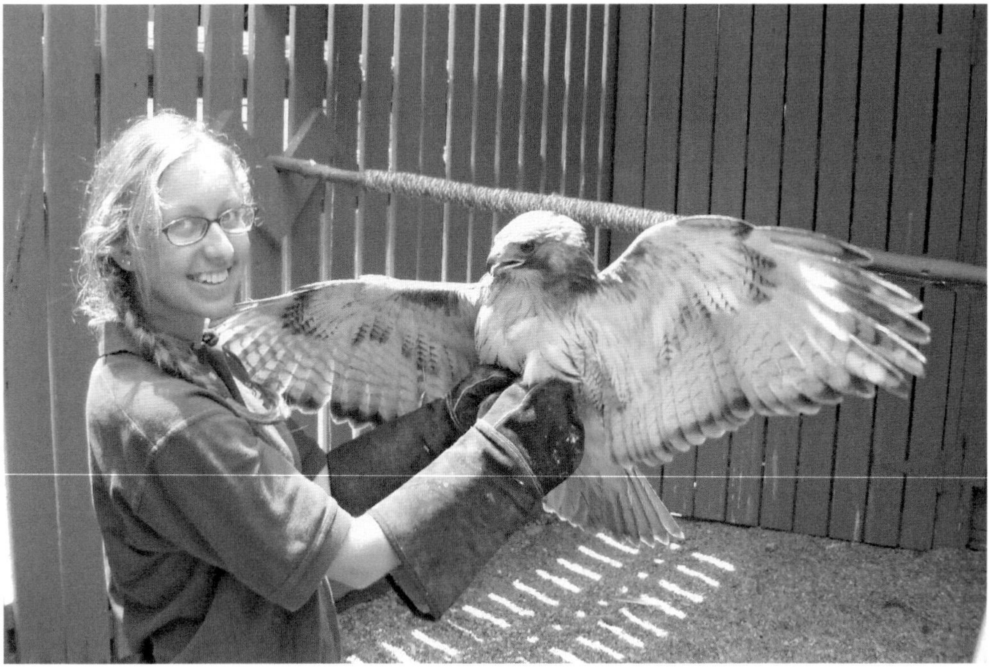

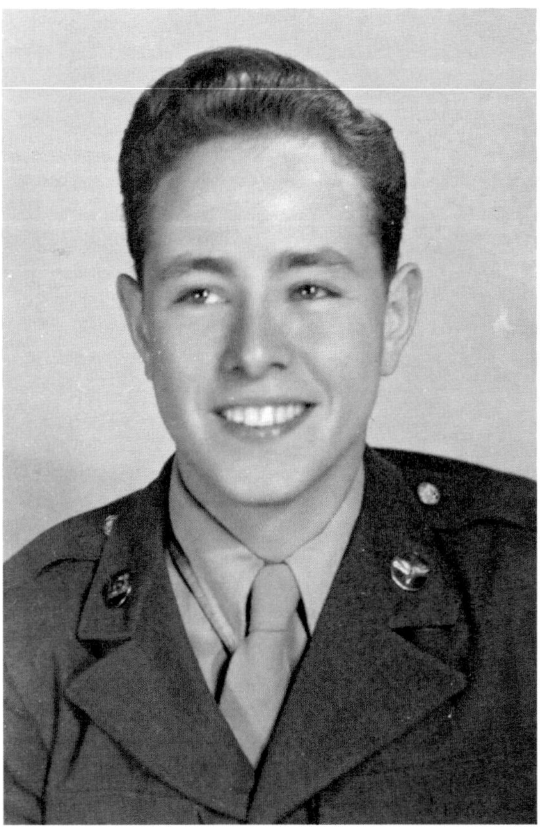

Taylor Hinton. Legend in the Making
Co-salutatorian of the class of 2010, Berea High School, Hinton's major at Allegheny College is environmental studies. During an internship at the Penitentiary Glenn Wildlife Rehabilitation Center in Kirtland, Ohio, she worked caring for wildlife and conducting public educational programs. Next, Hinton hopes to study in Kenya, concentrating on sustainable development in that country, which could include farming techniques, buildings, or energy generation. (Courtesy of Betsy Hinton.)

Robert Beach
An outstanding Baldwin-Wallace alumnus, Beach served the college "loyally and well" for 10 years as director of public relations. Pres. A. B. Bonds expressed disappointment at Beach's resignation to accept a position as assistant to the president of Antioch College. "Beach's combination of skill, insight, wisdom, and loyalty will be difficult to replace," said Bonds.

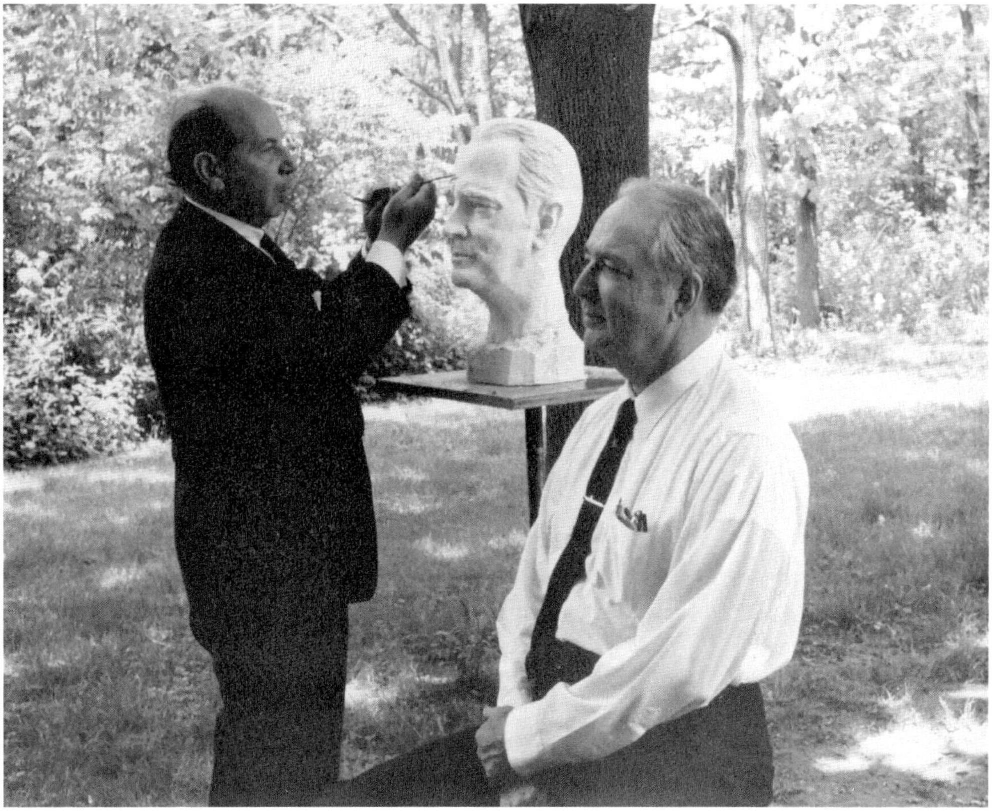

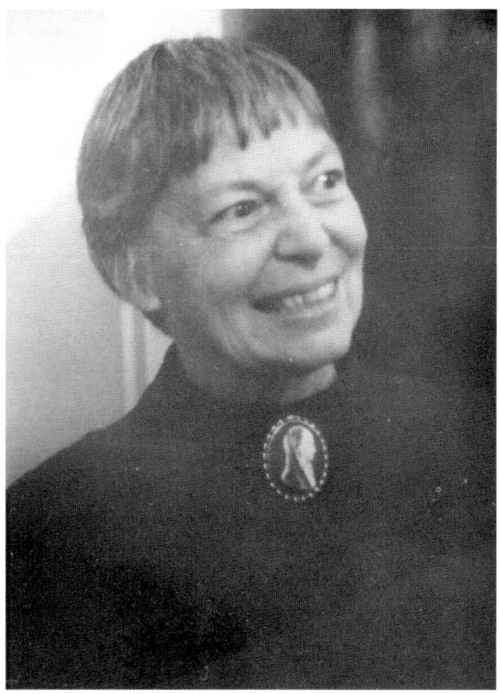

Dr. A.B. Bonds Jr. and Georgianna Bonds
In Alfred Bonds' 26-year tenure as president of Baldwin-Wallace College, his 15-year development plan resulted in an 85 percent increase in enrollment and a dozen new buildings. Dr. Bonds is pictured posing for eminent sculptor Felix de Weldon, a close friend of Bonds from their service together in the US Navy. De Weldon lived with Dr. and Mrs. Bonds in Washington, DC, when he first came to the United States. De Weldon is said to have mixed soft Johnson's floor wax with hard sealing wax on Georgianna Bonds' ironing board for the model of his Marine Corps memorial depicting the raising of the flag on Iwo Jima. After her husband had retired and their four children were grown, Baldwin-Wallace first lady Georgianna Bonds finished writing a family mystery her father had started 75 years before.

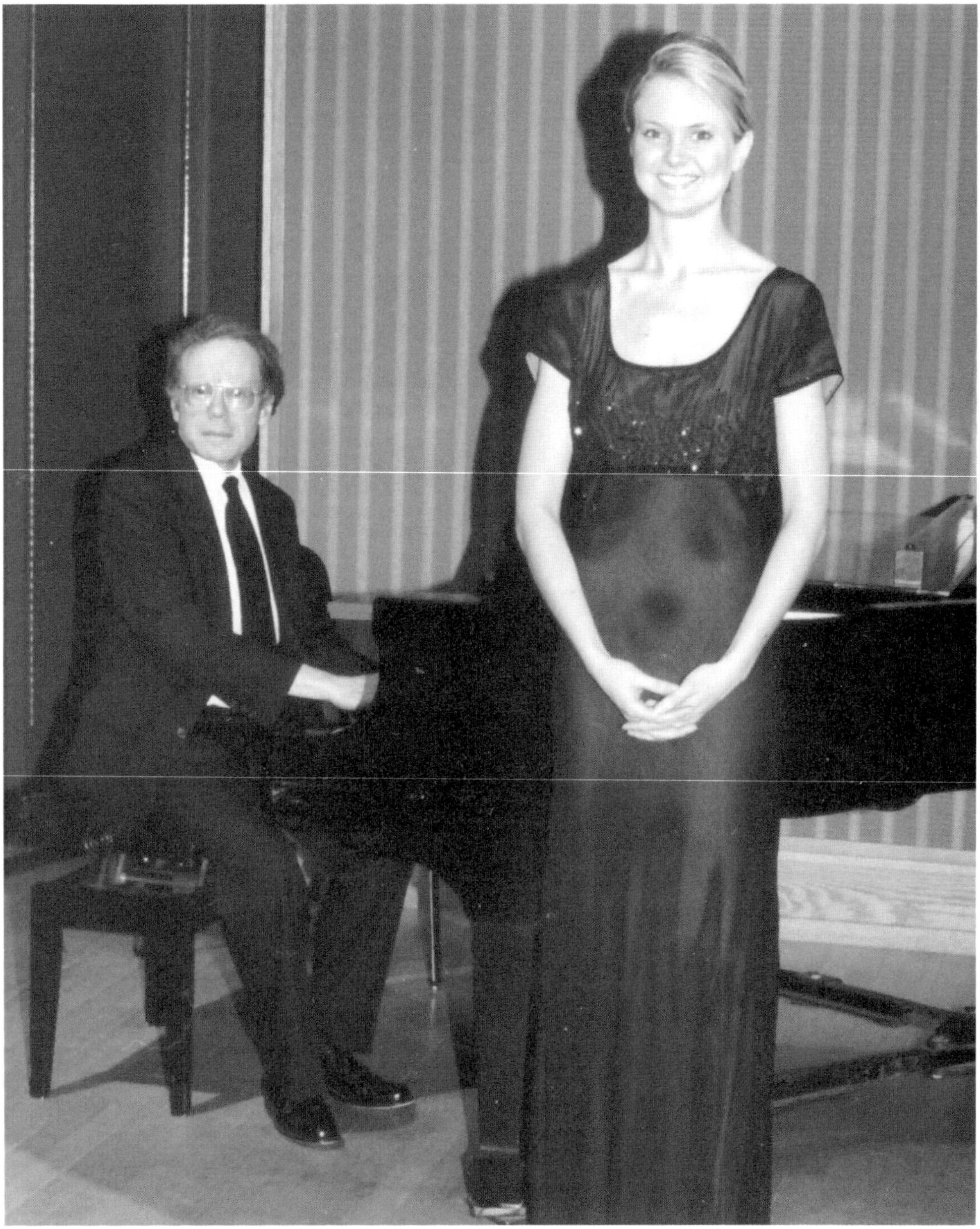

Dr. James Feldman

Feldman, music professor at Baldwin-Wallace College for 32 years, prepares to accompany Gloria A. Kostiuk in recital. When Feldman was stricken with amyotrophic lateral sclerosis (or ALS, more commonly known as Lou Gehrig's Disease), students and alumni organized a tribute and benefit concert in October 2008. Hundreds attended the event in the Berea United Methodist Church. Dr. Feldman was able to enjoy this moving outpouring of gratitude and loyalty. He dedicated his life's work to his students and family, and this was their way to reciprocate. One tribute: "He taught about the human spirit... art is not about mechanical performance but about presenting what is in one's soul." Dr. Feldman died on November 22, 2008. (Courtesy of Charlotte Feldman.)

CHAPTER FOUR

Medicine and Law

Dr. Alexander McBride was Berea's first resident physician. His home on North Rocky River Drive (then the old Rockport Road) is known as the McBride-Cushing home. Built in 1868, it has headquartered the Cleveland Pregnancy Center in recent years. In earlier times, many doctors had clinics or offices attached to their homes. The former home of Dr. Oliver Kechele still stands at the southwest corner of East Bridge and Beech Streets. The doctor's wife, Mrs. Helen Kechele, found this combined house and office to be a mixed blessing. Patients waiting to see the doctor often found their way to her kitchen to visit, keeping her from her household chores. Strange bedfellows were the Clark Cancer Clinic on East Bridge Street and a fossil museum. Dr. William Clark was widely known for his treatment of skin cancer, although he did not disclose his remedies. Clark also collected and exhibited fossilized fish.

The Berea Community Hospital (now Southwest General Health Center) stood at the corner of Front Street and Bagley Road. In 1920, the city purchased a home belonging to Mrs. Eva Sprague, widow of Milton A. Sprague, educator and businessman. Twelve hospital rooms were initially equipped with the stipulation from the Ohio State Hospital Board that a larger, permanent building would be erected in 16 months. This served the community until 1975. Administrator Helen Ott served the hospital for 34 years. The present ever-expanding hospital partners with University Hospitals of Cleveland and has several off-site facilities. It provides employment for many Bereans as well as countless opportunities for volunteers. The Southwest General Health Center Neighborhood Care Center, headed by Dr. Edward White, provides medical care to disadvantaged citizens of Berea and surrounding communities.

Many lawyers had their offices above businesses in the Triangle area. Sylvester Bobinsky, son of a quarryman, practiced law in Berea for 51 years. Bobinsky is said to be the only native son who became a Berea attorney. He lived in the area off South Rocky River Drive, colloquially known as the Hogsback. Active in many civic affairs, Attorney Bobinsky headed the Berea Chamber of Commerce in its early years. When Berea adopted a charter form of government in 1959, Bobinsky served on that commission, as did Judge Joseph Stangel. (see Chapter One).

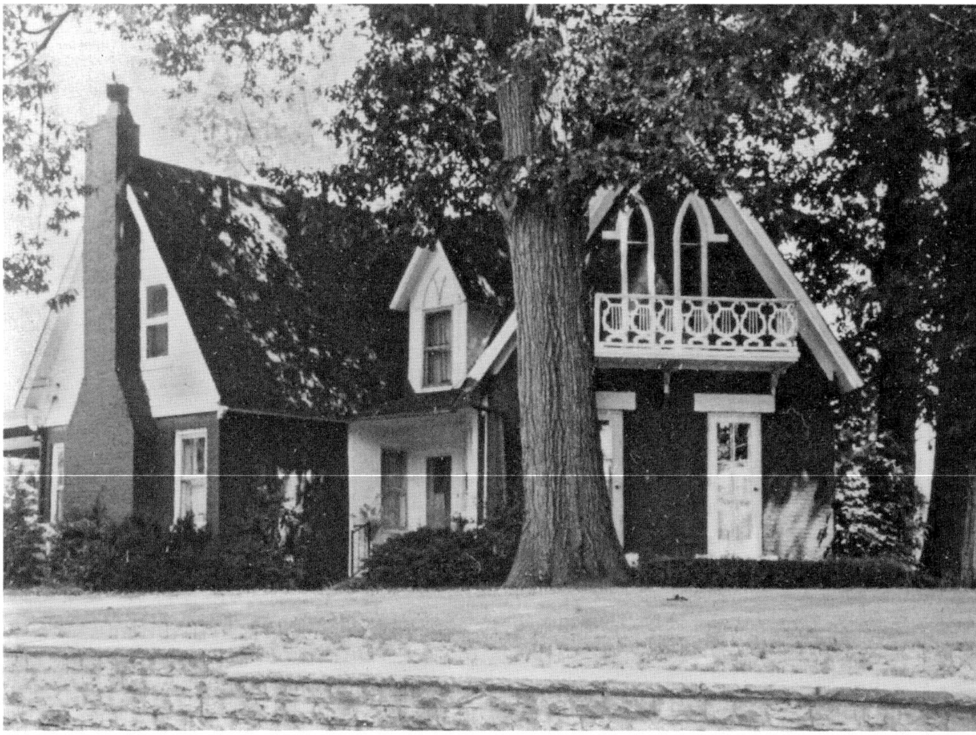

Alexander McBride Home

In 1847, McBride came to Berea, the first physician to locate in the area. He had graduated from the old Cleveland Medical College, a department of Western Reserve College. For 29 years, many families relied upon his skill, and Dr. McBride served many unable to pay. During the Civil War, he was an army surgeon. In recent years, his home (above), built in 1868, became headquarters for the Cleveland Pregnancy Center.

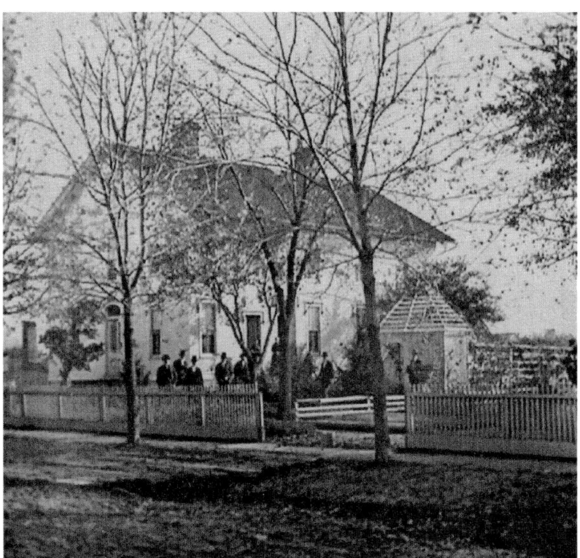

Dr. William Clark's Cancer Clinic

Known as a tireless investigator of ailments, Clark's determination often gave his patients incentive to recover. Besides his general practice, Dr. Clark made a specialty of treating cancers. Patients flocked to his cancer hospital (left) on East Bridge Street. Perhaps his greatest recognition, however, came later in his life when he became well known for his collection of fossils. Certain new species he discovered were named for him. He married Miss Jennie Hepburn after he moved here from Wooster. Two former marriages had ended in his wives' early death.

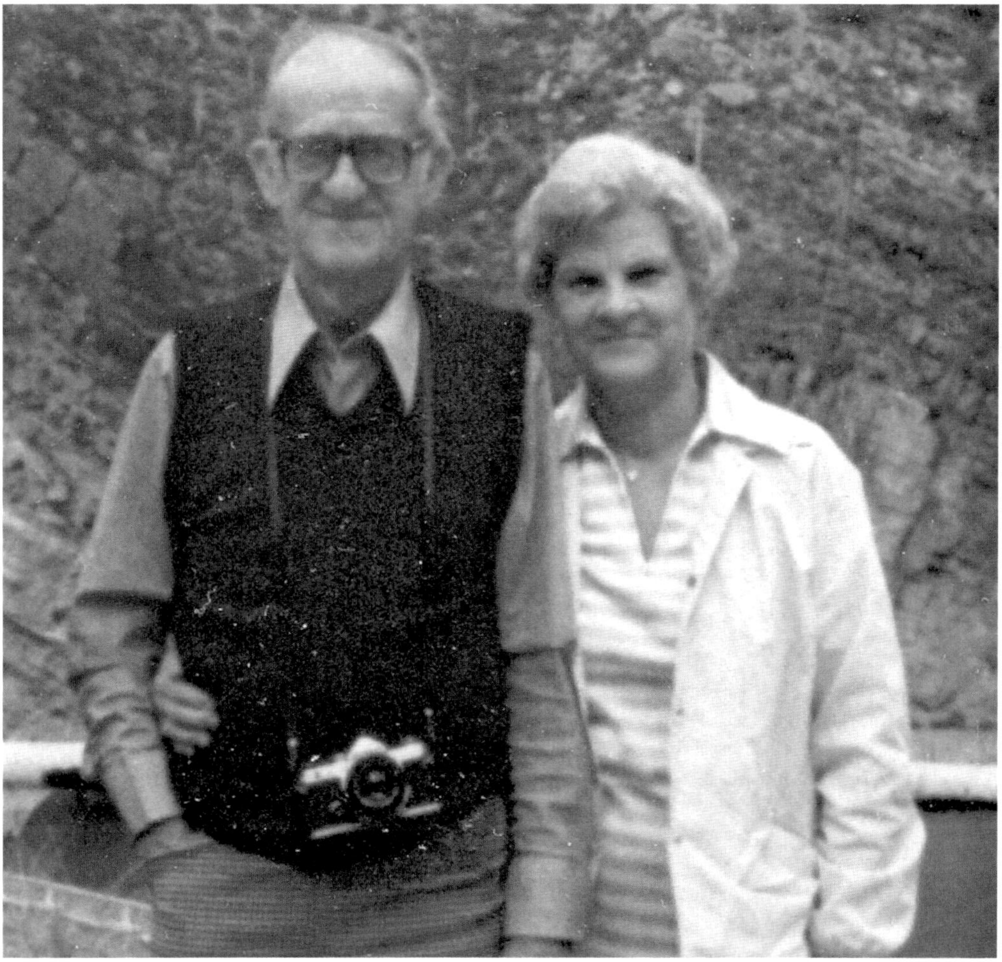

J. Elmer Barnum and Violet (Reicho) Barnum

Elmer Barnum's father, Thomas Barnum, was superintendent of Berea's sandstone quarries for the Cleveland Stone Company. As a boy, Elmer worked in the quarries as a water boy, fetching heavy buckets many times a day from a well 96 steps up a steep hill. His passion for playing the cornet helped put him through law school, playing with dance bands. In the 1930s, he opened his law practice on East Bridge Street and took an active part in community organizations, but his family—wife Violet and three daughters—always came first. He continued playing the cornet in drum corps and in band concerts on the Triangle. One of his favorite moments each year was opening the Baldwin-Wallace Bach Festival, playing his cornet from the tower of Marting Hall. Barnum was an avid horseman and served as president of the Western Saddle Club of America. And he loved a good game at Schuerlein's (or Skip's) Pool Hall on the Triangle, favorite haunt of Berea's movers and shakers. Violet Reicho made the front page of the Berea *News* on Friday March 23, 1928. At age 22, Miss Reicho, assistant to Mayor John R. Southam, became Berea's first police judge. City council passed an ordinance authorizing her to accept only parking and non-stopping tickets, plus $2. She was already well known in the community as she had been an outstanding member of the Berea High School girls' basketball team only a few years before. In August 1929, Miss Reicho traded her gavel for a bouquet of white roses and sweet peas. Wearing a dress of white georgette and a large white hat, she became the bride of Elmer Barnum at St. Mary's rectory. (Courtesy of Shirley Moon.)

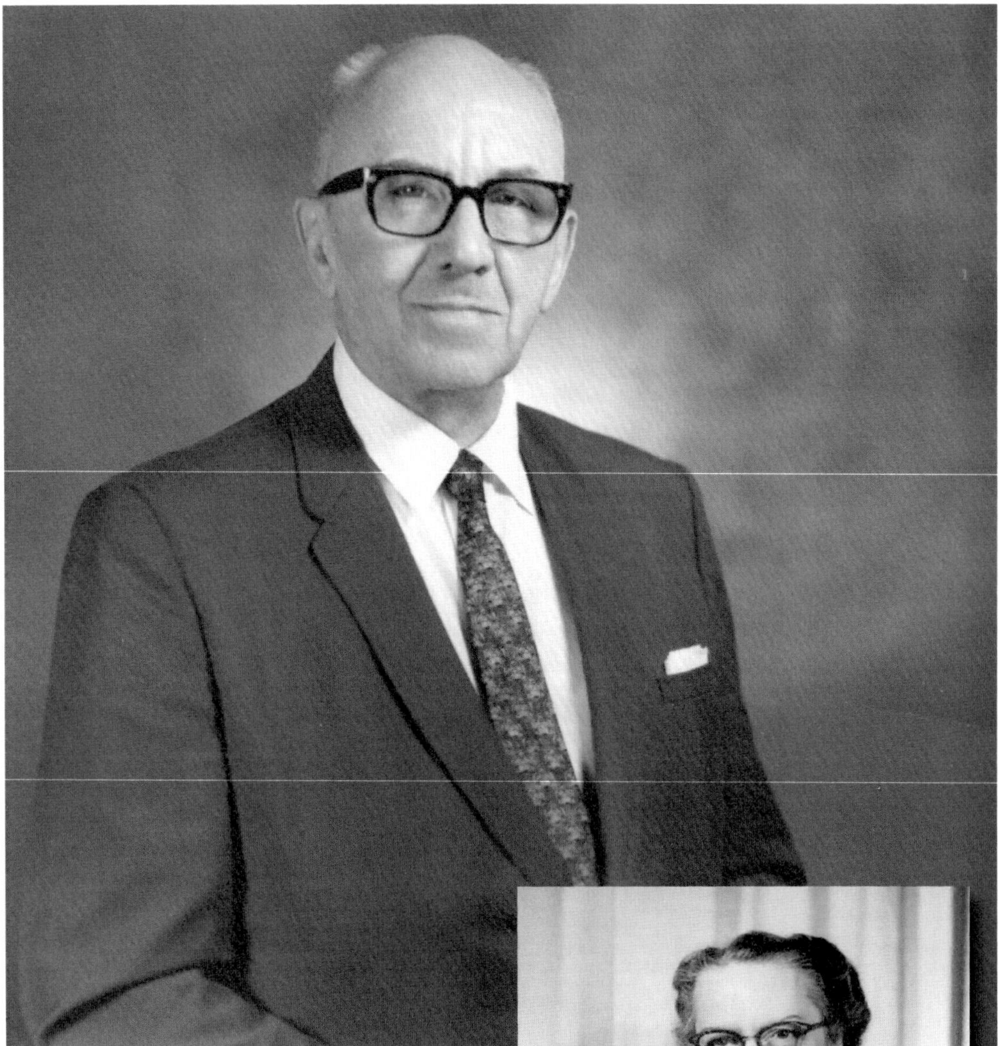

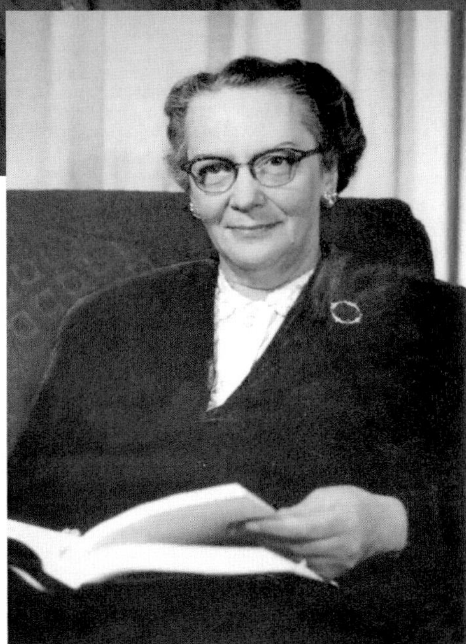

Dr. Oliver Kechele and Mrs. Helen Kechele
The big white house at Beech and East Bridge Street was home to Dr. Oliver Kechele, his wife Helen, and their two daughters. In an attached office, the doctor saw his patients. This was a common arrangement in those days. Dr. Kechele served in the medical corps during World War II. One city elected official claims he was told he was the last baby Dr. Kechele delivered before he went off to serve his country. The good doctor appeared at his patient's bedside and took care of the delivery—in his uniform! Helen Kechele kept busy working for the Red Cross, and she belonged to the guild at the local hospital. (Courtesy of Suzanne Simpson.)

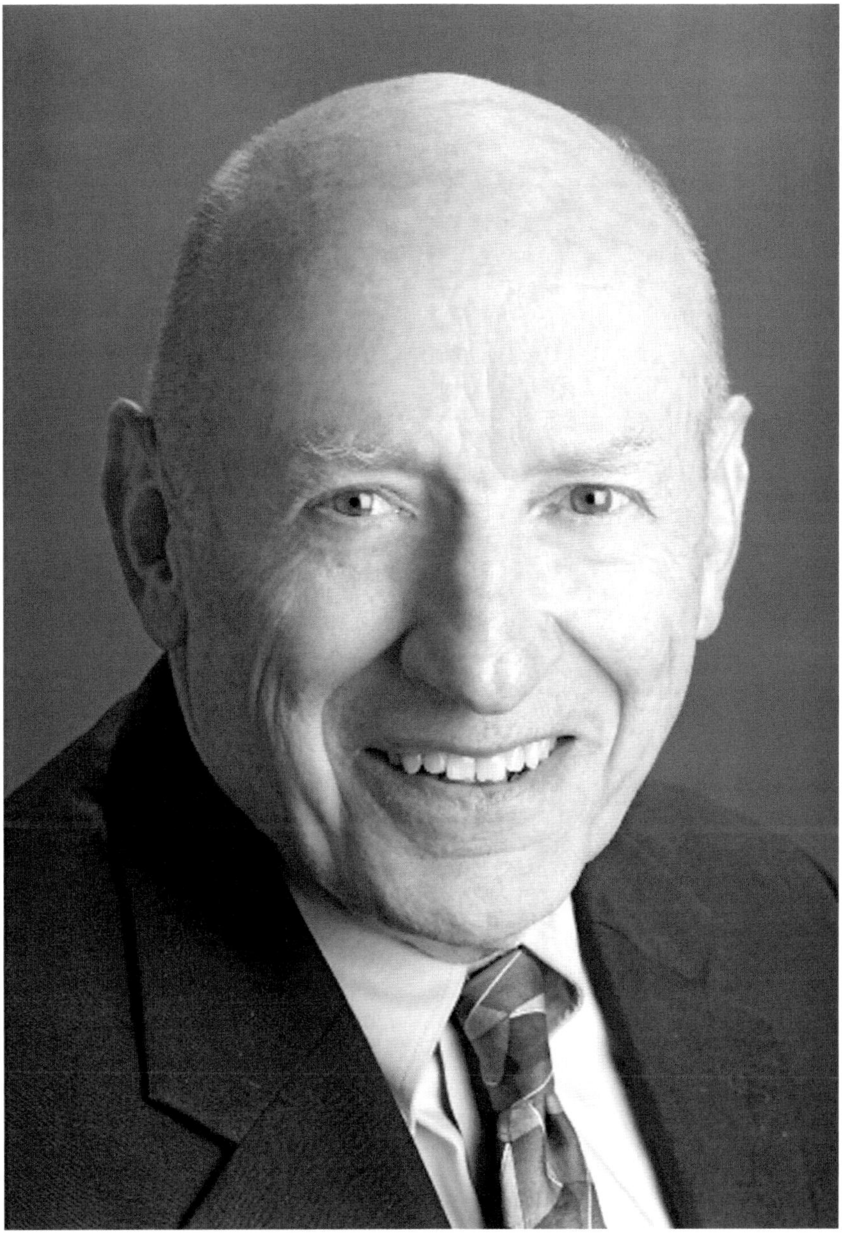

Dr. Edward White

In 1963, well-known Berea physician, Lechner, invited a young doctor to join his practice at 10 Beech Street. Edward White and his wife Diane soon realized that living and practicing medicine in Berea was right for them. Eventually, Dr. White became a member of Southwest Family Physicians. Community involvement has always been a major focus of Dr. White's life. He has been cited for his charitable work as well as for his longtime membership on the Berea schools' board of education and his service with the city's North End Foundation. After retiring from private practice, Dr. White became director of the Southwest General Health Center Neighborhood Care Center, providing medical services to economically disadvantaged citizens of Berea and surrounding communities.

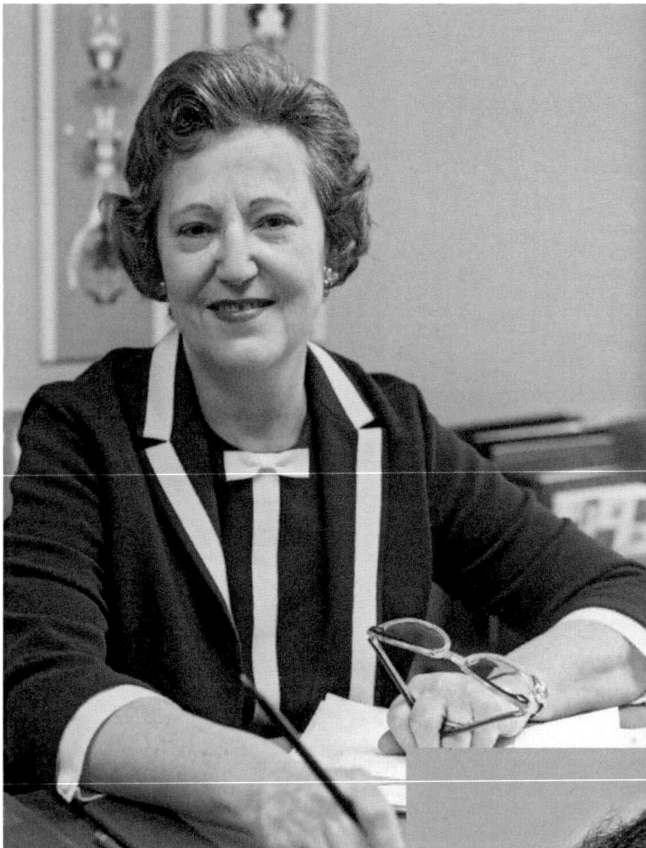

Helen Ott
Miss Ott was employed by Berea Community Hospital (now Southwest General Health Center) for 35 years, 25 of those as chief administrator. Under her leadership, the hospital underwent four major additions, growing from 32-bed capacity to 180 beds, and increased its staff from 50 to more than 475. She was a founder of the Berea Business and Professional Women's Club. (Courtesy of Southwest General Health Center.)

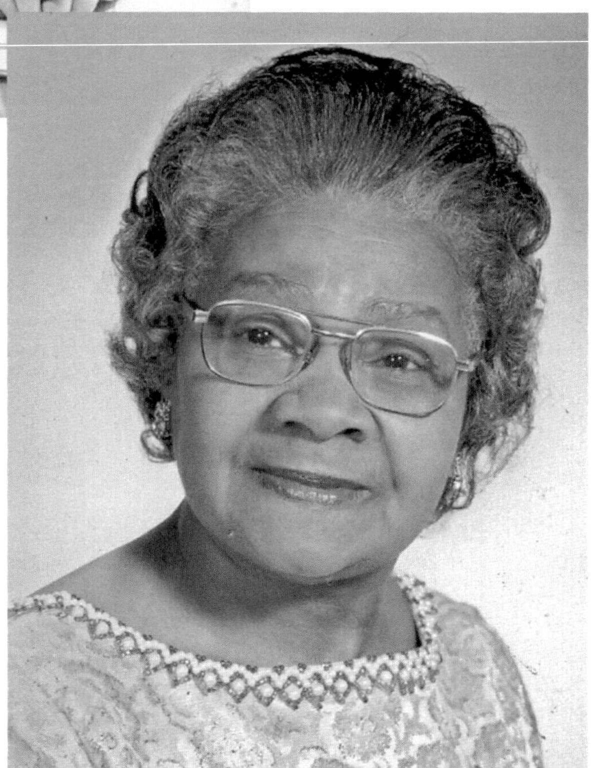

Ruth Taylor
Taylor, the first woman to be named Berea's Outstanding Citizen of the Year, was a licensed practical nurse at Southwest General Hospital for 24 years. Mrs. Taylor previously served several other hospitals as a dietitian and also operated a catering business. She had a home economics degree from Wilberforce University. Mrs. Taylor took a keen interest in others and was involved in civic affairs.

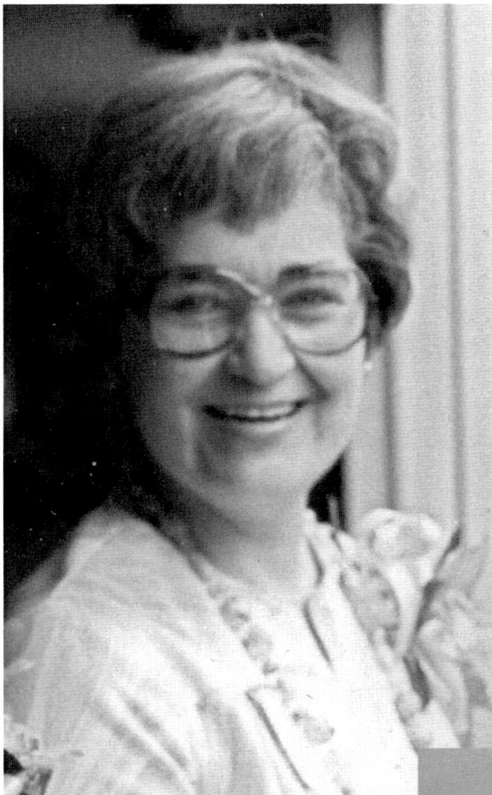

Patricia Boenker
At one time Boenker's volunteer recognition pin read 1,521 volunteer hours in a year at Southwest General Hospital. For many years, she was seen in the hospital corridors nearly every day. Boenker was chairman of the buyers for the Corner (gift) Shop for 20 years and president of the guild several times. "The only right we have is the right to be useful," she has been quoted as saying.

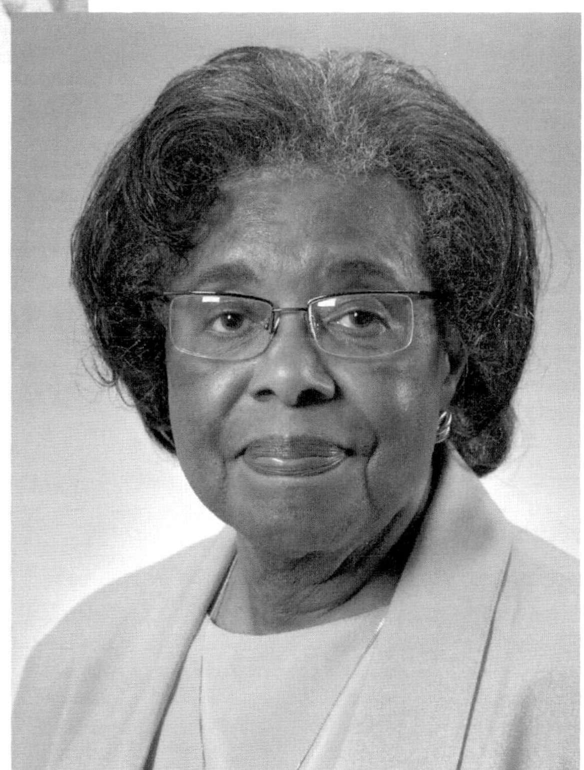

Daisy Collins Russell
Berea High School's 1954 valedictorian, Daisy G. Collins, graduated *cum laude* from both The Ohio State University and the Howard University of Law. After engaging in private practice for some years, she became an assistant US attorney for the Northern District of Ohio. Attorney Collins retired from her position as federal administrative law judge in February 1994. She has a passionate interest in reparations for African Americans. Now as a volunteer tutor at an elementary school, she has students repeat: "Knowledge is power. I can learn." Then she tells them, "I have great expectations for you to learn." Ms. Collins credits her parents, the late Luevinia and Booker T. Collins, for providing a stable Christian home and making it possible for her to succeed. (Courtesy of Daisy Collins.)

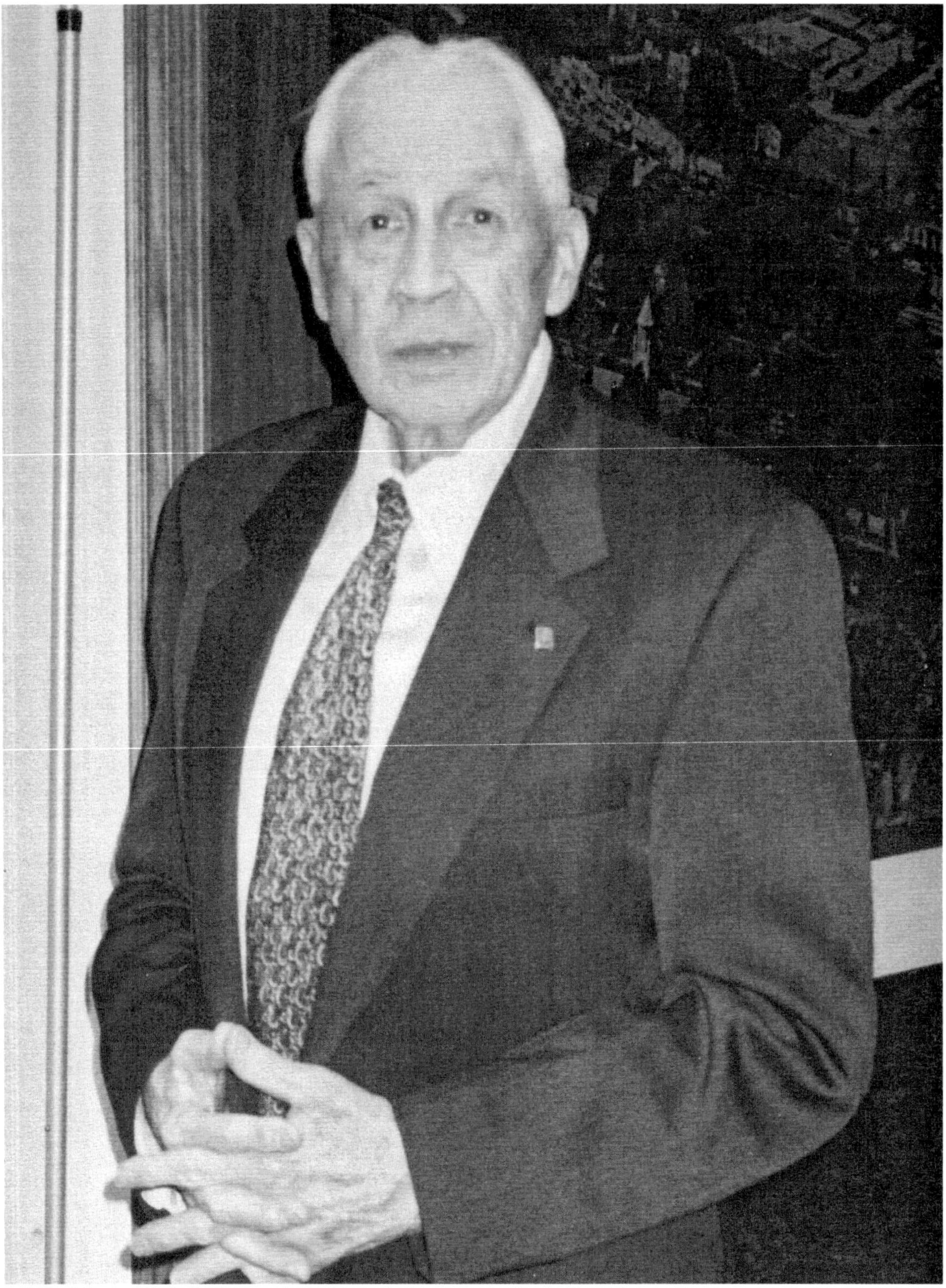

Sylvester (Syl) Bobinsky

Want to learn the history of that part of Berea once known as the Hogsback (off what is now South Rocky River Drive)? Syl Bobinsky's recorded interviews housed at the Berea Historical Society will fill you in. Bobinsky, whose father worked in the sandstone quarries, was born and raised in Berea. A Gold Bar alumnus of Case Western University School of Law, Bobinsky practiced law in Berea for 51 years.

CHAPTER FIVE

Business and Industry

Anyone who studies Berea's history will notice a remarkable occurrence: It would appear that some of the same families have been in business for more than 100 years. In a few cases, that is true: Shaft's Grocery and C.S. Johns Jewelry, for example. In a number of others, however, the owners have changed, but they chose to retain the original names. So a walk around the town in the early years of the 21st century will still take you past establishments named Baker, Gorman, and Brown. Yet these merchants have long since passed away. New owners either paid tribute to the founders of the business or were savvy about name recognition. Or common sense may have prevailed. Ken McCarthy, who bought Gorman's Photo and Art in the 1970s, says he preferred keeping the Gorman name since "McCarthy's sounded like a pub."

At the beginning of the 20th century, Berea business owners organized the Berea Board of Trade. Among the original officers were carriage maker (previously school superintendent) M.A. Sprague, E.S. Loomis, and Edward J. Kennedy. The membership consisted of nearly all Berea's business leaders. The organization's task was to promote industrial growth and attract manufacturers to the community by providing an environment favorable to business. The Dunham Company, founded by three Dunham brothers in the 1860s and maker of agricultural equipment, expanded to produce castings for auto manufacturers. Clarence Fox took over the toy manufacturing business from his father, John Fox. An educational spelling board, produced by Foxy Toyd on Lincoln Avenue, became a national success. The Ohio Nut and Bolt Company is still headquartered on Lou Groza Boulevard at Front Street. Their General Fastener Division is now located in the neighboring community of Brook Park. Ohio Nut and Bolt has enjoyed a long history of successful operation and has had many veteran employees. Several of its original officers were professors, namely J.C. Marting of German Wallace College and E.S. Loomis, former professor of mathematics at Baldwin University. This company, originated in the Berea Board of Trade, played an important role in the expansion of the civic and business life of the community.

By the 1950s, the Board of Trade had given way to the Berea Chamber of Commerce. Nearly all business owners took an active part in the community's activities, according to references in the Berea *Advertiser* (later Berea News). They put forth a model that business owners are following today. The Downtown Merchants and the Berea Chamber of Commerce sponsor many observances and activities designed to draw residents to the downtown Berea area.

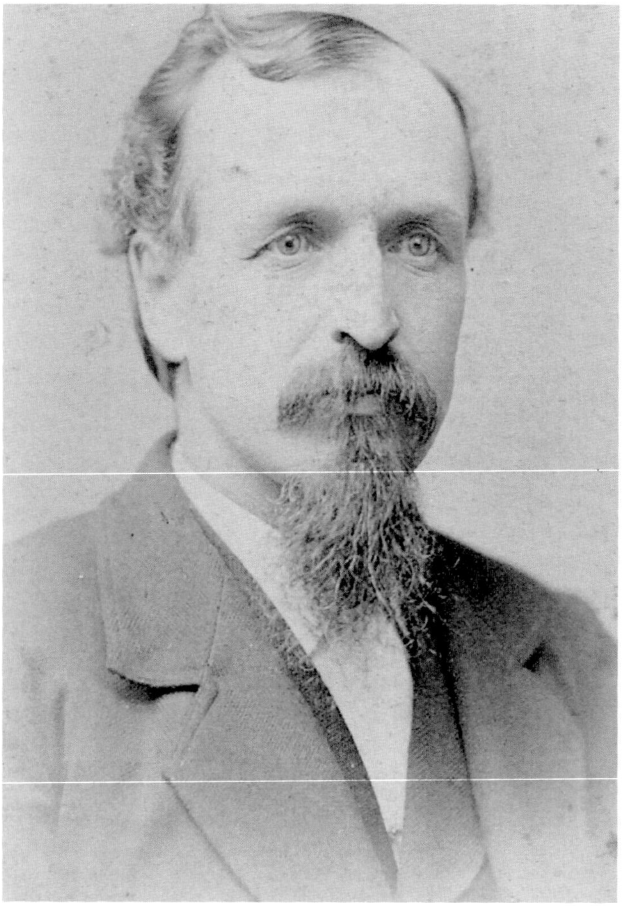

Milton A. Sprague

After teaching at the Union School from 1872 to 1882, Sprague purchased the Berea Carriage Works. The building was not new to him as it had been built for Berea's first high school, which he had attended. The shop and all its contents were destroyed in a fire that started in the Cleveland Berea Interurban car barns on Christmas Day, 1903.

Sprague Carriage Works

Mr. Sprague stated to the *Enterprise* that the burned building was worth $2,000 and the stock $8,500. A $3,000 insurance policy covered the harnesses, but they were not burned.

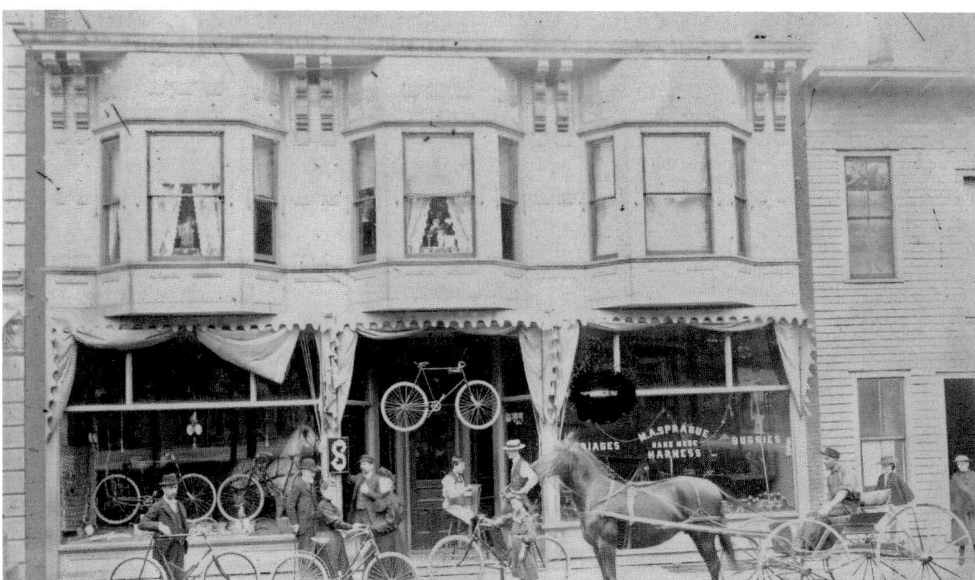

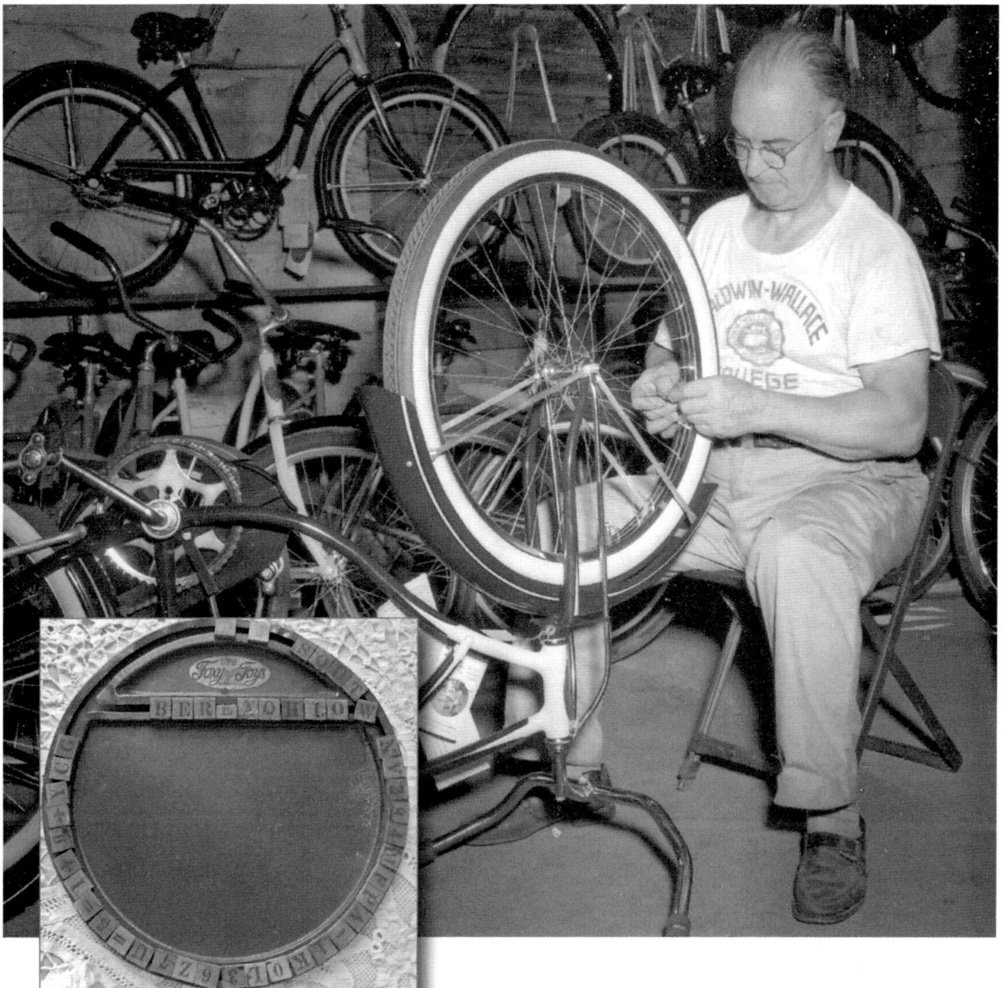

Clarence Fox and **Foxy Toys**

Fox was secretary and general manager of J.H. Fox and Son, a toy company founded by his father in 1903. Located at Lincoln Avenue and Columbus Street, the company expanded and added new equipment to meet the rapidly increasing demand. The company incorporated in 1920 and manufactured toys until 1935. Foxy Toys began by manufacturing novelties but became known for educational toys. The most popular toy was the spelling board. Others included a wall-hung blackboard, an easel blackboard, and a device to test manual dexterity. It was a box with dents in the bottom. The object was to roll the marble to the correct depression. Clarence Fox was a governor of Ohio District Kiwanis and a Berea village councilman. One cold January day in 1933, he was a hero in a $35,000 robbery of the Commercial and Savings Bank on Front Street. He wrested the gun from one of the two robbers as they were making their getaway. Fox shot at him five times, and two of the bullets wounded the robber, and he fell to the pavement. He was taken to the prison ward in City Hospital, Cleveland. The other robber commandeered a truck and escaped with the cash but was later captured. Fox had another career as owner of Campus Cycle Shop. He started out repairing bicycles and renting them to college students and then added new bike sales. He and his son John operated the business on Beech Street. Clarence Fox was a familiar sight, making his daily trip to the Triangle on his bicycle for lunch, coattails flying. (Photograph of spelling board by Susan Lee.)

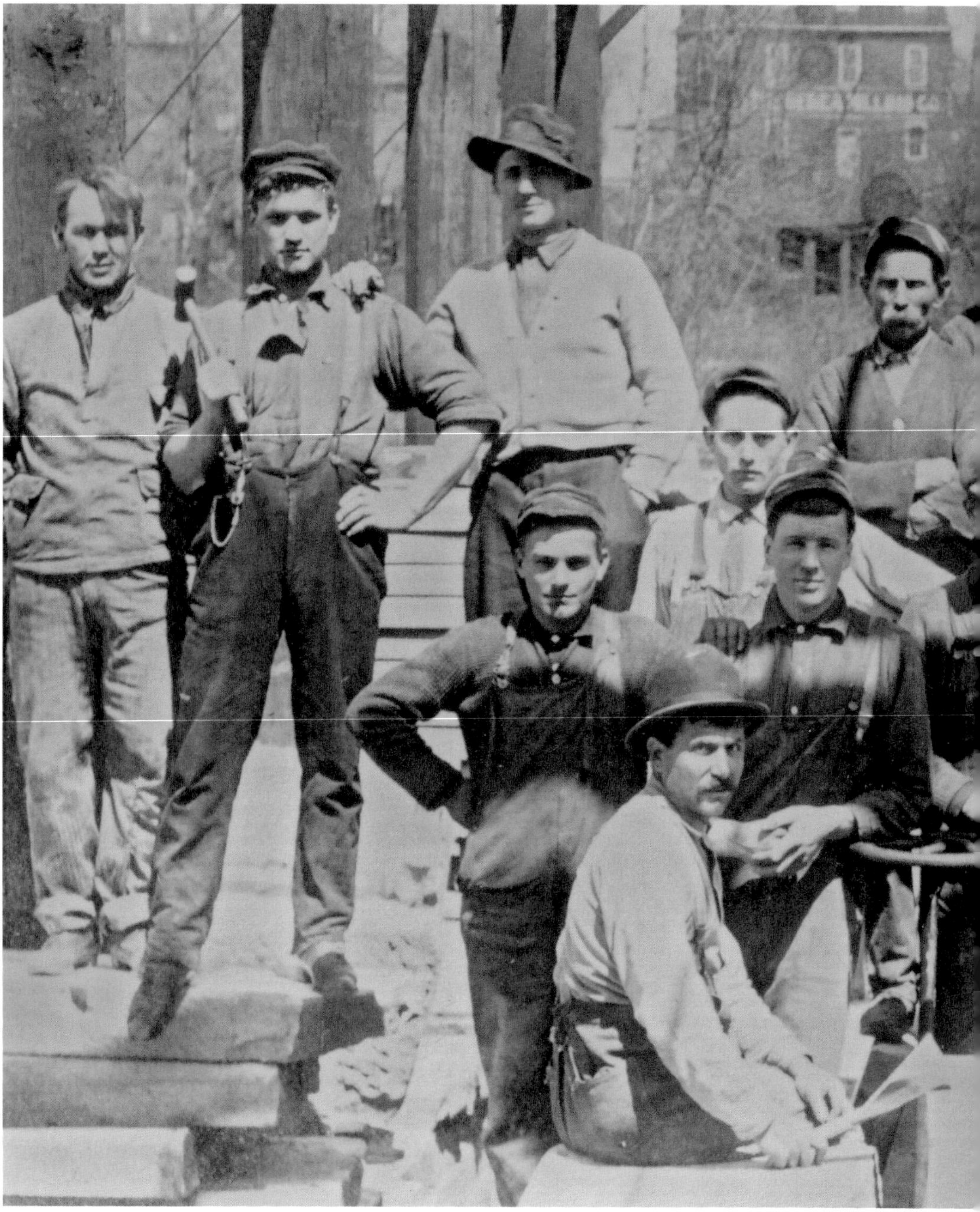

Quarrymen of Berea

Most immigrants to Berea came from southern and eastern Europe. They sought a better way of life for themselves and their families. Quarrying was treacherous work, though. Accidents were frequent and often fatal. And there was that Berea dust. Yet they were strong, courageous folk who loved their families and their churches and left an indelible stamp of greatness on this growing community. Many descendants still live here.

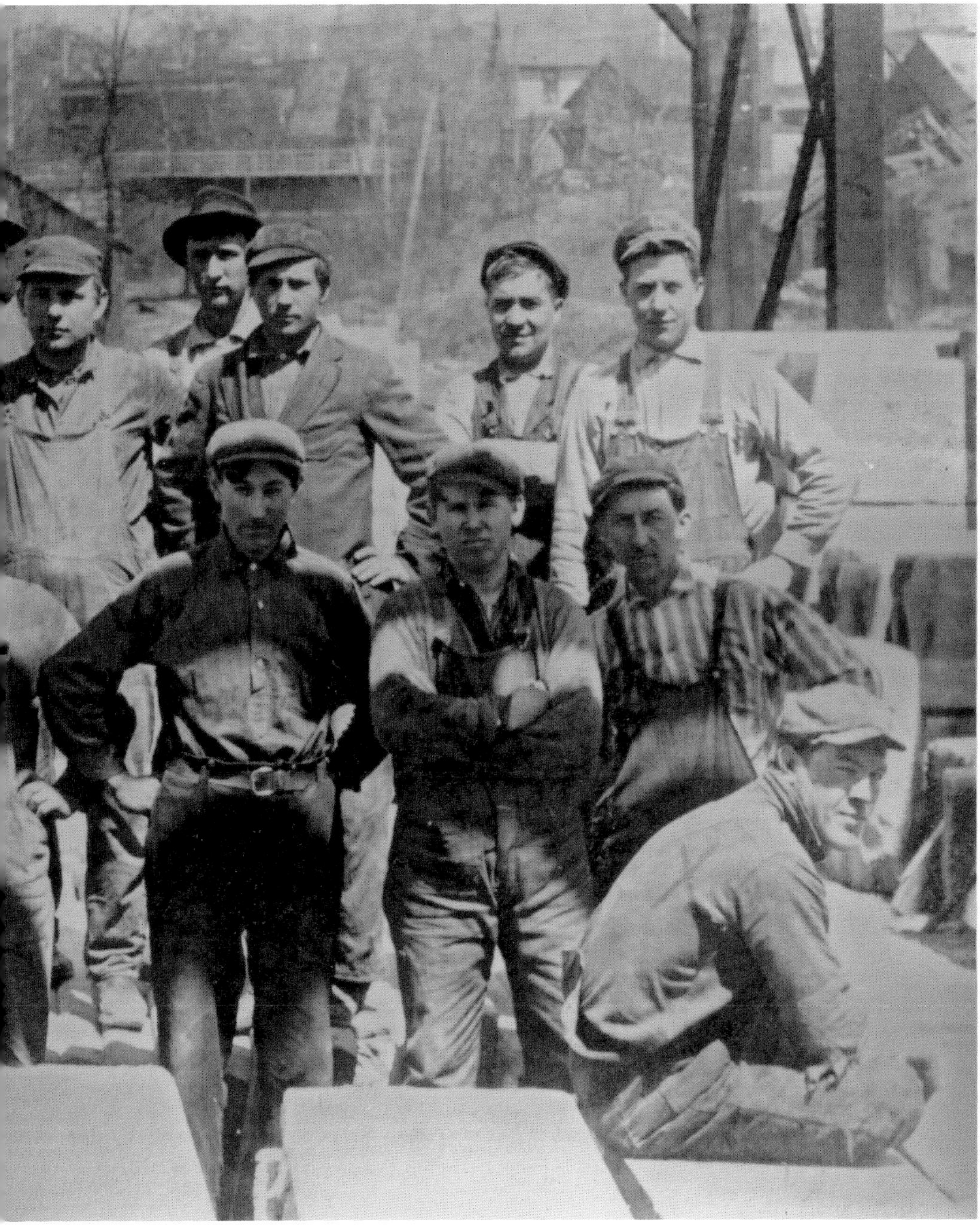

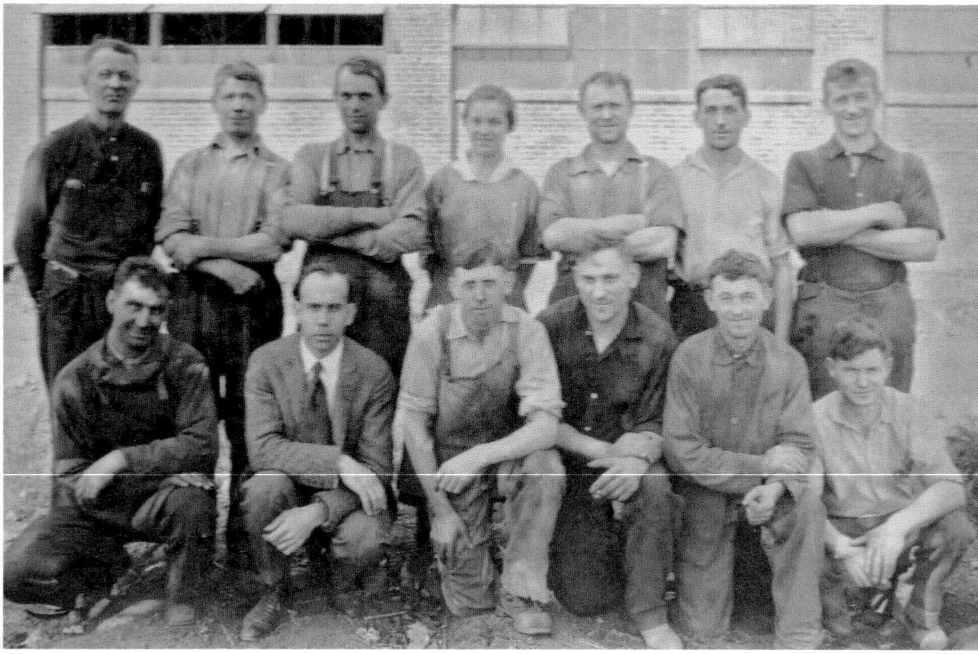

Dunham Company and Culti-weeder

Until the Dunham Foundry arrived in 1890, the quarries represented Berea's only sizable industry. The Dunham Company, owned by several generations of Dunhams, patented the "culti-packer" and "culti-weeder" and eventually made castings and flywheels for the auto industry. Although it failed during the Depression, the company had expanded the area's economy. This photo from around 1920 shows the size of the Dunham Company's payroll at that time.

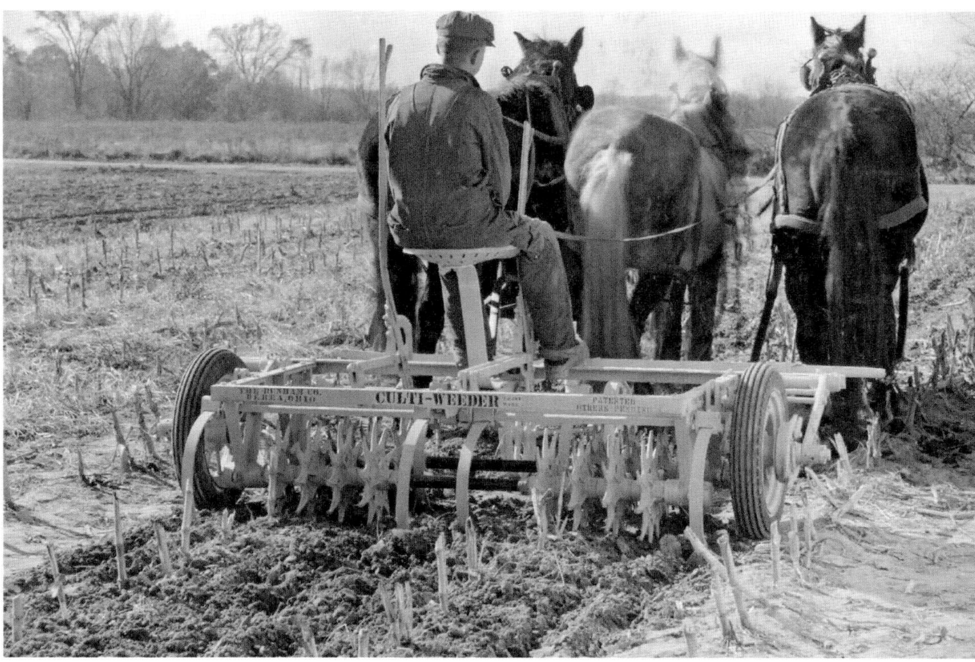

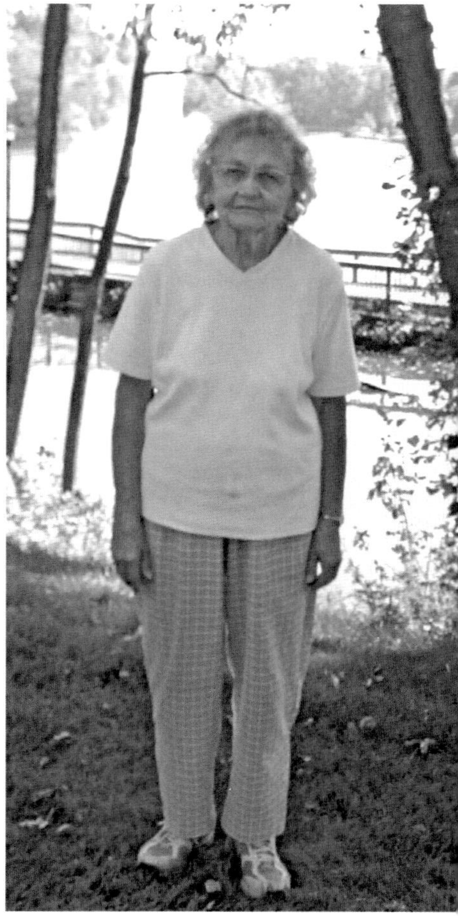

Sophia (Sophie) Golinski

Golinski came to Berea as a bride in 1946 when her husband Ralph took over the grocery his father, Joseph, operated. Through the years of raising four children, Sophie helped in the store until customers dwindled to a mere handful a day. Supermarkets were sealing the doom of many "Mom-and-Pop" stores. A few months after Ralph died in 1969, Sophie closed the doors of Golinski's Grocery. It had been a landmark and gathering place in Berea's North End for 40 years. Neighborhood children cried when they heard "Aunt Sophie" would no longer be selling them penny candy from the old glass candy case. Customers said they would miss the homey atmosphere. But Sophie Golinski didn't just sit down and rock after she closed her store. She worked for many years in the food service department of Fairwood School, and her life has always been filled with ways to help others. She speaks fluent Polish and often was called on as a translator by hospitals and the courts. When Baldwin-Wallace College began its Institute for Learning in Retirement, Sophie walked Berea streets, searching out locations for the classes. She has always been active at St. Adalbert's Church, still helping to make hundreds of nut rolls at holidays, for instance, and singing in the choir. She enjoys meeting for lunch each month with other retired staff members from Fairwood School. Although she is now past 90 and lives in a retirement home, Golinski is grateful it is near scenic Coe Lake. Using a wheeled walker ("just for security," she says), Sophie Golinski walks two miles every day. "I've never been one to sit and do nothing. A few years ago, friends and I were walking to Strongsville and back every day. That was eight miles." (Photo by Patricia Mote.)

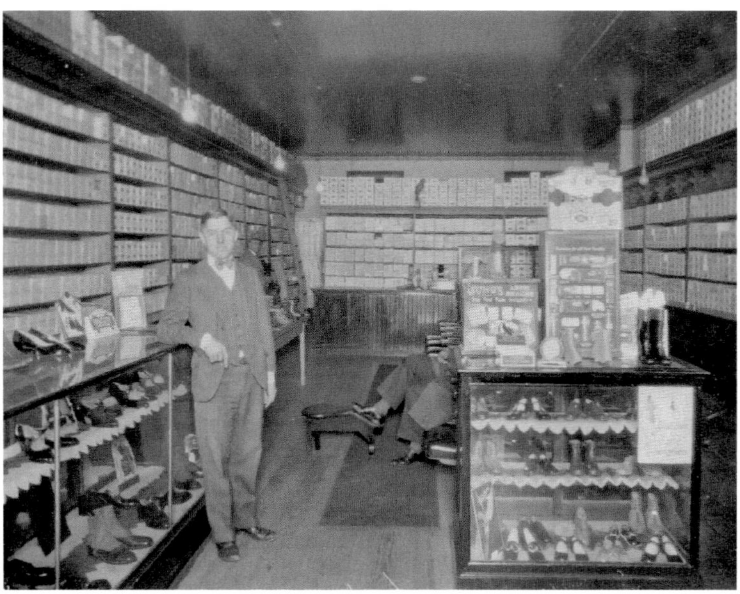

Fred G. Schuerlein

In 1910, Schuerlein was an errand boy at the Neubrand Shoe Company. He worked up to clerk and then manager. In 1937, after 10 years as manager, he owned the thriving Front Street business established in 1859 by George Neubrand, a German bootmaker. Schuerlein added a foot x-ray machine as a free service in 1959 to aid in fitting shoes more carefully.

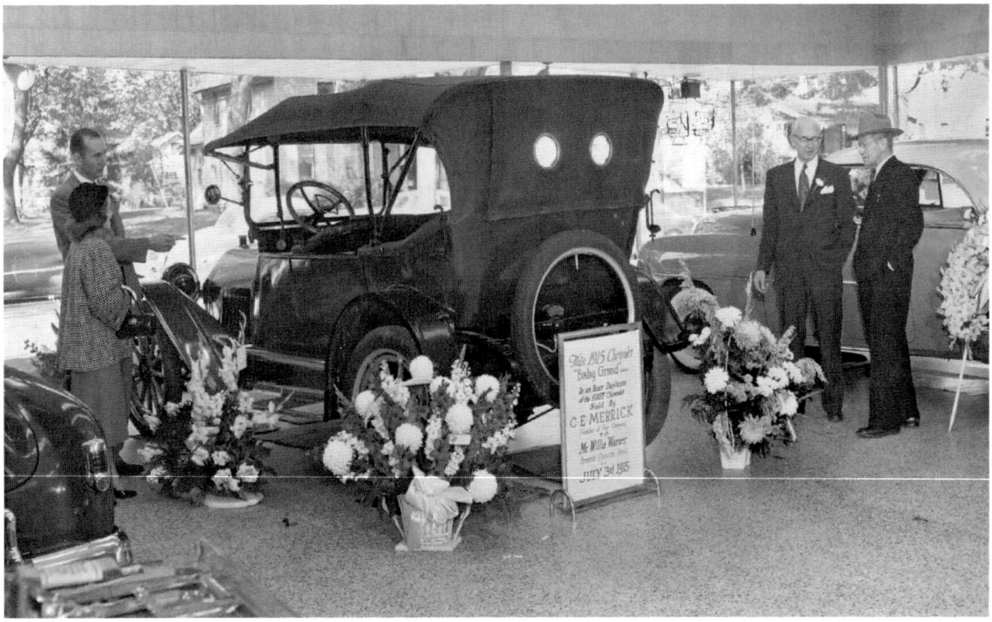

William H. Ragg

Throughout his youth, Ragg (left) worked at the Merrick Chevrolet agency founded by his grandfather, Charles Merrick, in 1915. Ragg became a leader in the auto sales industry, both locally and nationally. He attributed his success to working under his father, Wilbur Ragg, (right) in every facet of the business. The 1915 Chevrolet on display celebrates the firm's 75th anniversary.

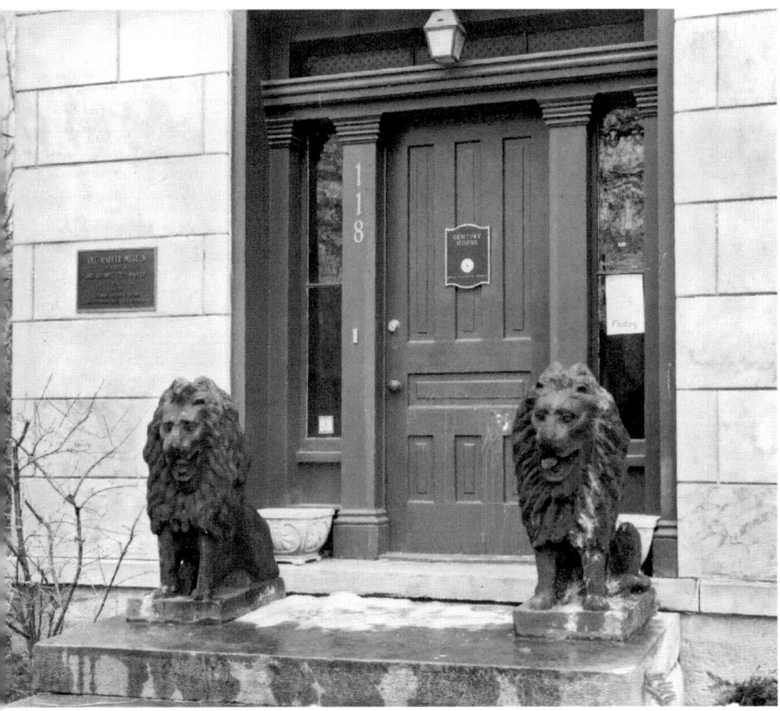

Fred and Rosie

These sandstone lions, carved by Gus Barendt, a stonecutter from Germany, once looked over downtown Berea from the top of the Bullinger Block. Bullinger's stone building and the lions survived the 1899 fire that destroyed most of Berea's businesses that were built of wood. Affectionately named for Fred and Rosina Bullinger, today they stand at the entrance to the Mahler Museum.

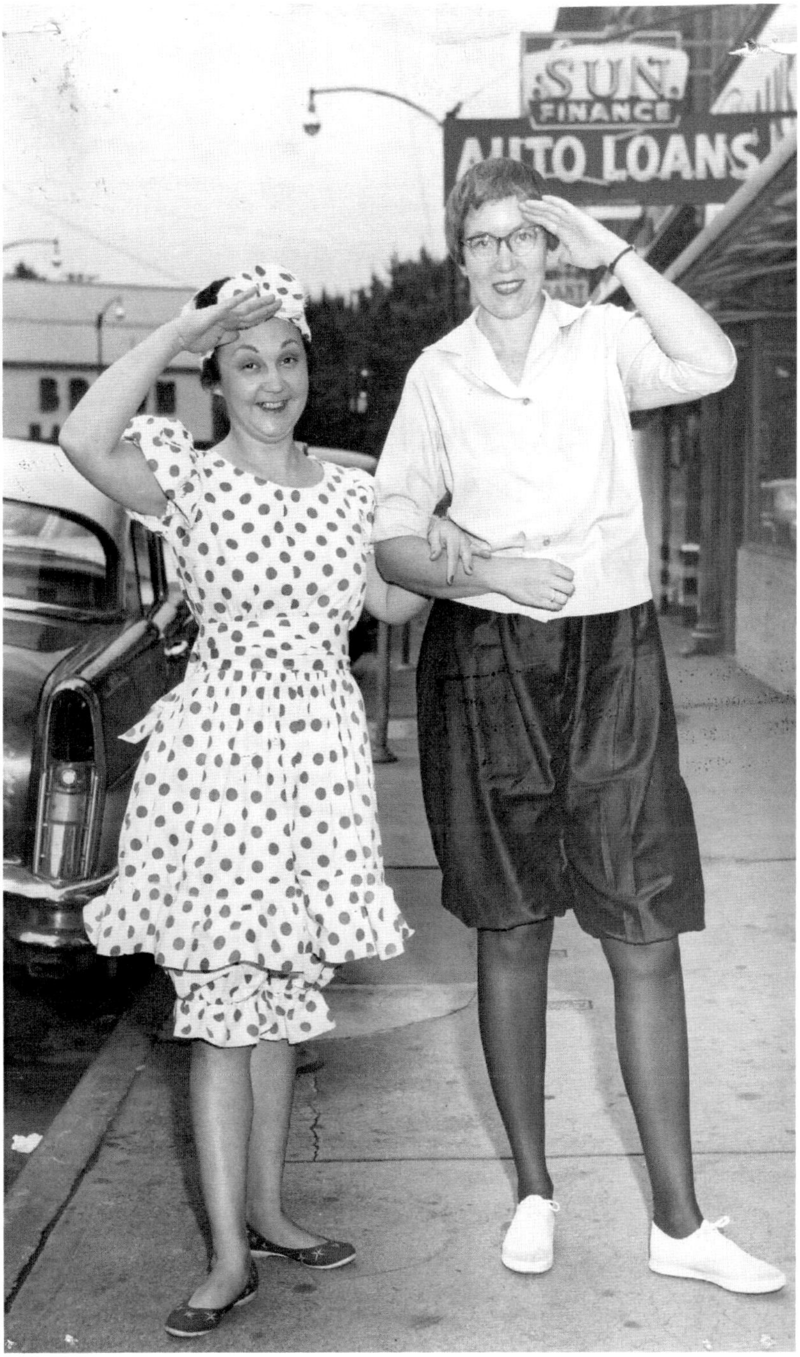

Elizabeth Ragg

For 37 years, this veteran Berea businesswoman owned and operated Elizabeth Ragg Gifts. One of the first tenants of the Parkway Shops, she was always active in community affairs. Ragg (right) poses as an 1890s bloomer girl with Mary Jane Gorman as an 1890s bathing beauty. The occasion was an old-fashioned street bazaar in downtown Berea.

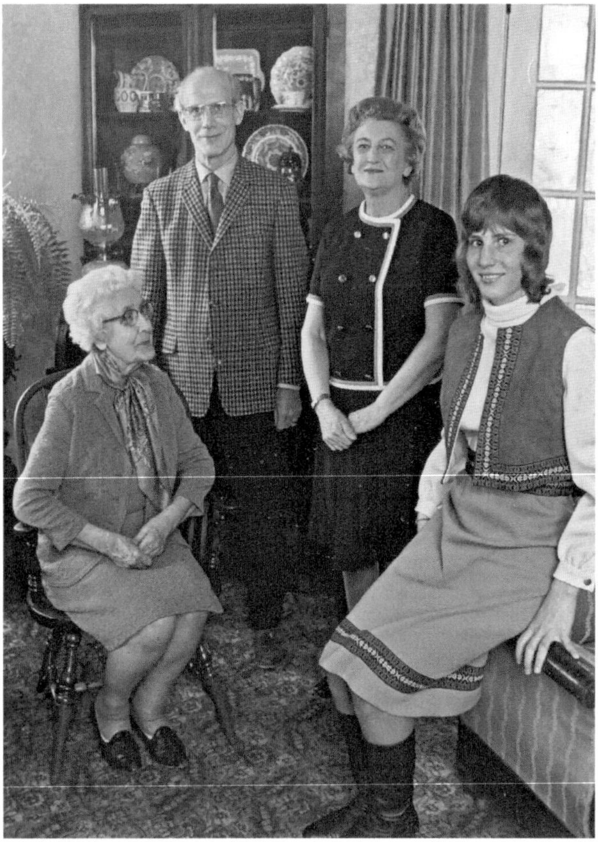

Eldon P. and Arlene J. Roe

E. P. Roe's Inc. women's millinery and accessory stores had 17 retail shops located from Buffalo to Chicago. After retiring from his business in the early 1980s, Roe established the Roe Millinery Museum to display his collection of more than 200 women's hats. He was well known in local politics and as a peace activist, a musician, and a collector of antique farm tools. In 1952, the Roe family purchased the historic home that John Baldwin Jr. built in 1859 (below). The Roes were the first owners who were not descendants of the Baldwin family. Arlene Roe, Baldwin-Wallace graduate and May Queen of 1934, devoted her life to her family, her community, and her alma mater. (From left) Mrs. Elias Roe, Eldon Roe, Arlene Roe, and Jane Roe in the early 1960s.

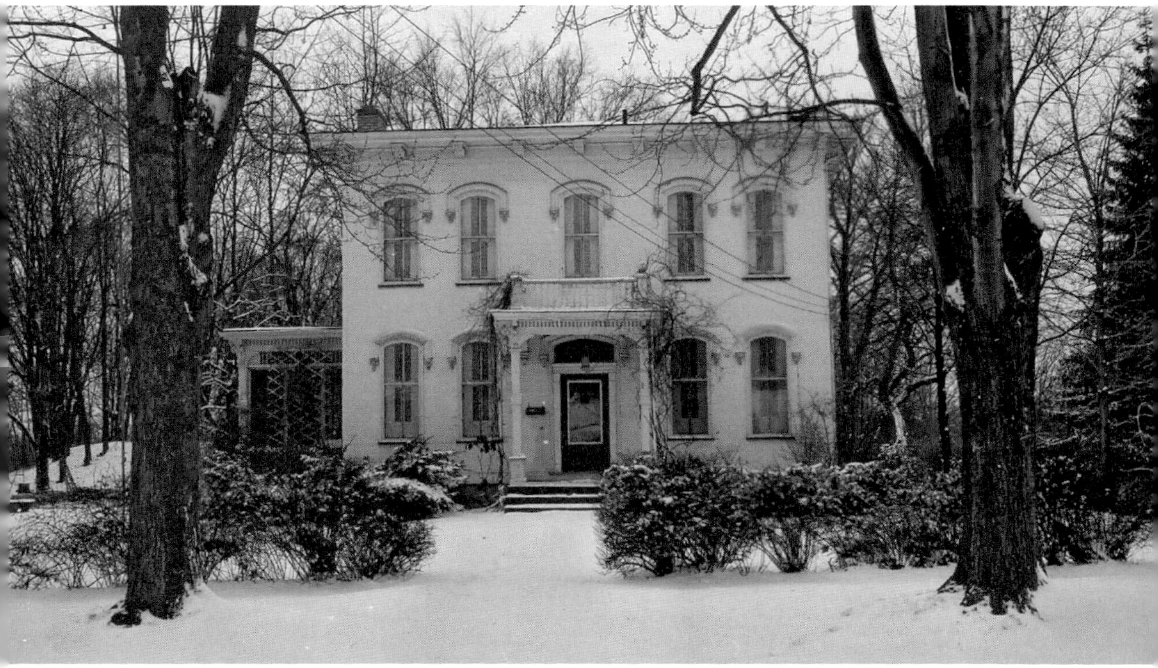

George Pritchard

Although he had an auto business in Medina, Pritchard's marriage to a young lady from Berea caused him to move. For a while he worked for Williams Motors, then as a clerk at Brown Hardware Co. (below) for $22.50 per week. After serving in the armed forces in the South Pacific for three years, Pritchard became part owner of Brown's, along with J.G. Ramsey. Later, Pritchard was elected president. Pritchard continued the policies of Fred Brown, who founded the business in 1877. Brown built his business on honest dealing, and that policy has never changed throughout the years. Pritchard did not limit his inventory to quick turnover articles. The needs of the customer have always come first. Customers can find attention given to help them find the smallest screw or to find help in locating a competent repairperson. Brown Hardware Co. escaped burning in the fire of 1899 when Fred Brown nailed sheet iron over his storefront. He replaced the wooden building with a two-story brick building on the Triangle. In the 1970s, community redevelopment caused Brown's to relocate on Sprague Road. Present owner of the still-thriving-after-all-these-years business is Gary Dilley.

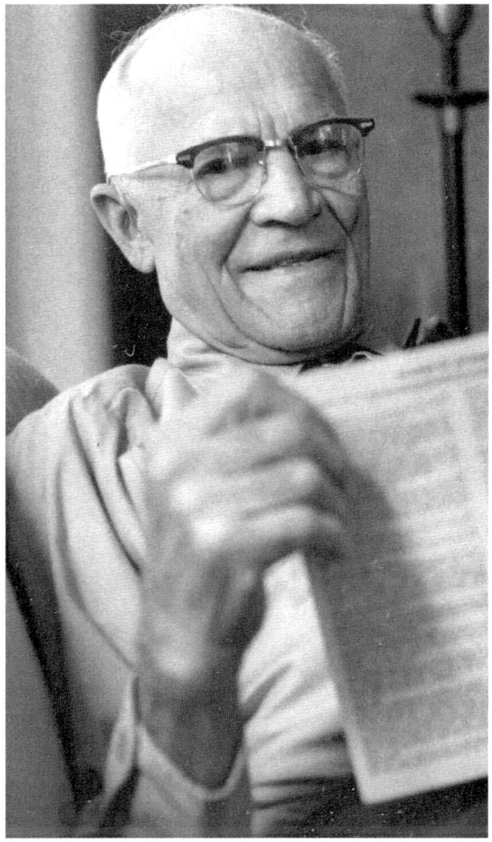

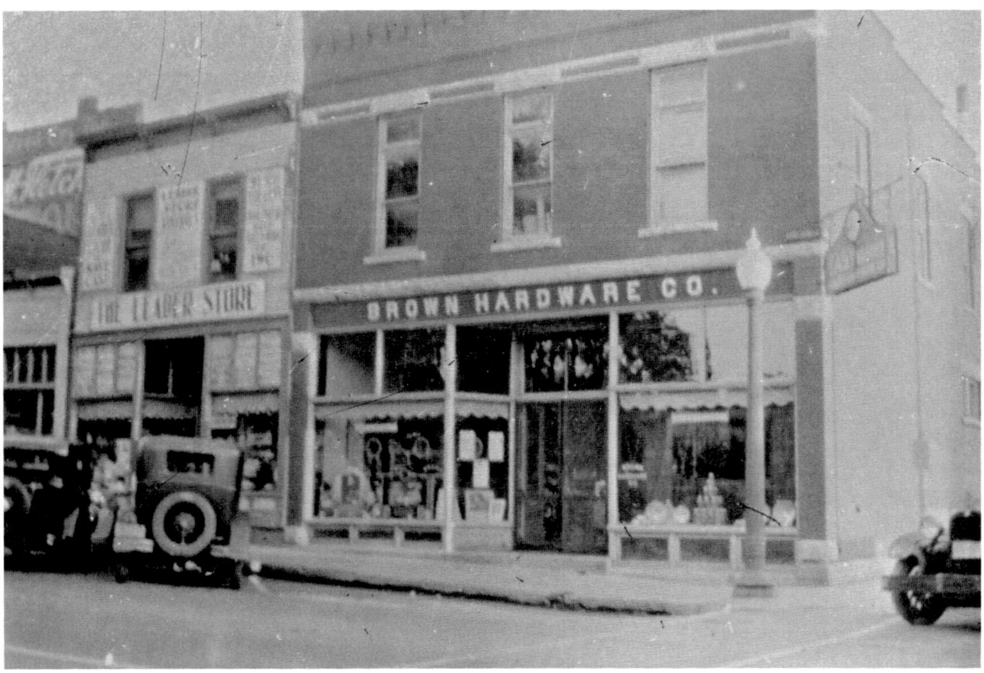

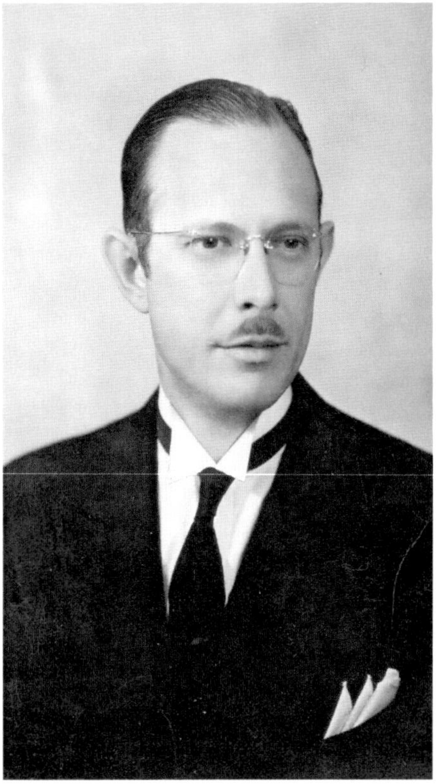

Wesley Baker Sr.

Founder of one of Berea's oldest businesses, Baker first gained experience in mortuary work assisting funeral director Earl Jenkins during the 1918 influenza epidemic. Baker started his own business in 1934 on Seminary Street. Baker Funeral Home moved to its Front Street location in 1936. Baker's wife Eleanor assisted in the business, and three sons followed their parents as licensed funeral directors and embalmers.

William (Billy) Simpson

On display at the Mahler Museum is the gasoline-powered car Simpson built in the 1890s. It was carefully crafted and actually ran. Simpson's real business was a jewelry store located near what is now the Berea Commons. At his home, he had a shop where he was a fervent tinkerer, although many townspeople regarded his inventions as a joke. He did invent two other vehicles—a 5-horsepower steam wagon/tractor and a street sprinkler—and an array of smaller items. Unfortunately, only a toy gun, sold to Berea-based Foxy Toys, and a mop were ever patented. He was a town councilman and also one of the original members of the First Businessman's Association. (Below) Billy Simpson (seated) is ready for a ride in John Baldwin Jr.'s "horseless carriage."

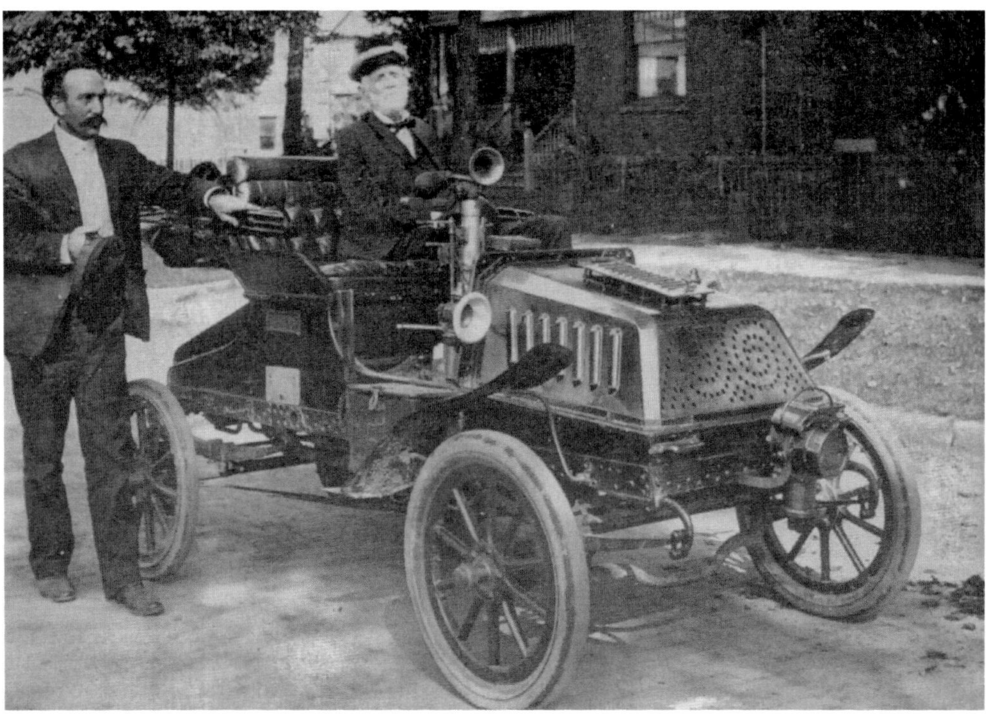

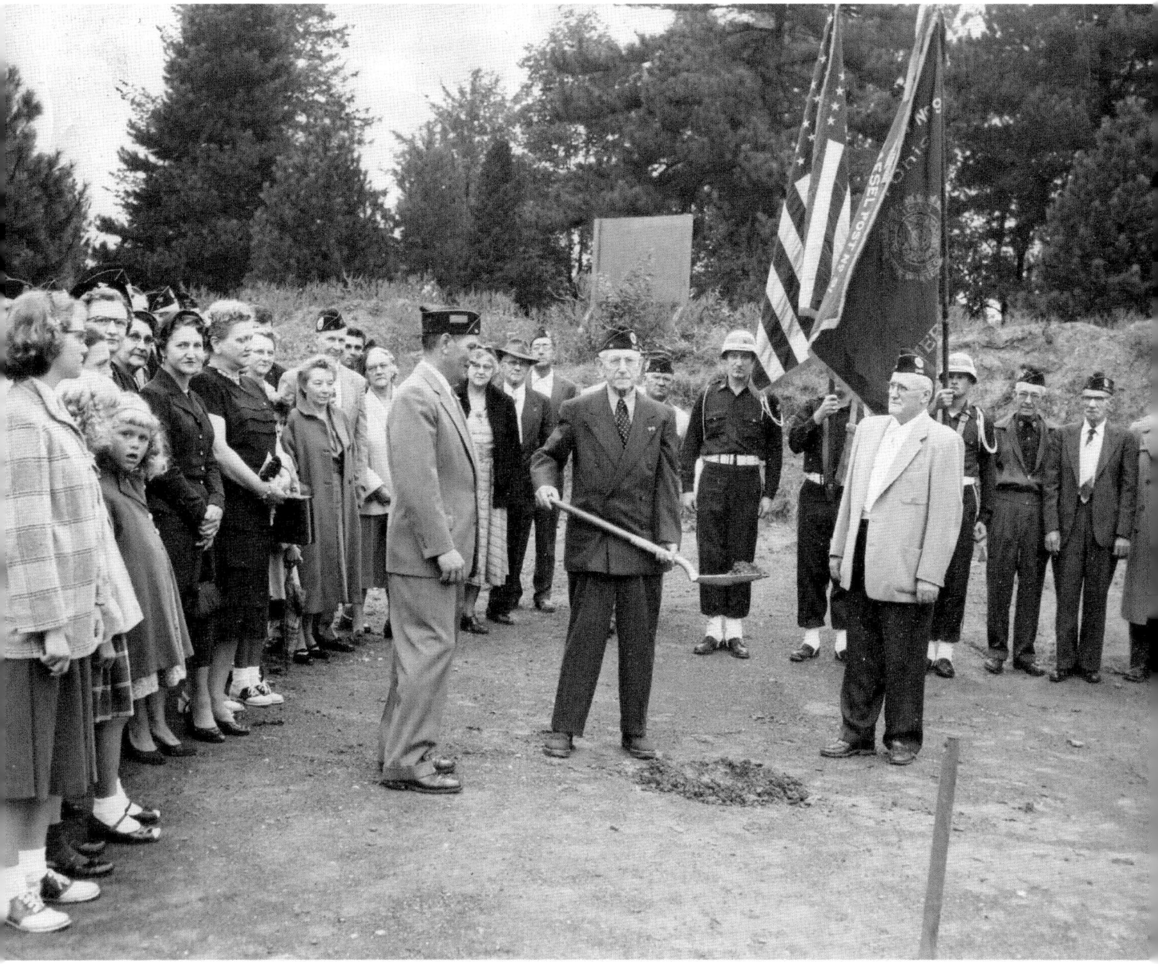

Rudolph S. Ursprung

With a German surname meaning "the beginning of all things," Ursprung's success as a builder was not surprising. Buildings in Berea and Cleveland stand as testimony to his ability to finish things as well—Berea High School, Parma High School, the original Hopkins Airport Terminal, and many buildings on the Baldwin-Wallace campus, including the gymnasium named for him. Ursprung was a trustee of the college for 25 years. "I conducted my business between wars," Rudolph (Rudy) Ursprung often remarked. A decorated veteran of both World Wars, Ursprung (right), chairman of the building committee, supervises the ground breaking for the Albert Baesel Post 90, American Legion in 1955. At left is Bernard McEwen, then-commander of the post. Wielding the shovel is Thomas Marks, first commander of the post.

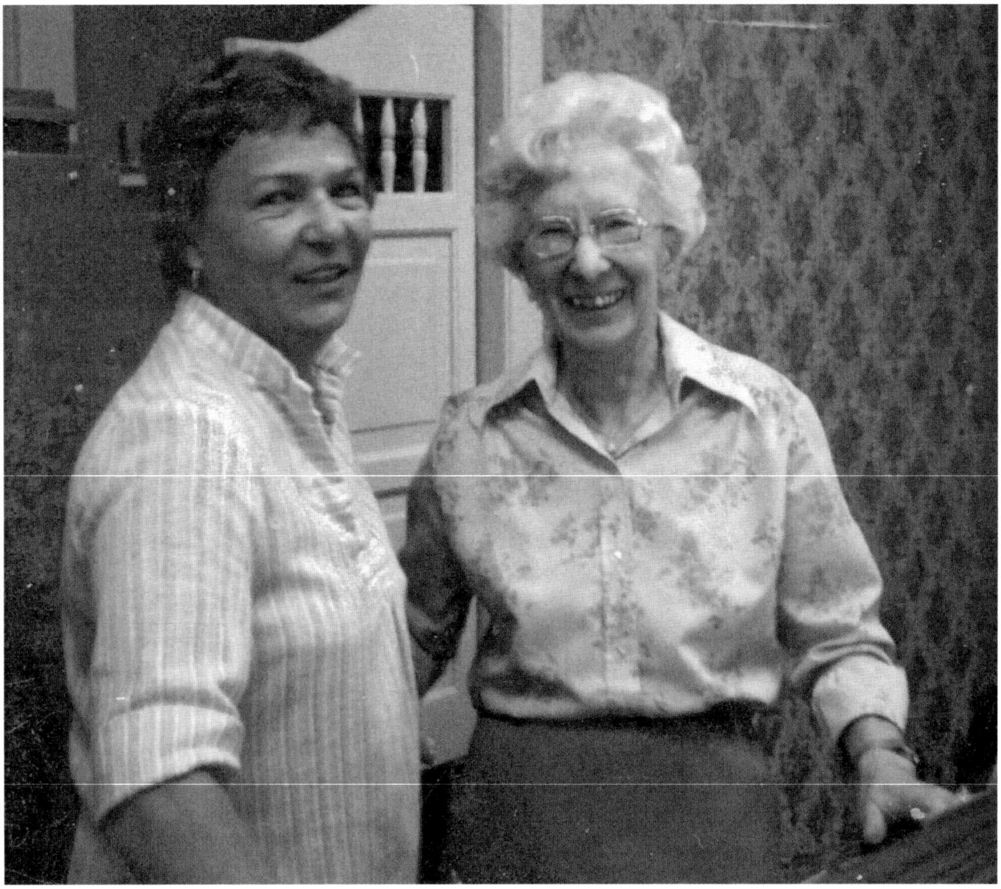

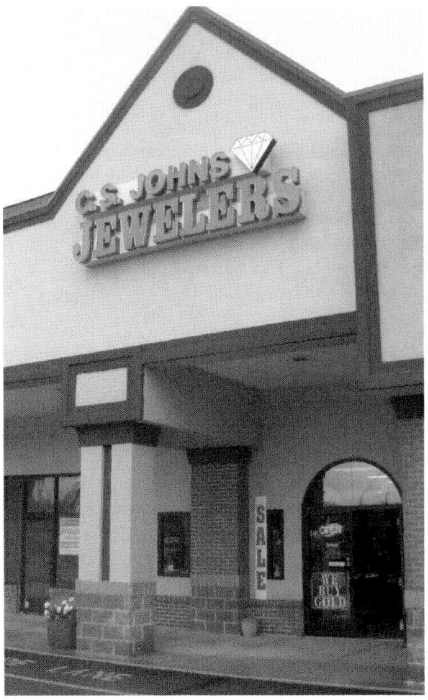

Elizabeth Johns (RIGHT)

In 1932, Clifford S. Johns died at age 36. What she described as her "confounded stubbornness" convinced Elizabeth (Beth) Johns to carry on the jewelry business she and her husband had started successfully in 1928. He had established a firm foundation on which to build. In March 1978, Mrs. Johns celebrated her 50th year in business, having weathered the Depression, World War II, and Berea's urban renewal. She was always active in community affairs. One of her able assistants was Mary Jean Fisher (above, left). Mrs. Johns chaired the Berea Library Committee that obtained a commitment from city council for a new library. After she died, the Berea Library received a check for 10 percent of Elizabeth Johns' estate. The jewelry business, now owned by Mark and Matt Regatti, still bears the name C.S. Johns. (Courtesy of C.S. Johns Jewelry; left photograph by Susan Lee.)

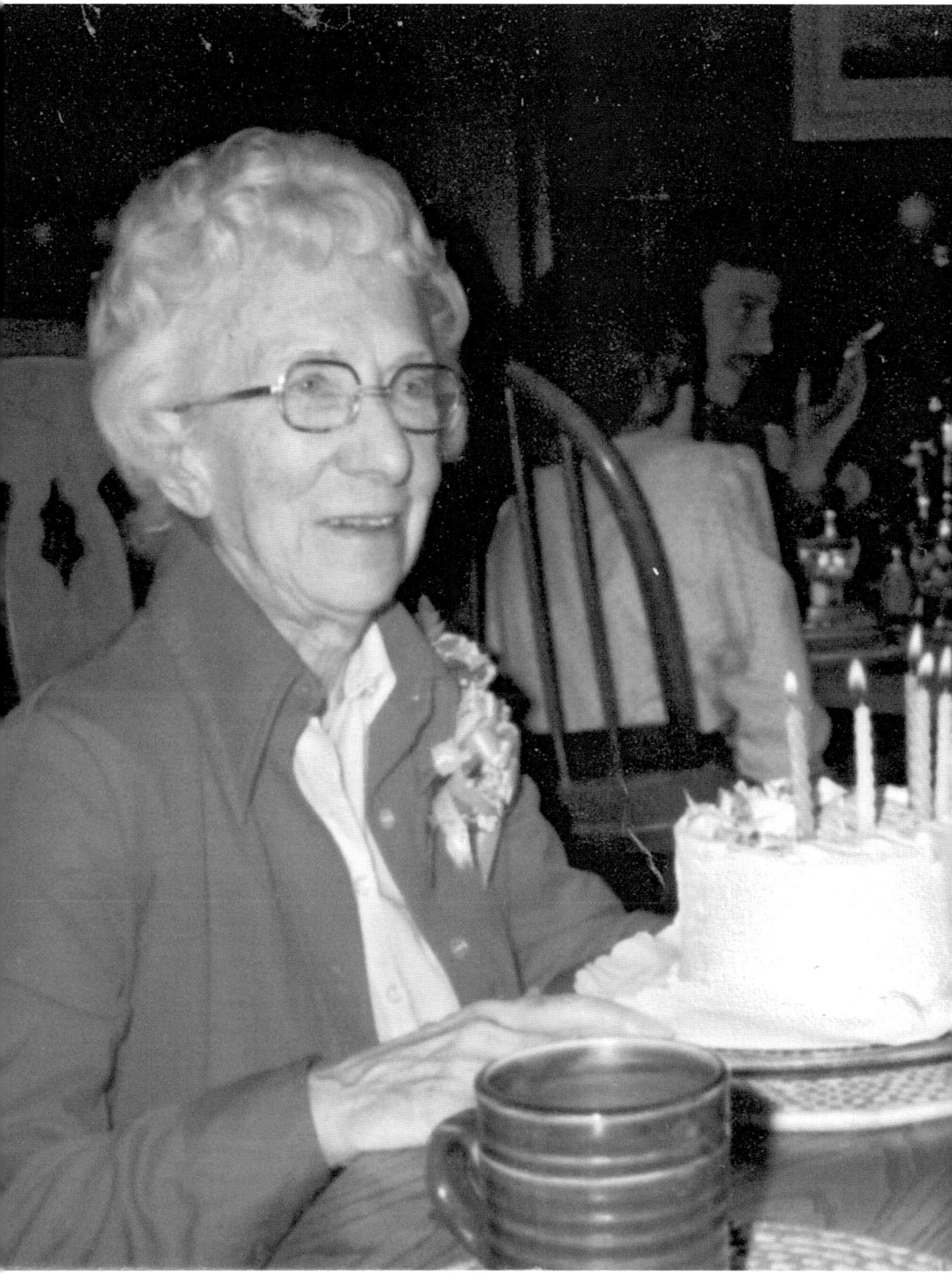

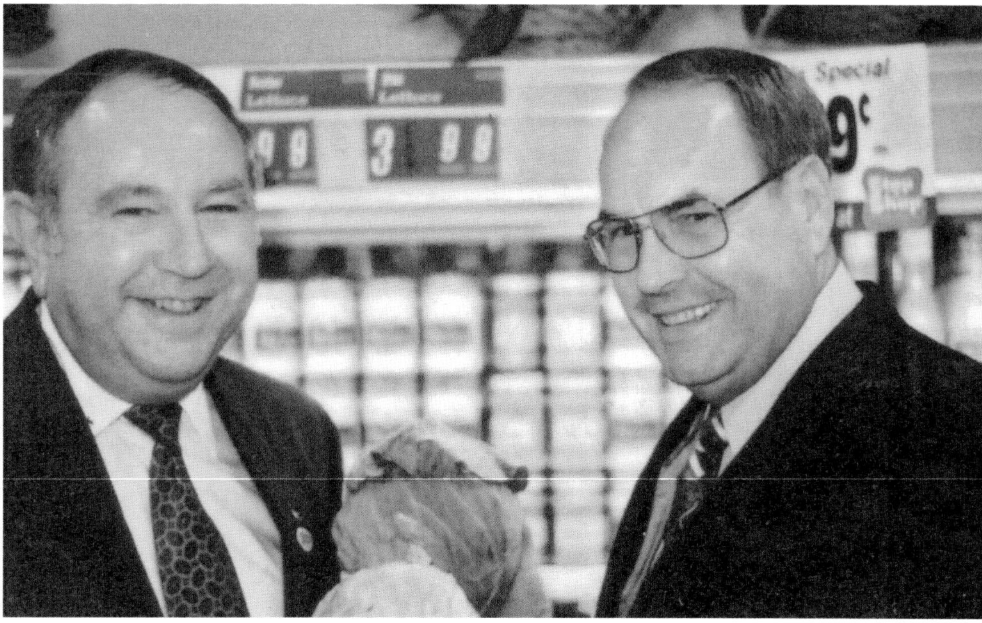

Clint Williams and H. Allen Tadych

Two successful real estate brokers announced their combined 60 years of experience by appearing at Rego's supermarket and declaring, "Lettuce Show You How 2 Heads Are Better than 1." Williams (right) received the Herrick Memorial Award from the Early Settlers Association for his restoration of the turn-of-the-century village, Grand Pacific Junction. Tadych, virtually a fixture in community affairs, was regarded as fundraiser *extraordinaire*. (Courtesy of Clint Williams.)

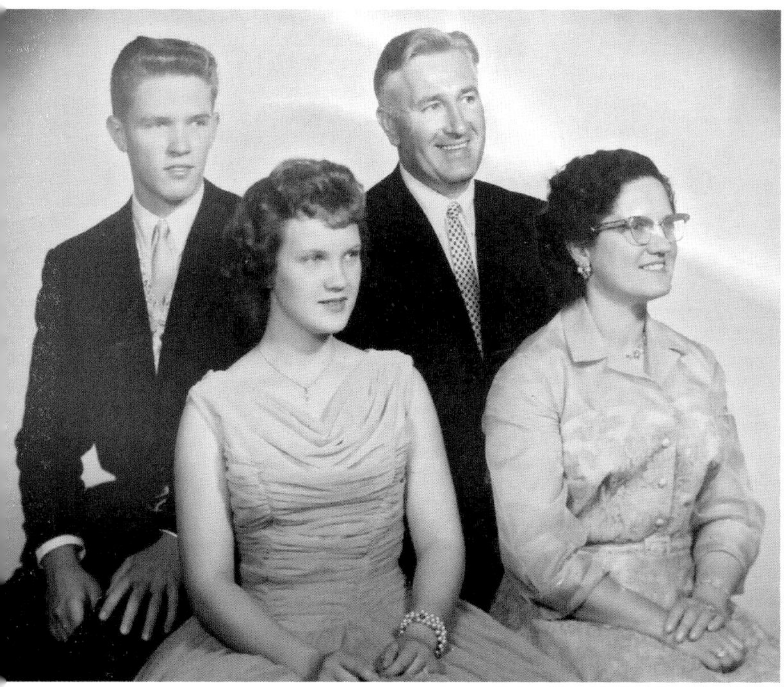

John C. Siodla Family

Siodla, son of a quarryman, like many young Berea boys, worked as a water boy in the quarries. He became president of Personality Homes, which built many Berea homes during the 1950s. The Siodlas celebrated their 25th anniversary with a mass at St. Adalbert's Church, followed by an evening reception. (Back left, Gene Siodla and John Siodla. Front left, Connie Siodl, and Berniece Siodla.)

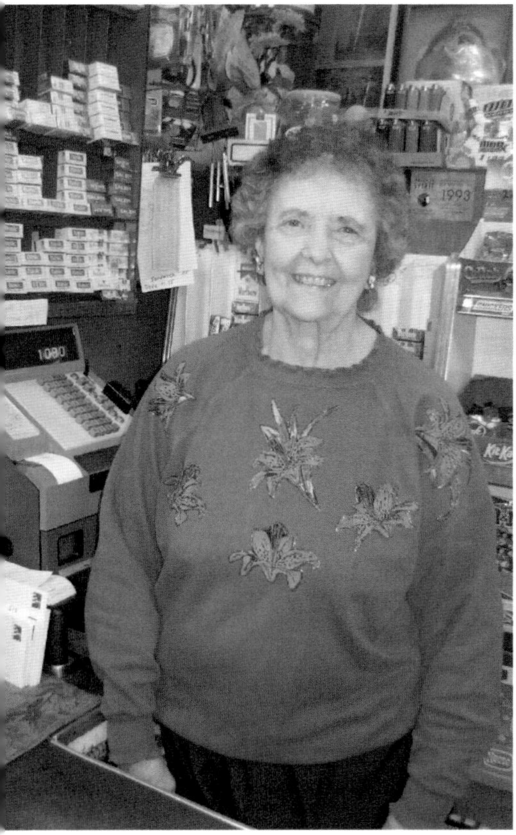

Loretta Juergens
Just as her grandmother, Mary Shafts, minded the grocery store while her husband Joseph worked in the sandstone quarries, Juergens continues the tradition with the help of family members. She treats her customers like neighbors. Entering the unhurried atmosphere of Shafts' Grocery is like taking a step back in time. "No, we don't have a scanner," Loretta tells curious children. (Photograph by Susan Lee.)

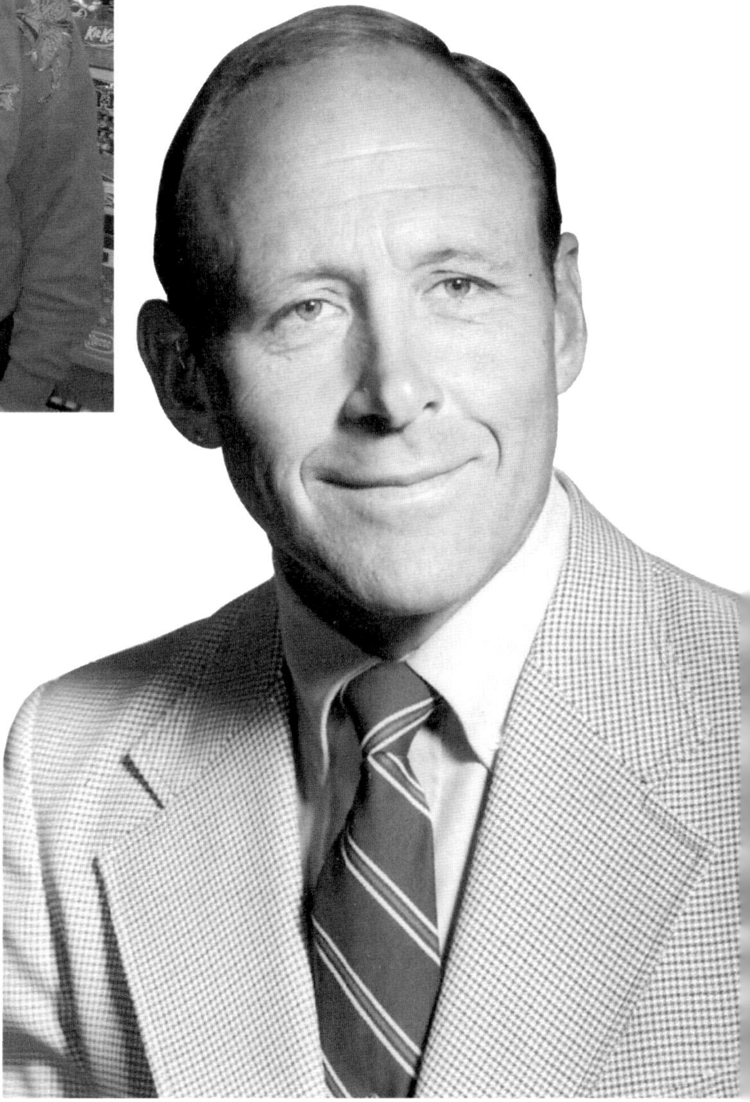

William H. Beyer
A lifelong Berean, Beyer's public-spirited dedication to his community has always been a vital part of his life. He has undertaken leadership roles in community service and volunteerism but always in a quiet and unassuming way, whether for the schools, the city government, the hospital, or civic groups.

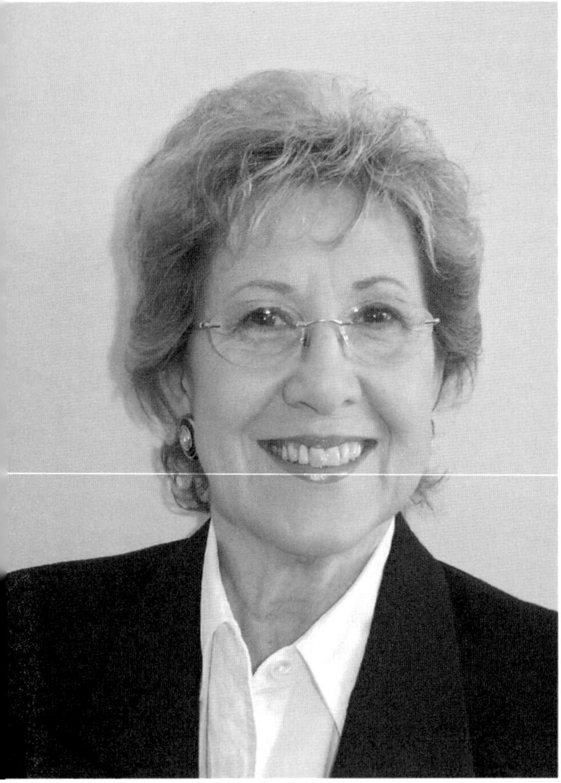

Judy Stull

Stull's great-grandfather, Lawrence Walczak, lost his life in an accident at Big Quarry. She credits the "Berea grit" in her veins that gives her strength when facing challenges. (Berea sandstone was known as "Berea grit" because of its strength and durability.) From 1967 to 2001, she and her husband Ralph operated Spudnuts, a popular doughnut business. Since selling the business, Stull's name appears on the active volunteer list of many organizations—the Berea Historical Society, the Berea Rotary Club, the Berea High School Alumni Association, and Church Street Ministries, to name a few. As a fourth generation Berean, she takes pride in sharing her knowledge and love of the community by leading trolley tours for the Berea Historical Society. The Berea Rotary Club named her its first female member; in 1994–1995 she was named Berea Rotary's first woman president. Stull has led her Berea High School Alumni Association since 2002, and she has volunteered for 10 years at the Second Mile Shop operated by Church Street Ministries. A fellow Rotarian described her as a dynamic, energetic, and strong supporter of Berea. "She lovingly speaks of Berea like one of her children, like it's home," he said. (Courtesy of Judy Stull.)

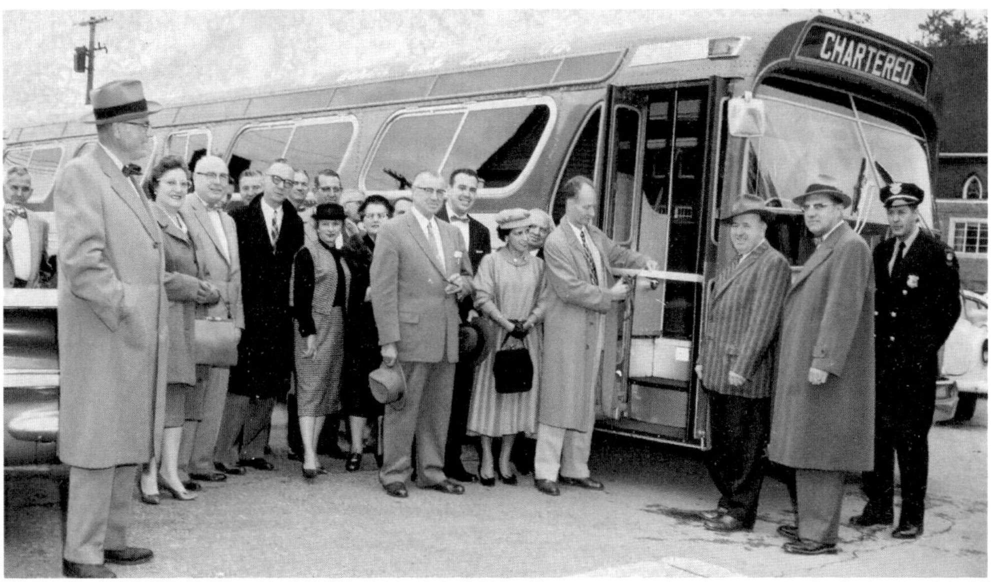

Rudolph (Rudy) Weber

Weber, president of Berea Bus Lines Co., watches (third from right) with a tour group as Mayor Ernest Quackenbush cuts the ribbon on a new bus. When he was 18, Weber began working at the fledgling Berea bus line as a mechanic's helper and driver. By the mid-1940s, he was president of the company.

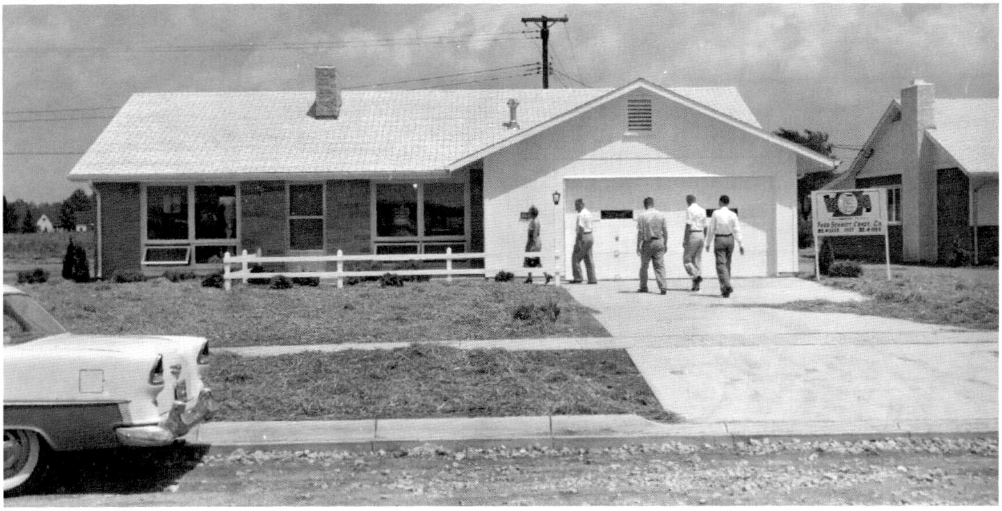

Schmitt Homes

One-story ranch-style homes boasting family rooms, woodburning fireplaces, and plenty of storage—these were some of the desirable features of Bob Schmitt Homes. An ambitious builder, Schmitt began building developments in Berea in the late 1950s. He expanded into neighboring towns, and the firm has won countless awards of excellence in homebuilding.

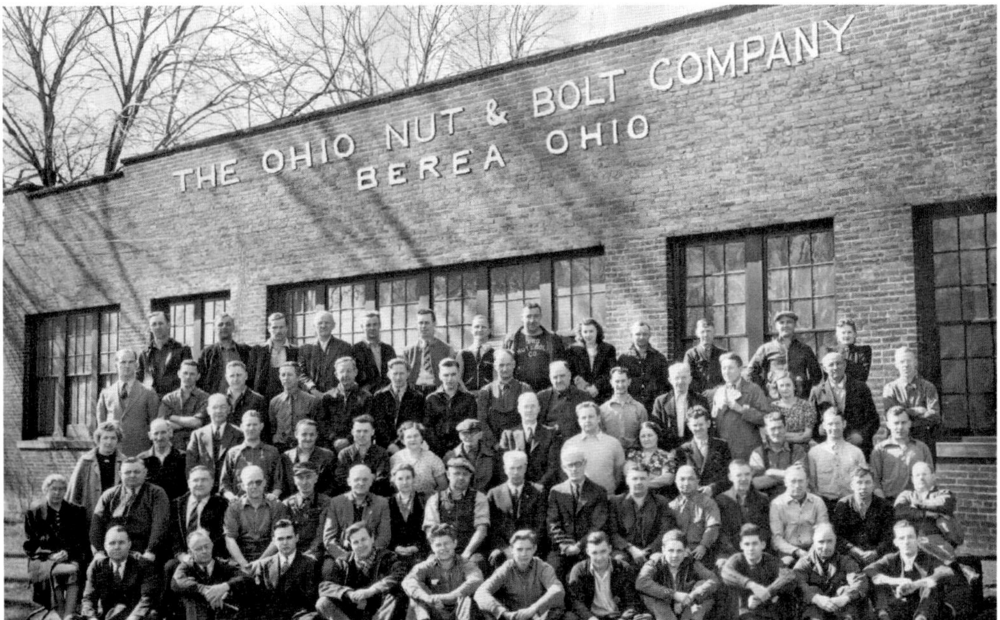

Ohio Nut and Bolt Co.

This firm incorporated in 1905 as successors to Ray Automatic Machine Co. Fourteen Berea businessmen took over the bankrupt Ray firm. By 1958, Ohio Nut and Bolt was Berea's largest and oldest industry, and a number of employees had worked there for more than 35 years. The company still operates on the original six-acre site. (Courtesy of Jack Shumway Collection.)

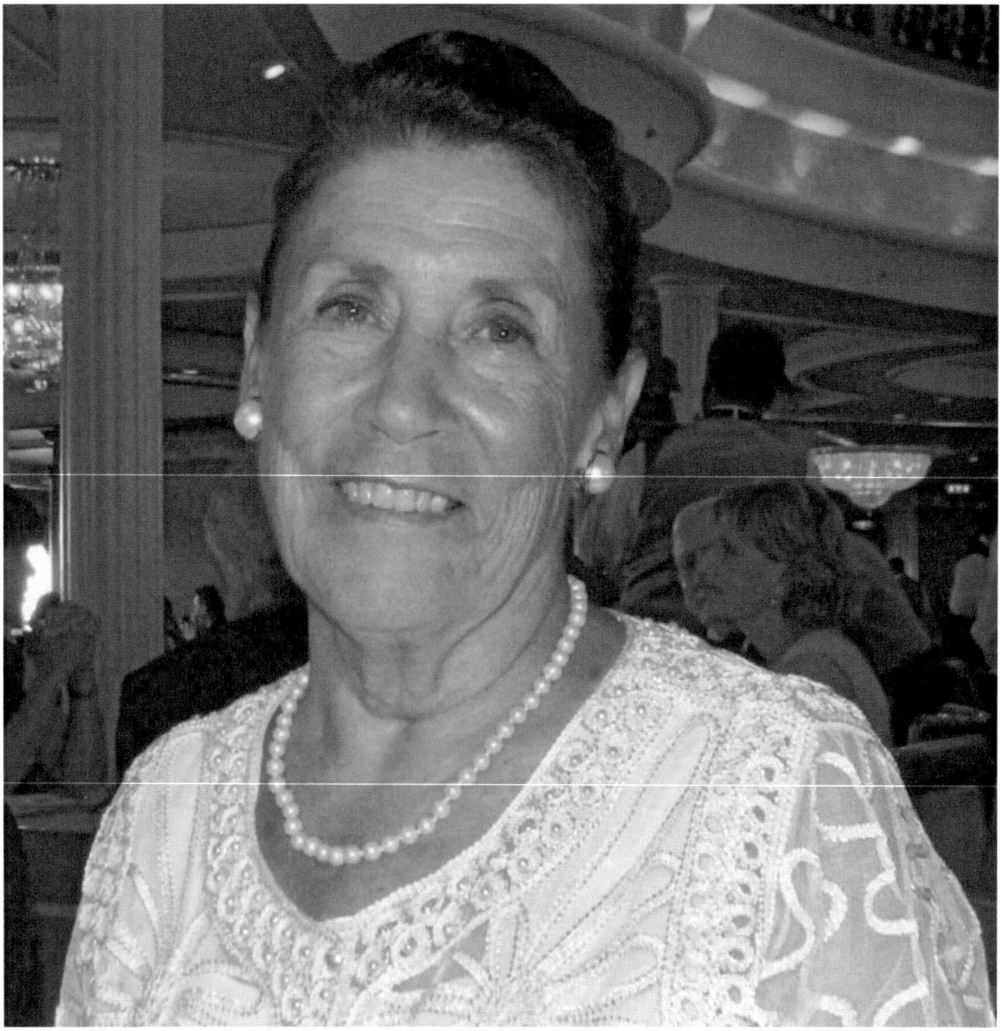

Mary Ellen Posze

Posze may have booked a vacation for you or sold a house to you. She had two separate, very successful careers and raised two daughters. She opened Village Square Travel in Berea in 1976. In the early 1980s, Art Modell and the Cleveland Browns became co-owners with Posze in Village Square Travel. With this investment, she was able to expand the operation and open offices in Baltimore, Jacksonville, Florida, and the Greenbrier at White Sulphur Springs, West Virginia. The headquarters remained in Berea. By 1987, the travel industry was changing; more people owned computers and were making their own travel arrangements. She sold Village Square Travel to Bank One in 1987. By 1990, she had returned to college and finished her undergraduate degree at Baldwin-Wallace College. Posze then turned to selling real estate, primarily in Berea, the community she knew and loved best. Whether representing individual buyers, the college, or the city, she always kept aware of the market in Berea, both residential and commercial, and could match buyers with desirable properties. However, the needs and wishes of her clients were always foremost. An active Rotarian and chamber of commerce board member, Posze could be counted on to lend her support to "all things Berea." Founder and Queen Mother of the Berea Bonnet Belles (Red Hats), she was a loving, caring grandmother, her most cherished role of all. (Courtesy of Vanessa Prince.)

CHAPTER SIX

Religion and Philanthropy

Driving into Berea from any direction you will see the almost-twin spires that dominate the skyline from the near-downtown area. These were once familiarly called the "Brick Church" (First Congregational) and the "Stone Church" (German Methodist). Although today these buildings function differently than they once did, their architecture has been preserved, and they stand as reminders of the solid Christian values upon which this community was founded. Early Methodist pastors included William Pierce, the town's first resident pastor, who also rode a four-week circuit, and William Nast, who traveled more widely and attracted settlers to Berea. Gifted pastors of other denominations settled in Berea also. Represented here are the colorful Fr. John Garrity of St. Mary's Roman Catholic Church and Rev. Charles Kuck, First Congregational Church (now United Church of Christ). By 1860, there were a number of other congregations established in a town of slightly more than 3,000. These offered not only a spiritual direction but also centers for social life. The German Methodist Orphans Home (now the Berea Children's Home), located at the center of town, spoke a daily reminder, since Civil War times, of the need to be our brothers' and our sisters' keepers.

Not surprising, then, that history set the stage for a town that as it grew, would take a firm stand on the Golden Rule, or "doing unto others. . . ." Strong service clubs, such as Kiwanis and Rotary, took the lead and attracted "doers" like Donald Williams, Mary Ellen Posze, and Larry and Elaine Myers. Dedicated and inspired individuals such as Frances Millward, Wendy Nelson Crann, and Rev. Leroy McCreary have founded ministries that serve special populations. Generations of Bereans, such as Howard and Gladys Wyles, Glenn and Jean Snow, and Robert ("Robbie") Robinson, have stood ready to lend support and promote worthy causes. These people are included as examples of hundreds more with similar values and enthusiasm.

Perhaps this is the place to mention tolerance. Every community seems to have its "characters," who are legendary in that they are frequently seen about town but not really understood. Berea has had its share of these: Walkin' Willie, Safari Jane, and Scissors are nicknames recalled from the second half of the 20th century. These people were recognized and respected as being different somehow, but they were part of the community even so. Who doesn't remember seeing Willie (Tadych) having a free cup of coffee handed to him at a restaurant? Or noticed someone helping Safari Jane (Myna Davis) in her pith helmet) up the post office steps with her pushcart at 4:30 in the afternoon? And housewives always listened for the pushcart and ringing bell that meant "Scissors" (Ira Hostetler) would soon stop by to sharpen their utensils. These folks lived in a world of their own, but the town looked out for them, nevertheless.

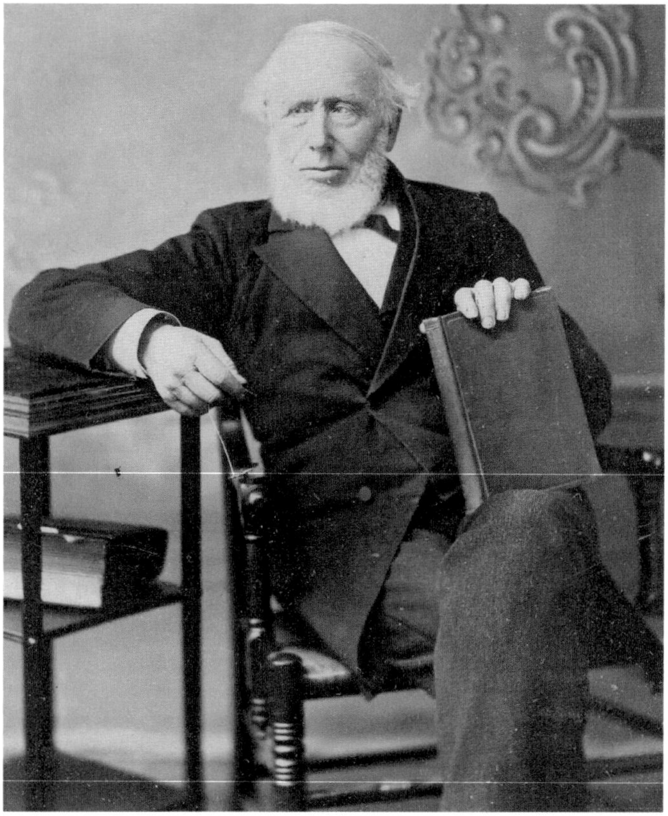

Dr. William Pierce
When Pierce became Berea's first pastor in 1846, his four-week circuit lay between Sandusky, Marion, and Medina, including Olmsted and Hoadley's Mills (later Westview). He was connected with the Baldwin Institute as trustee or professor throughout his career. Dr. Pierce was regarded as a "man of an unusual degree of taste and culture" and gave a "stamp of culture to the community."

Rev. Henry O. Sheldon
Berea might have been called *Tabor* if Rev. Henry Sheldon's flip of a coin had not come down "heads" for *Berea*. Sheldon, an influential Methodist circuit rider, and John Baldwin, early settler of Berea and founder of the grindstone industry, thus settled the town's official name. Sheldon became the town's first postmaster. His diaries describe the town's early years.

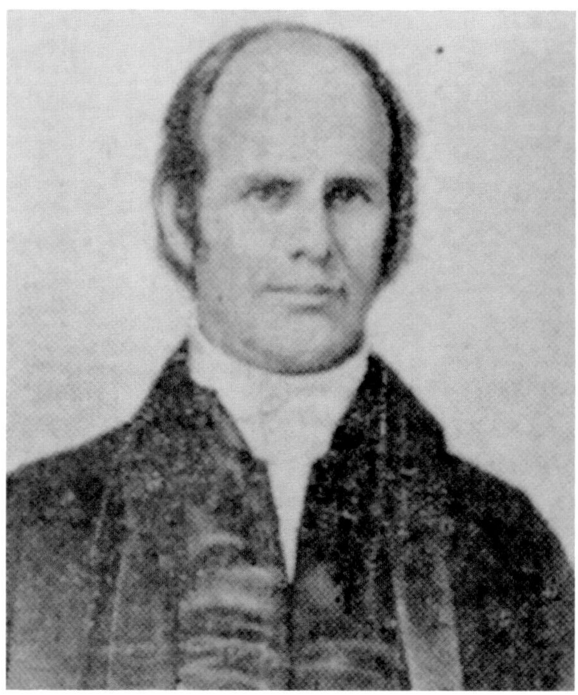

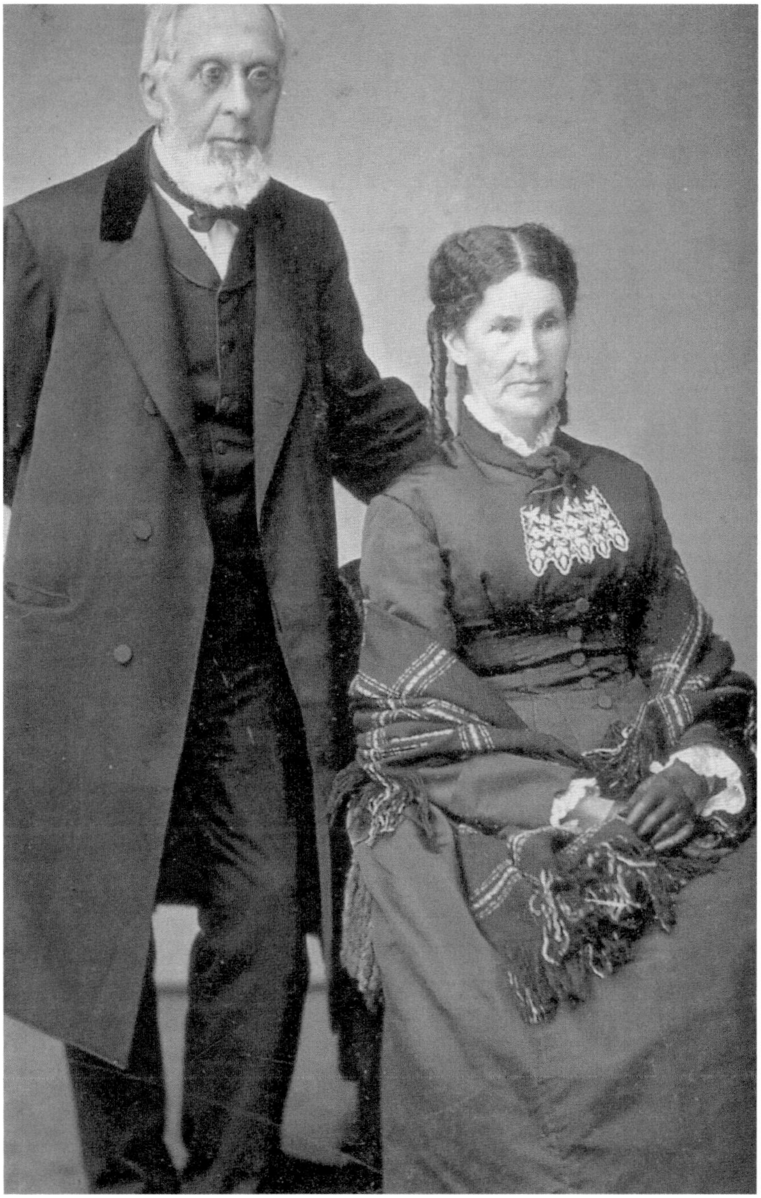

Mr. and Mrs. William Nast

A prominent leader of German Methodism in America, William Nast and his wife, Margaret Eliza Nast, traveled widely, promoting Berea as a desirable place to settle. Nast became the first president of German Wallace College, a post he held for 30 years. Their daughter Fannie Nast Gamble was the first woman to graduate from German Wallace College. The Nasts and their daughter, Fannie were instrumental in founding the German Methodist Orphans Home (now Berea Children's Home). Fannie donated money to establish the Conservatory of Music, now affiliated with Baldwin-Wallace College. She also donated $10,000 to the orphanage to build a chapel and dining room, which were named in honor of her mother. Fannie was married to William Gamble, grandson of James Gamble, founder of Procter & Gamble, Cincinnati.

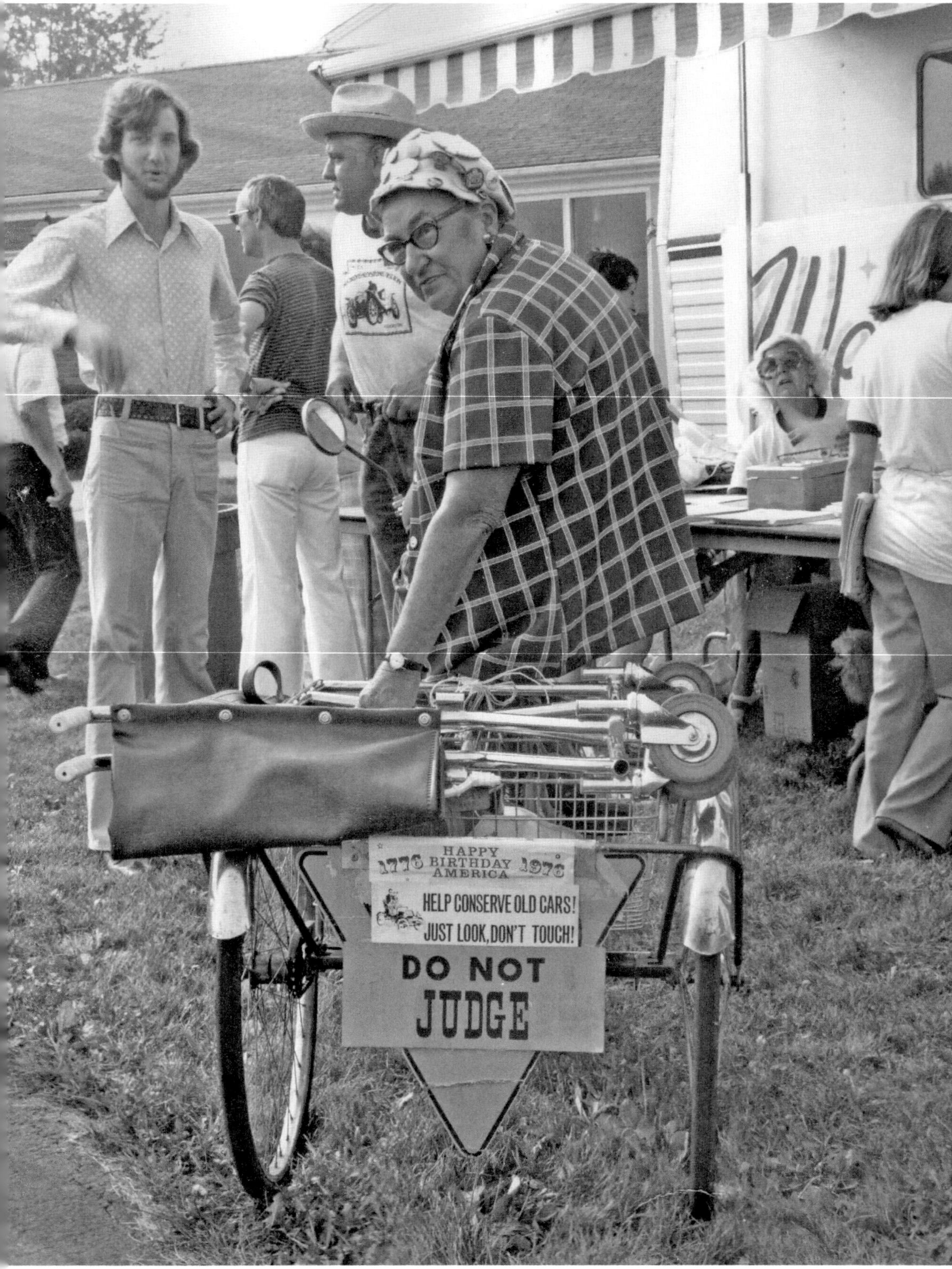
HAPPY
1776 BIRTHDAY 1976
AMERICA
HELP CONSERVE OLD CARS!
JUST LOOK, DON'T TOUCH!
DO NOT
JUDGE

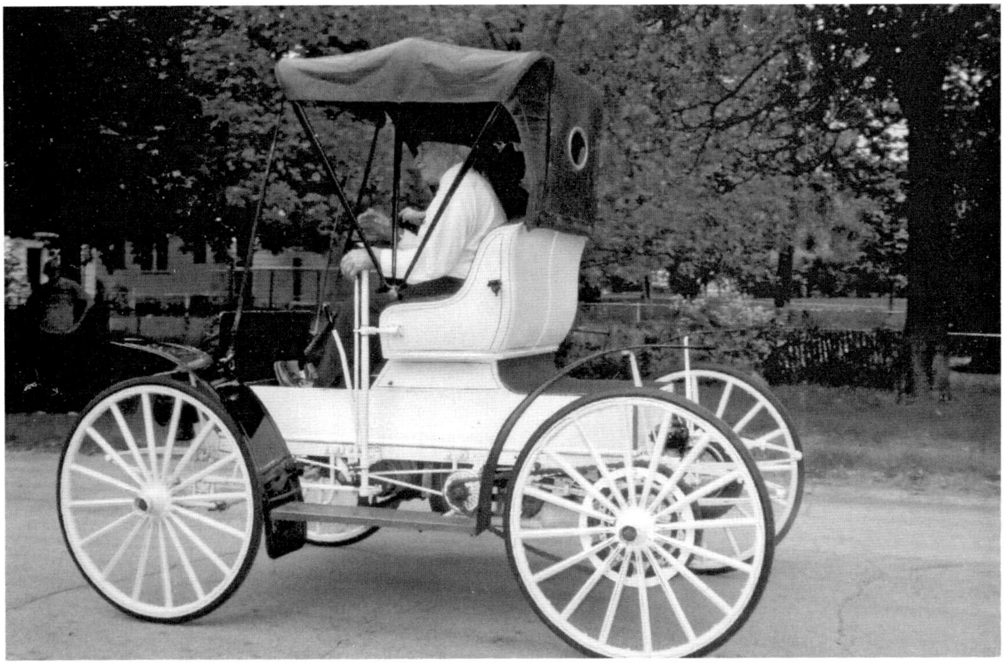

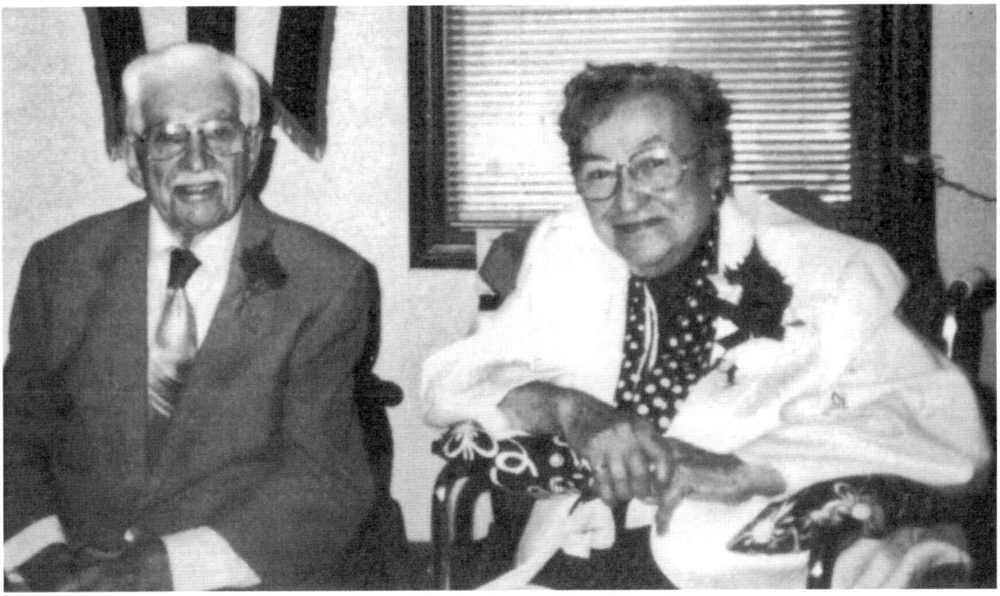

Howard and Gladys Wyles

Professionally, Gladys Wyles was a nurse at the old Community Hospital, and Howard was a successful contractor. But both became enthusiastic, able, and caring supporters of community efforts. To name a few, Howard became a leader in promoting fair zoning laws and revising the city charter, while Gladys was active with the Fairwood School PTA, the Berea Summer Theatre, and the Mahler Historical Museum. The Wyles were well-known antique car buffs who participated in Grindstone Festival parades and car shows. Although Gladys pursued her busy schedule from a wheelchair for some 30 years, she did not regard this as a handicap.

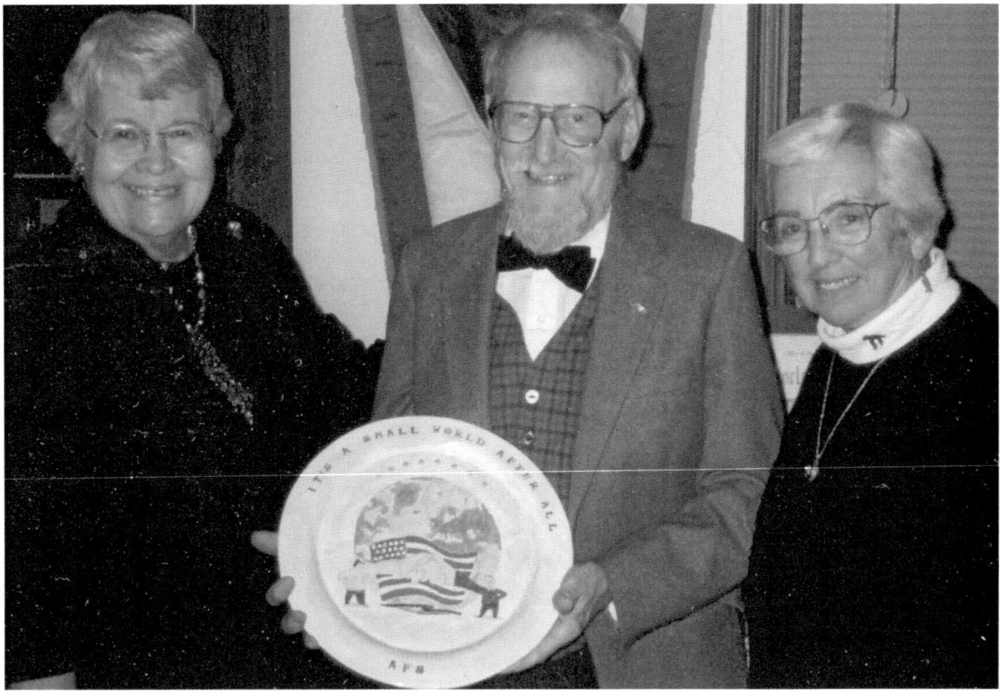

Robert ("Robbie") Robinson
A chemical and patent engineer for Union Carbide Corporation until retiring in 1980, Robert (Robbie) devoted his attention to the ministries of the Berea United Methodist Church as lay minister and the American Field Service (AFS) as senior volunteer coordinator at Berea High School. Here he presented an AFS award to officers of the Berea Historical Society.) From left, Barbara Sherwood, Robinson, and Eloise Tressel).

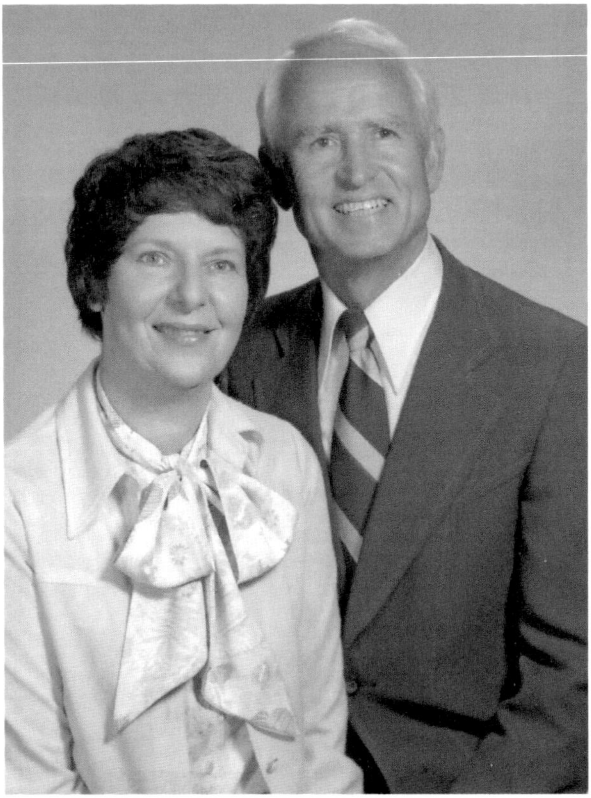

Glenn and Jean Snow
When they moved to Berea in 1950, both Jean and Glenn Snow found countless ways to help make Berea a better place to live. Glenn, an engineer and developer, chaired the Berea School Task Force to find ways to resolve school problems. Jean helped found Learning Resources Unlimited. They established the J. and. G. Snow School at the Berea Children's Home.

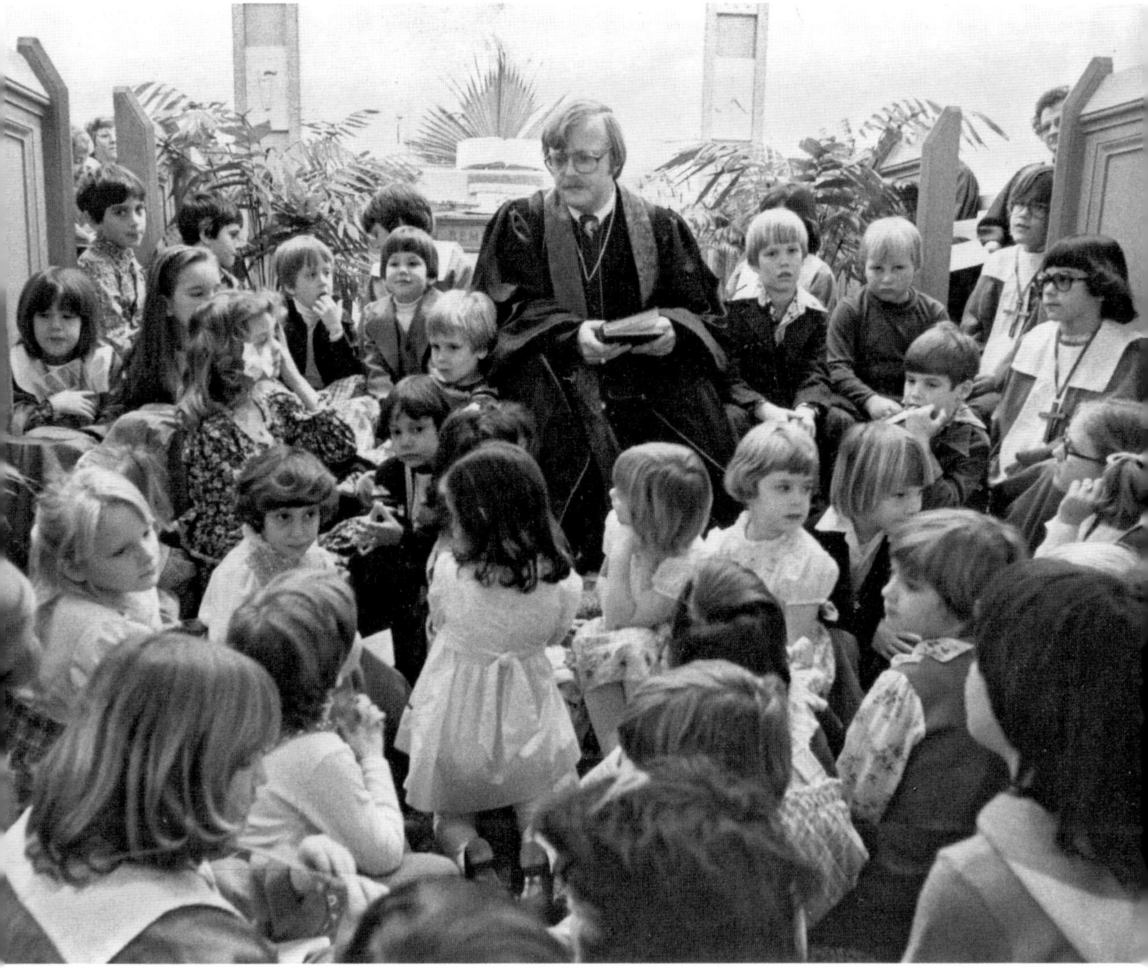

Rev. Charles Kuck

When Reverend Kuck came to Berea, he came to serve a church bitterly divided over social issues—civil rights and the Vietnam War. The pastor who preceded him had died after six months of service. Kuck not only brought about healing to the First Congregational United Church of Christ of Berea, but remained as pastor there for 16 years. Under Kuck's leadership, "First Church," founded by a group of abolitionists in 1855, once again became, in the reverend's words, "...pilgrims, caring for the poor, the hungry and the disabled as well as preaching the gospel." Contributions and volunteer efforts for those less fortunate grew as church members followed their beliefs in the "social gospel." "At one time," Kuck told the Berea *News-Sun,* "First Church was known as the church that was always having problems. Now people say, 'Oh, you're the church that does so much for other people.'" Reverend Kuck tempered his ministry with liberal doses of humor and good-natured banter, but he never lost sight of the aim of his calling—demonstrating and finding love through helping others. His ministry knew no bounds—from the youngest of his flock to persons outside his own congregation. In addition, as chaplain of the Berea Fire Department for 15 years, Kuck was called on day or night to minister to families suffering loss of property—or life. Reverend Kuck moved on to accept a pastorate in Dublin, Ohio, that, like Berea's "First Church," was having difficult times and looking for unity. He remained at the Dublin church until his retirement. In 2005, he returned to Berea to celebrate the 150th anniversary of the First Congregational United Church of Christ with his former congregation.

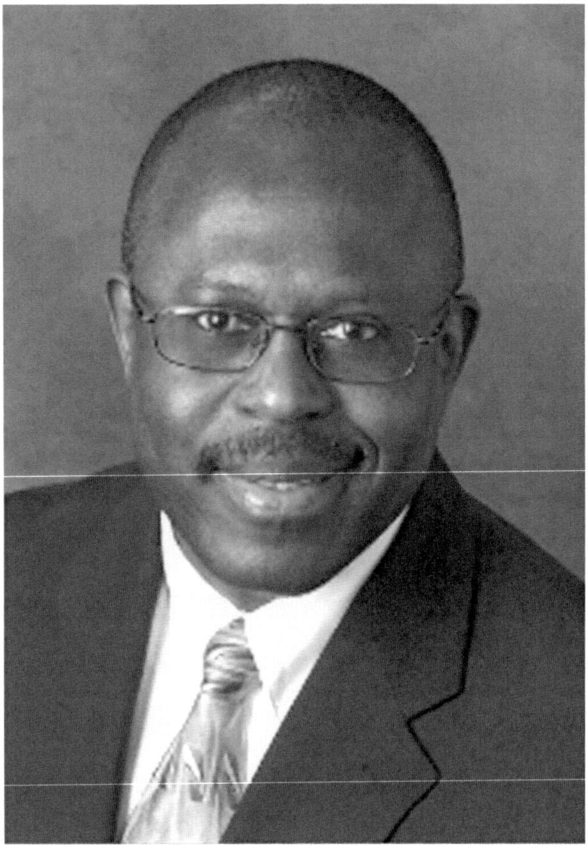

Rev. Leroy McCreary

Pastor of People's Community Church since 1975, Reverend McCreary has applied his organizational and management skills to the Berea City school board. He most recently was chairman of the Board of Trustees of Southwest General Health Center and founder and president of the North End Foundation. Employed 37 years at NASA Glenn Research Center, McCreary retired as chief operations officer of human resources. (Courtesy of People's Community Church.)

Fr. John M. Garrity

A beloved pastor of St. Mary's Catholic Church for 25 years, Garrity was known for a keen sense of humor and for a St. Patrick's Day celebration that attracted more than 1,200 people each year. Under his leadership, the church acquired a new school site and developed adjacent real estate for residences. During his tenure, the congregation grew to nearly 8,000 members.

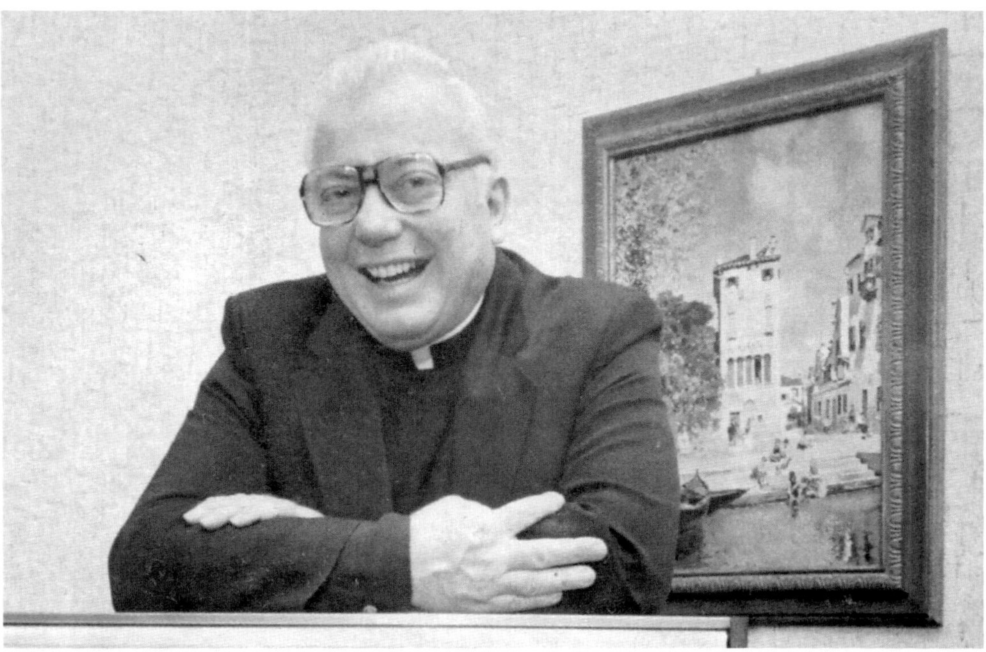

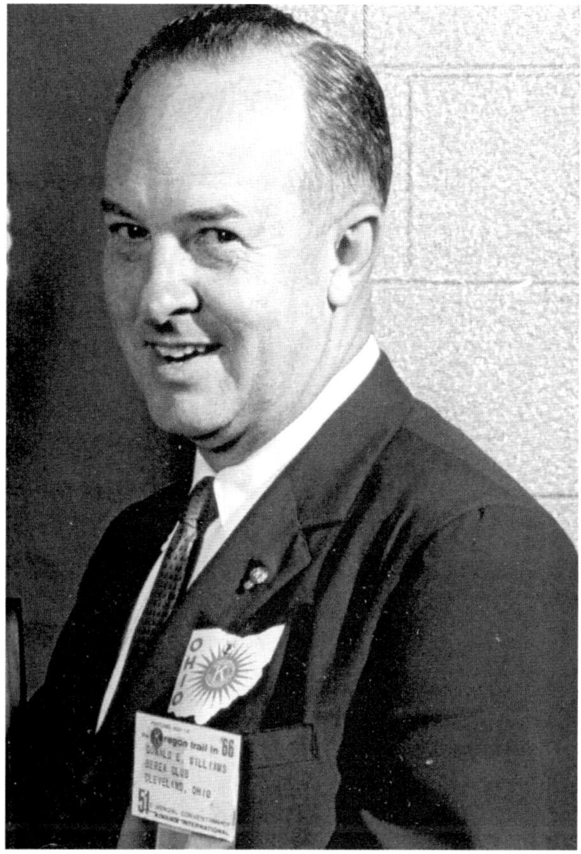

Donald E. Williams
"I just have this strong feeling we're put on this earth to do more than eat, sleep, and work," Williams once said. Kiwanis was one way he chose to contribute to his community. Williams served in many local and state positions and, eventually, as president of Kiwanis International in 1985–1986. He also was a board member and president of the Board of Trustees of Southwest General Hospital (now Southwest General Health Center.)

Mac Bright
All smiles, Mac Bright and Doris Hecht show off the T-shirts bearing the Berea logo that Mac designed for theechamber of commerce The logo has been in use since 1977.

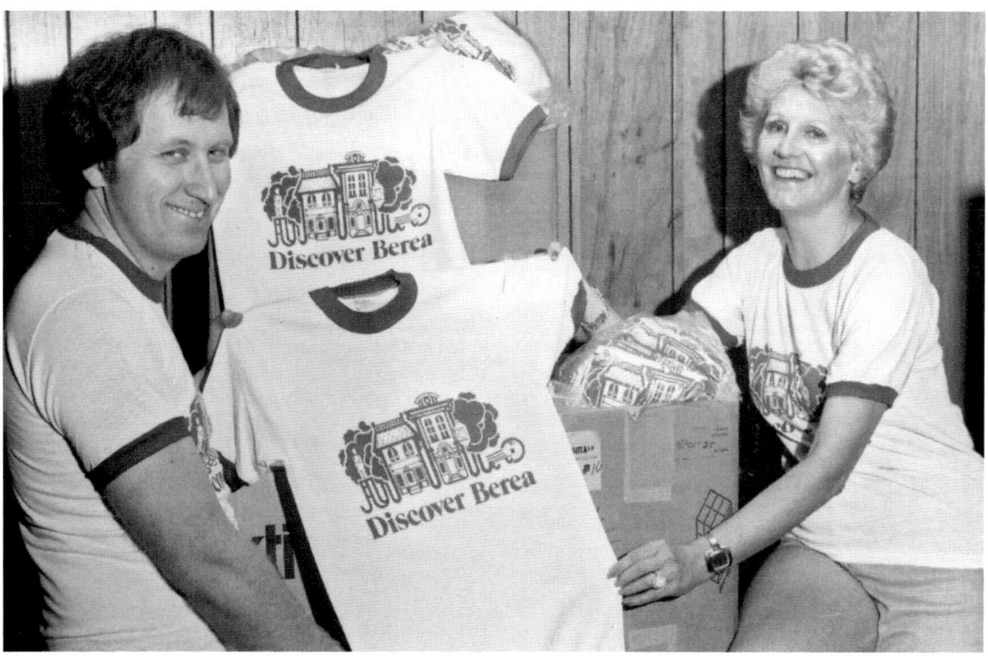

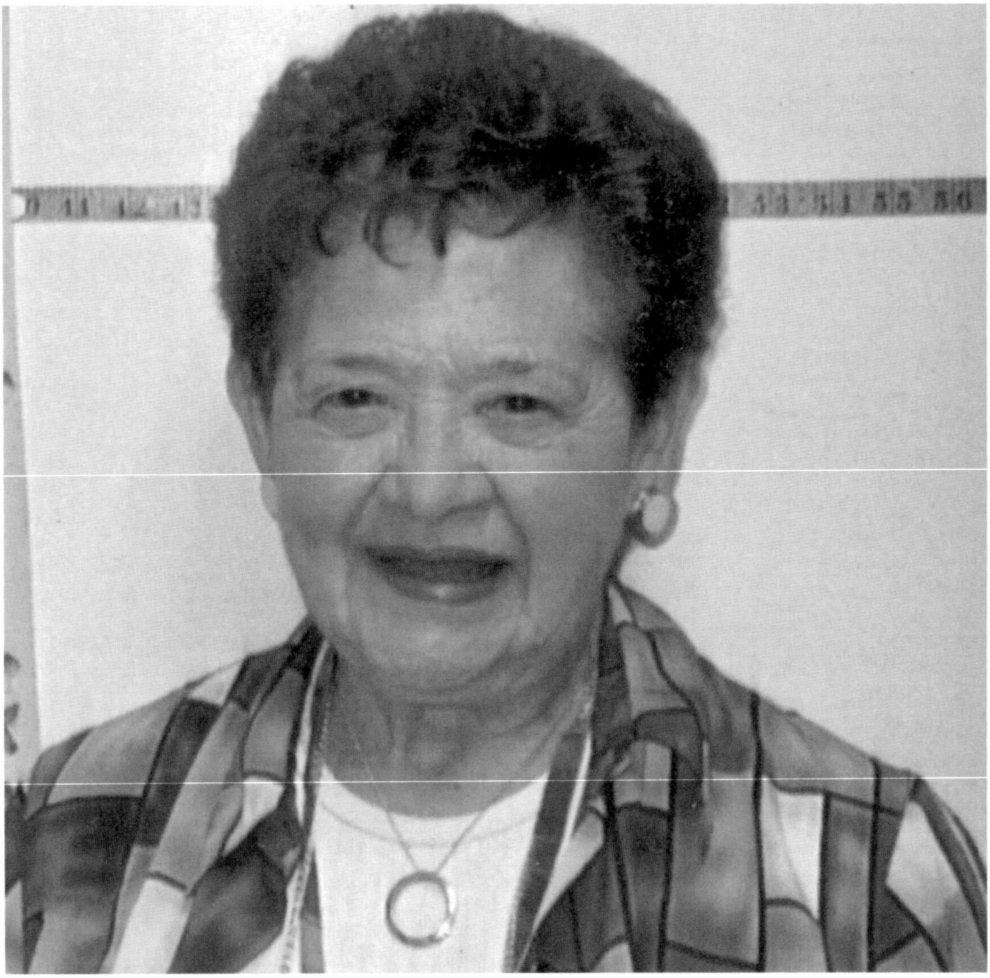

Frances (Frannie) Millward
Her official title is Minister of Outreach, but Millward is sometimes called "Berea's Mother Teresa." With oversight of the First Congregational United Church of Christ of Berea, she founded Church Street Ministries in 1986. Supported by two thrift stores, many churches, civic groups, and generous individuals, the ministry offers a food pantry, emergency financial assistance for rent, utilities, and medical expenses, plus support groups and counseling services for persons in emergency situations. Although she is in her mid-80s, Millward's energy and compassion seem boundless. She has devoted all of her adult life to social services, both as a professional and as a volunteer. Her compassionate, one-on-one approach, her long hours, including weekends, and her innovativeness and selfless dedication characterize Millward's devotion to those in need. In earlier years, Millward worked in several different churches in Christian education, particularly with youth. She still is involved with a group she founded in the 1970s called TORCH (Teen OutReach through Community Help). Young people work together to assist local agencies at shelters and nursing homes. For more than 30 years, she has gone every summer with a group of young people to Lotts' Creek, Kentucky, for a week-long work camp. These experiences offer opportunities for young people to understand and respond to the needs of those less fortunate. Millward talks the talk and walks the walk that Jesus taught his disciples: "As you did it to one of the least of these my brethren, you did it to me." That's Matthew 25:40. For Frannie Millward, it's the foundation of her life's work. (Courtesy of Church Street Ministries.)

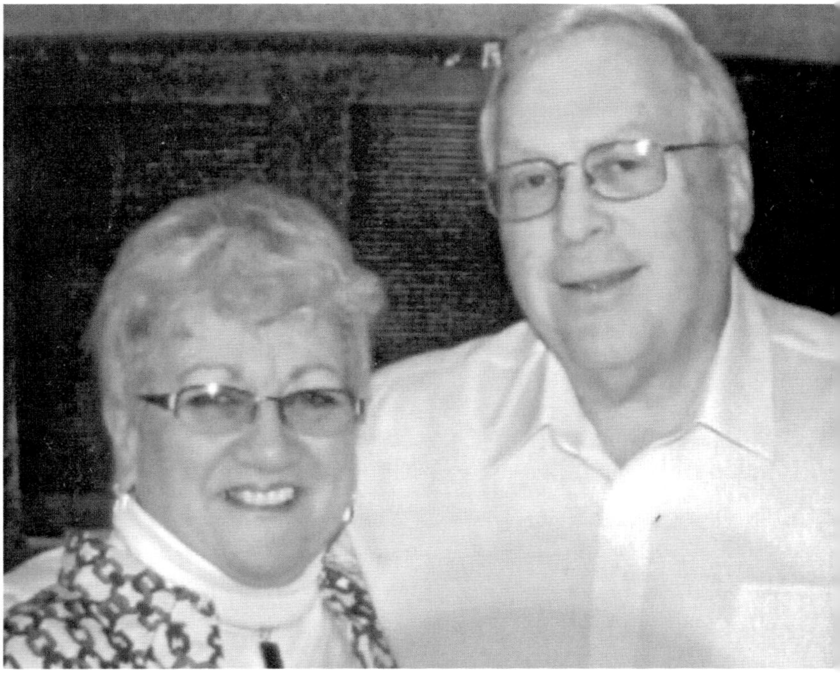

Larry and Elaine Myers
The Berea Kiwanis Club is said to be their first love. Both have held offices and worked tirelessly at Kiwanis events. But their efforts toward making Berea a better place to live impact many organizations. For example, Larry Myers organized the Berea High School Athletic Hall of Fame in 1981. Elaine Myers volunteers regularly in high schools in the Suicide Prevention Education Alliance (SPEA). (Courtesy of Elaine Myers.)

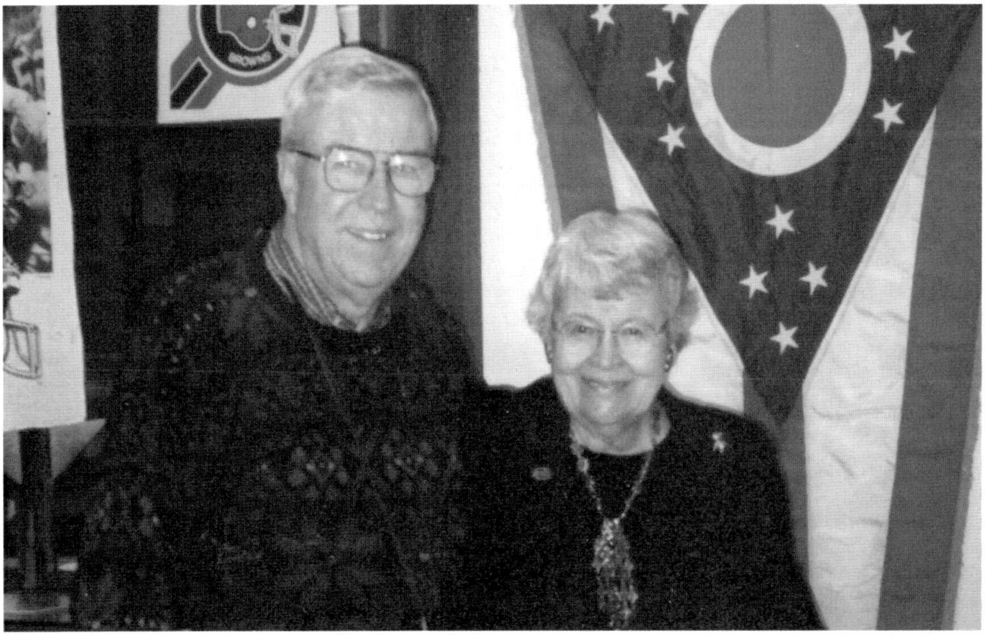

Barbara and Richard Sherwood
Barbara Sherwood was president of the Berea Historical Society and columnist for the Berea *News Sun.* Richard is a World War II veteran. Their daughter Betsy and husband Robert Bradshaw are Wycliffe Bible translators. They serve the Doromu-Koki people of Papua New Guinea by translating the Bible into their native tongues. The Bradshaws have raised their children, Jon, Jessica, and Christopher, in Papua New Guinea.

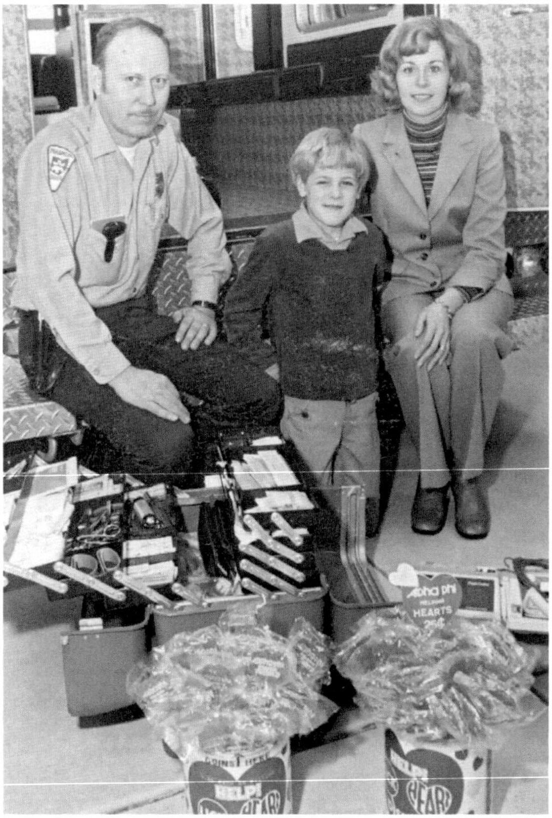

Heart Association Fundraiser
Jack Cicak, assistant fire chief, is pictured with John VandeVisse and Kathy VandeVisse at an American Heart Association fundraiser in 1980. Fundraisers are frequent happenings in Berea, whether by police or fire departments, civic organizations, churches, or young people's school or church groups.

WAGS 4 Kids, Legend in the Making
A Berea-based, nonprofit organization founded in 2004, WAGS (Work Animals Giving Service) 4 Kids provides mobility service and skilled companion animals to Northeast Ohio children with disabilities. Founder and director Wendy Nelson Crann states, "Workers in the WAGS 4 Kids 'Cell Dog' program engage in weekly sessions at a correctional institute with a select group of inmates who learn how to train the dogs." Pictured is Andrew Prince with Kip. Andrew is the grandson of Mary Ellen Posze. (Courtesy of Vanessa Prince.)

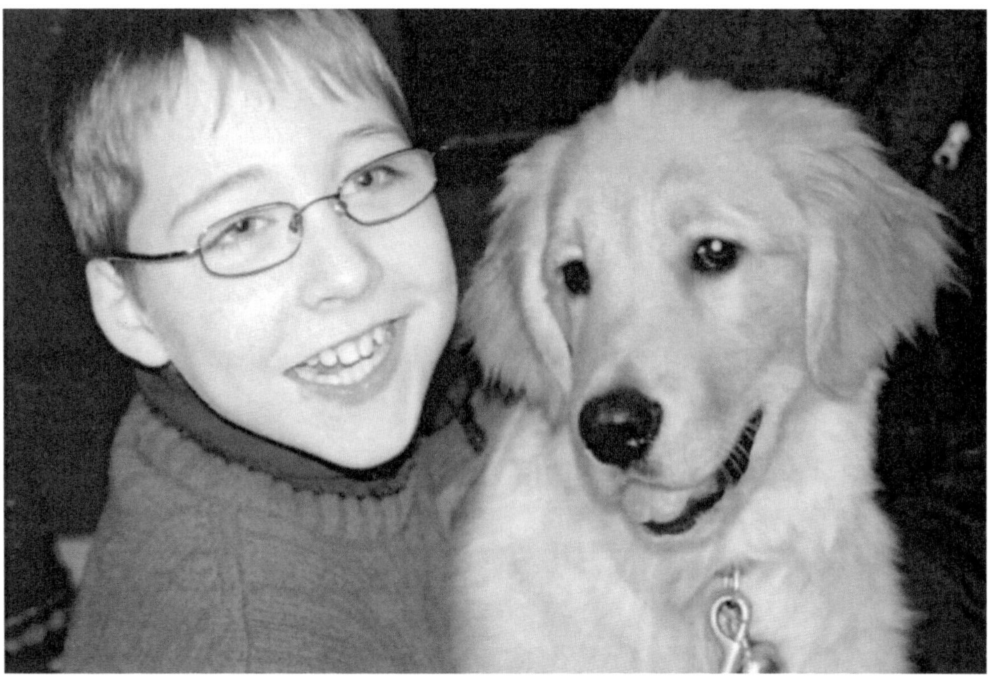

CHAPTER SEVEN

Fine Arts

As the German Methodist Orphans Home (now the Berea Children's Home) may have set the stage for philanthropy in this small community, so the annual Bach Festival at the Baldwin-Wallace Conservatory perhaps initiated an emphasis on fine arts that persists today. Even those whose tastes lie outside the classical music realm take pride in the performers and patrons who arrive in Berea each spring. During the school year, weekly concerts are offered at the conservatory's Kulas Hall by students and faculty. Summer concerts by popular groups at the Coe Lake Gazebo draw families who enjoy an eclectic mix of music against a backdrop of what once consisted of clanging derricks and burrowing drills in a stone quarry.

The Berea Little Theatre first performed in the Fairwood School auditorium and later in upstairs rooms on the Triangle. Baldwin-Wallace College professor William A. Allman founded the Berea Summer Theatre that delighted patrons from throughout the area during the 1970s and 1980s. Well-known music and drama productions by the two high schools, Berea and Midpark, approach a professional level in their staging and talent. The annual Berea Arts Fest held in September, also in the Coe Lake area, and several art shows each year by the Berea Fine Arts Club, give residents a chance to display their talents to the public. Several book discussion groups exist; some have been meeting for decades. Mary Ellen Nichols, adult service director of the Berea Branch of the Cuyahoga County Library, assists these groups in suggesting selections and obtaining materials.

Individuals from Berea have excelled in the fine arts. Some you will meet on these pages are Edward Kuekes, Pulitzer Prize-winning cartoonist for the Cleveland *Plain Dealer*; Henry Barr, outstanding photographer who left a treasury of his work to document the history of Berea; John-Michael Tebelak, author of *Godspell*; Dan Waugh, whose newspaper ramblings about nature inspired readers for years; and, most recently, Rebecca Pitcher, Berea High School and Baldwin-Wallace Conservatory graduate, who played the leading role of Christine Daaé in the touring company of *Phantom of the Opera.*

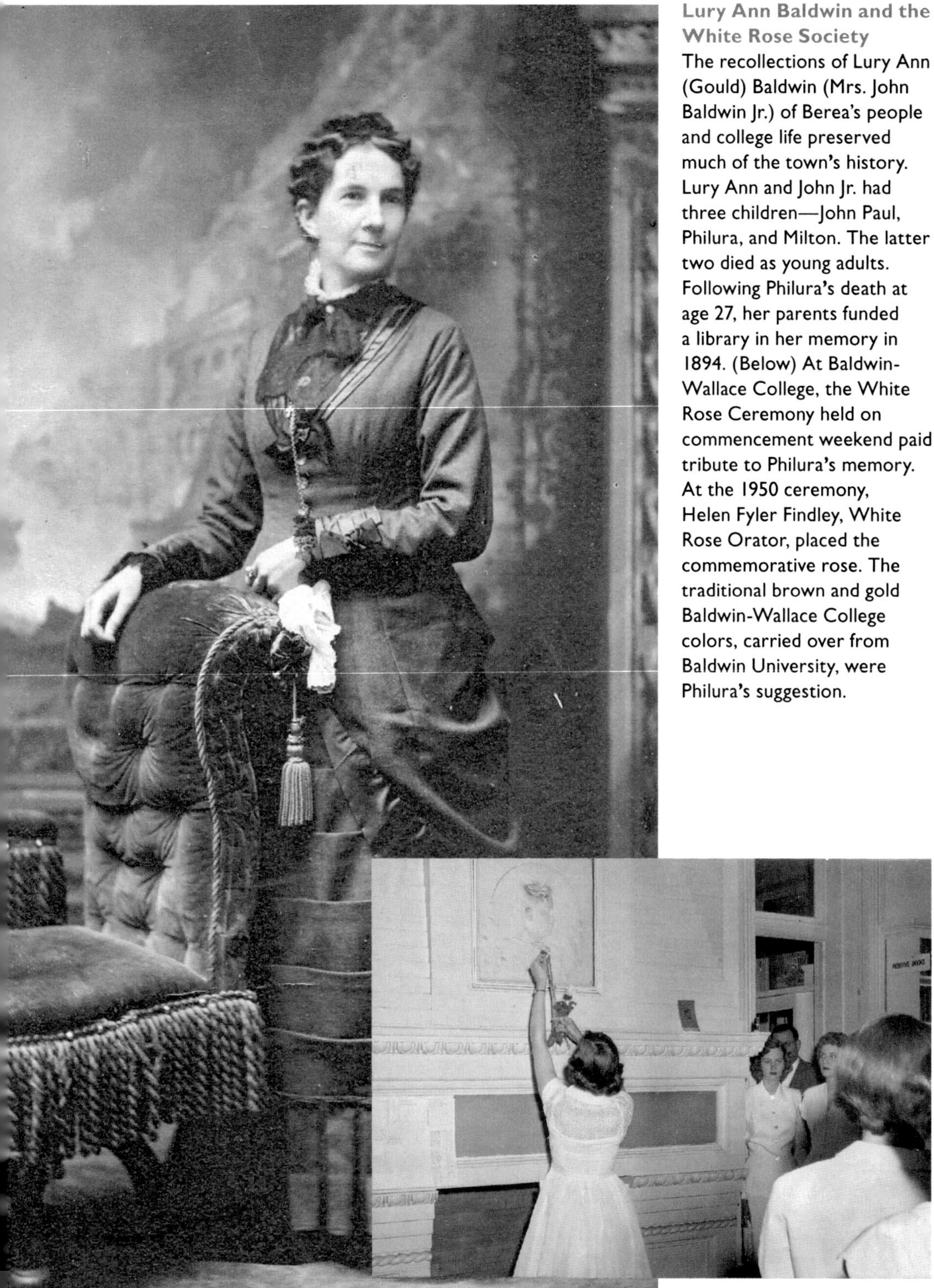

Lury Ann Baldwin and the White Rose Society

The recollections of Lury Ann (Gould) Baldwin (Mrs. John Baldwin Jr.) of Berea's people and college life preserved much of the town's history. Lury Ann and John Jr. had three children—John Paul, Philura, and Milton. The latter two died as young adults. Following Philura's death at age 27, her parents funded a library in her memory in 1894. (Below) At Baldwin-Wallace College, the White Rose Ceremony held on commencement weekend paid tribute to Philura's memory. At the 1950 ceremony, Helen Fyler Findley, White Rose Orator, placed the commemorative rose. The traditional brown and gold Baldwin-Wallace College colors, carried over from Baldwin University, were Philura's suggestion.

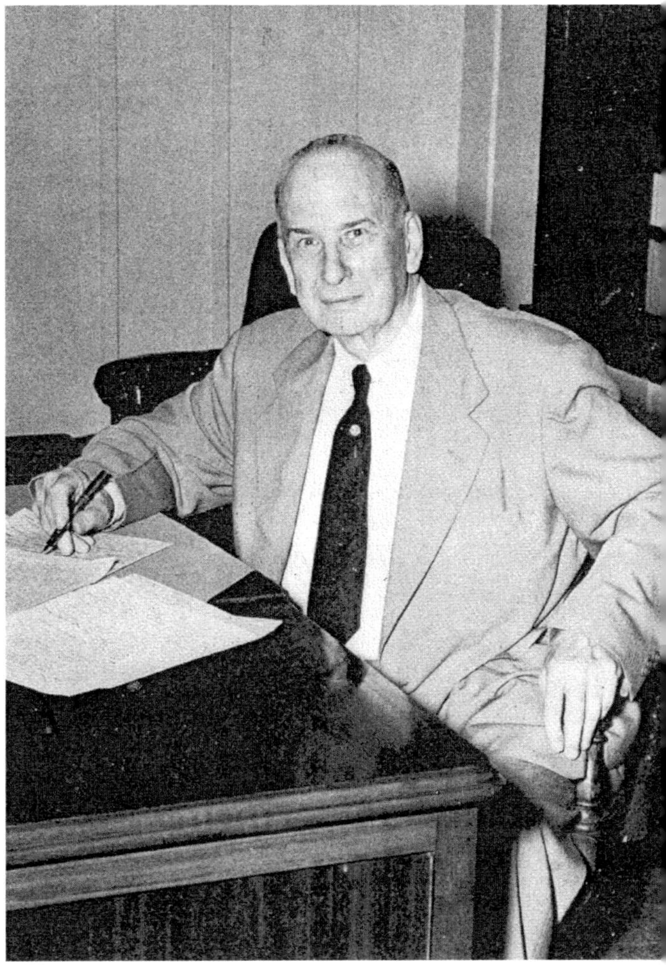

Albert and Selma Riemenschneider
The Riemenschneiders were founders of the renowned Bach Festival at the Conservatory of Baldwin-Wallace College. Classical music lovers and noted performers come to Berea for this event held each spring. Baldwin-Wallace performing groups join with faculty members, students and local professional musicians in the three-day, multi-event program. Soloists are internationally known artists, and lecturers are distinguished Bach and Baroque scholars. The Bach Festival has been held annually since 1932. Dr. Riemenschneider, a professor of piano and organ, was director of the conservatory for 35 years from 1913 to 1948. He also served as acting president in 1949. Riemenschneider made seven trips to Europe to study with Bach scholars and collected an extensive library of Bach's works, including rare editions. Sometimes he would hide the paperback mysteries and westerns he loved to read behind a large Bach manuscript.

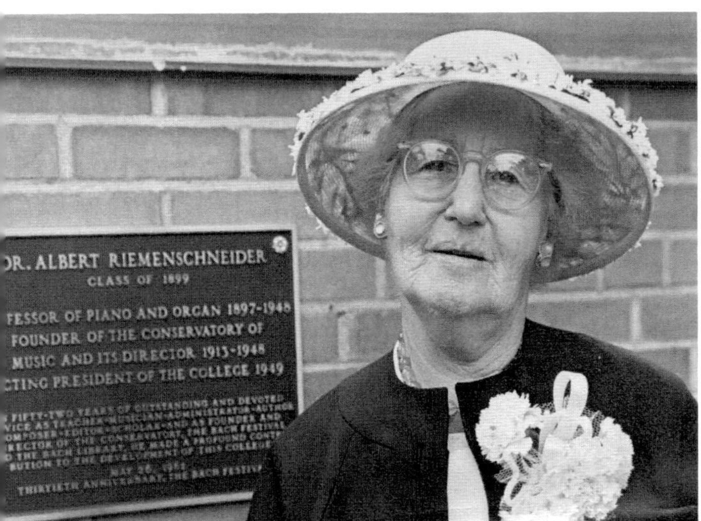

Mrs. Selma Riemenschneider
On the 30th anniversary of the Bach Festival in 1963, Selma Riemenschneider unveiled a plaque recognizing her husband's service and leadership. Following his death in 1950, Selma Riemenschneider continued to live in Berea and to participate in the management of the Bach Festival. In 1951, she donated her husband's collection of rare Bach manuscripts to Baldwin-Wallace College, founding a library that became the Riemenschneider Bach Institute.

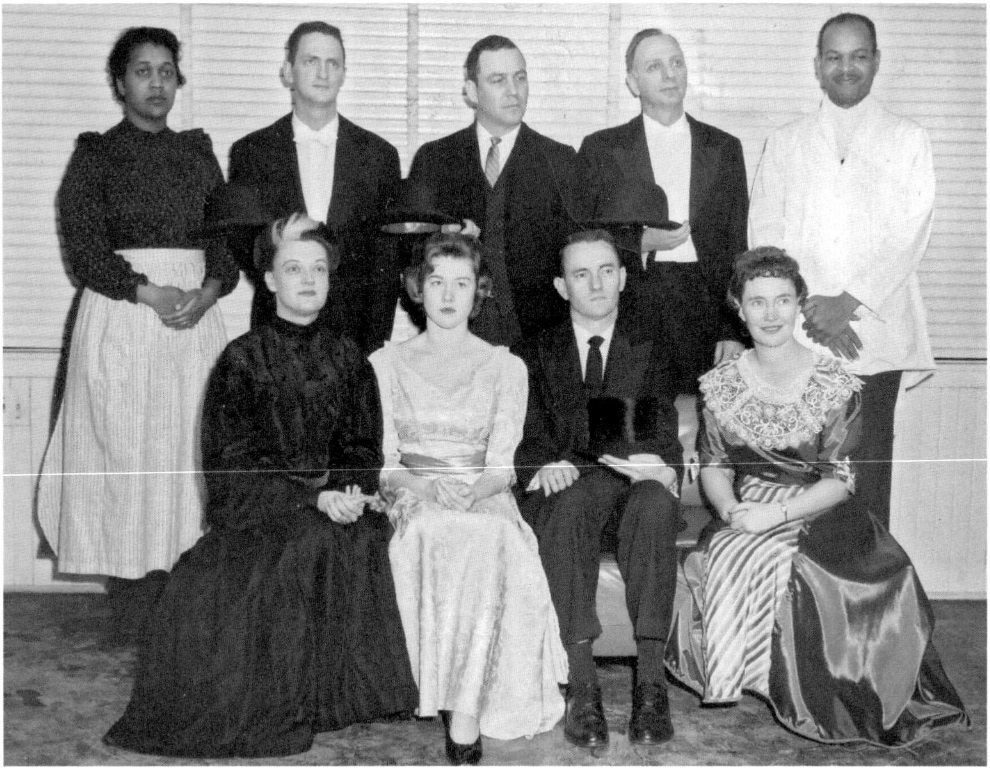

Berea Little Theatre
This active group of thespians performed in the Fairwood School auditorium and later in a building on the Triangle in the 1960s. The cast of *The Little Foxes* posed following dress rehearsal. Row 1, from left, Jo Green, Betty Sandhoff, Bill Stevens, and Martha Vranek. Row 2, from left, Nora Kellog, Dick Babbitts, Don Murray, Austin Beach, and Charles Grimes. The director was Clyde Stevens.

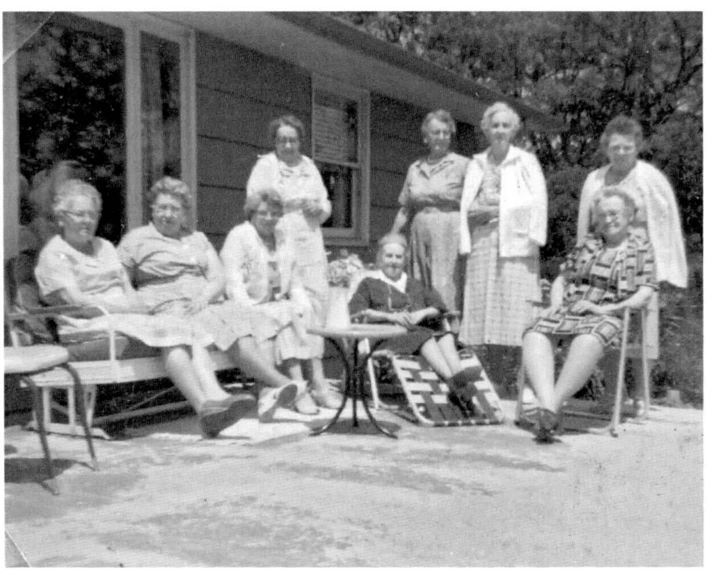

H2O Club
Its name had nothing to do with Berea water. Instead, the club's name stood for Home, Health, and Other Things. Members met after lunch at one another's houses and were home when their children arrived from school. Meeting on Laura Phillips' patio are from left, Laura Phillips, Jessie Schmidt, Olata Smith, Irene Stull, Pauline Clough, Anna Squire, Esther Adams, Hilda Chapman, and Harriet Lansinger.

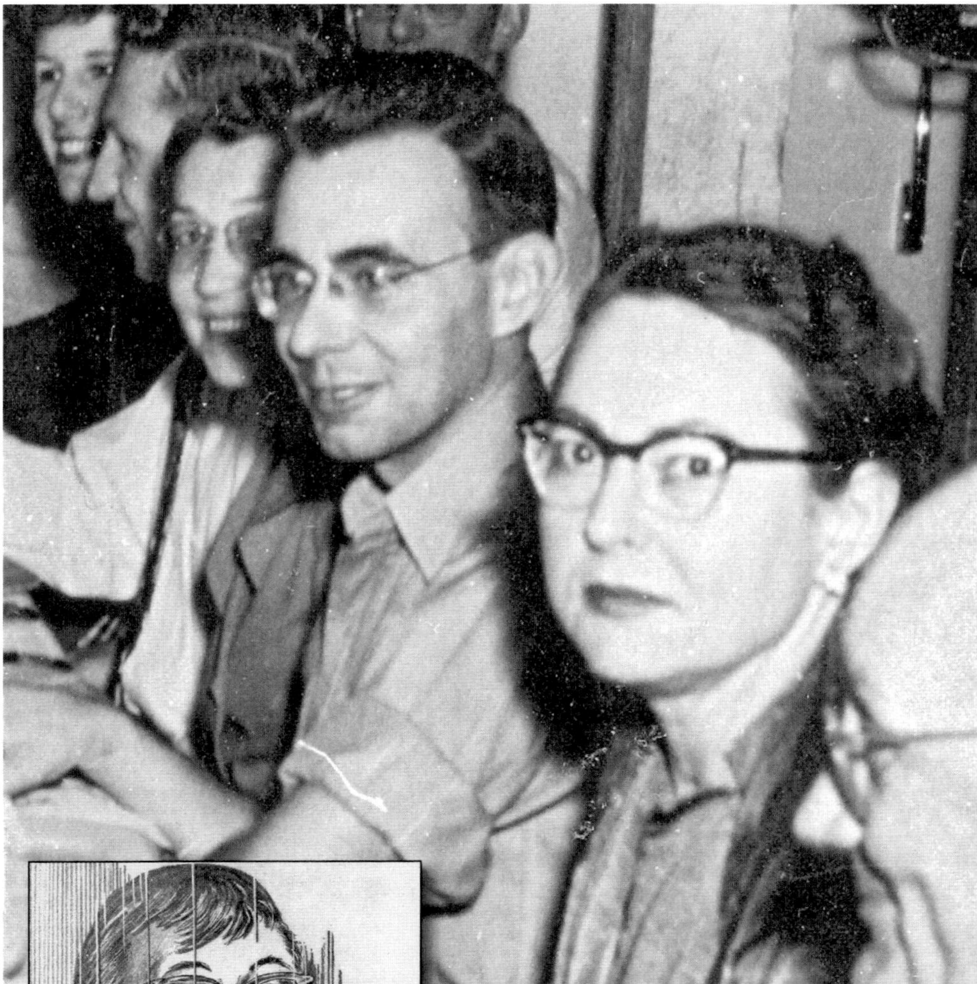

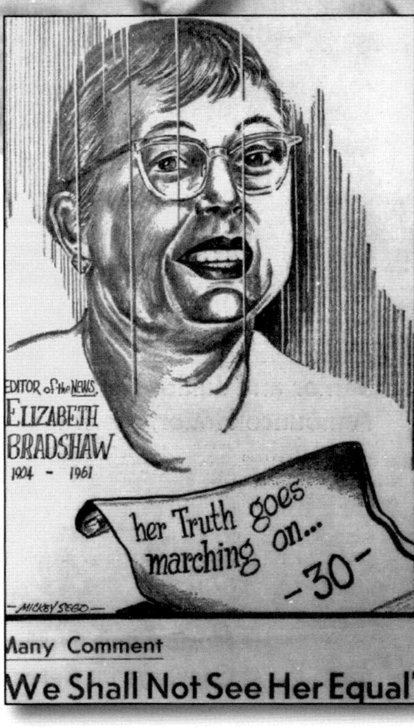

Elizabeth Bradshaw

From a small farm on Sheldon Road near Lake Abram, after graduating from Baldwin-Wallace College *cum laude,* Elizabeth Bradshaw pursued her journalism career in her hometown. Starting as society editor in 1932, then assistant editor, then editor of the Berea *News* in 1945, she remained with the paper until her death in 1961. She became well respected in the community as well as state and national publication circles, and the Berea *News* publications won numerous awards for excellence under her leadership. Miss Bradshaw was noted for her keen mind and forthright opinions. (Cartoon by Mickey Sego.)

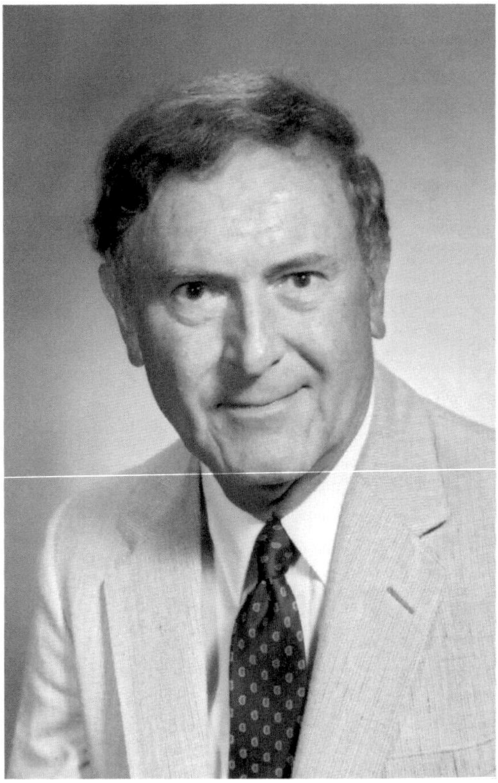

C. Bruce Hardy

Many of Hardy's community activities involved music. He sang in the Baldwin-Wallace College Bach Festival choir for 16 years, in the United Methodist Church choir for 40 years, and in the Grindstone Four, a local barbershop quartet. Roles with the Berea Little Theatre and the Berea Summer Theatre expanded his love for the fine arts. Active in many civic affairs, Hardy also taught evening extension classes at Baldwin-Wallace. Eventually, he turned to politics as his father, Alva, had done. He served one term as city councilman-at-large and two terms as council president. Professionally, Hardy spent most of his career in the advertising business in Cleveland. In later years, he was a self-employed marketing consultant in Berea.

Front Street Five Plus Two

In 1971, this popular group entertained at the Antique Automobile Show in Berea. (From left, Leroy Cramer, drums; Milt Hines, trumpet; Bruce Hardy, clarinet; Dr. Myron Welty, trombone and leader; Bill Miller, piano; Amos Battenfield, bass guitar, and Bill Fiske, banjo. (From Charlotte Fiske collection.)

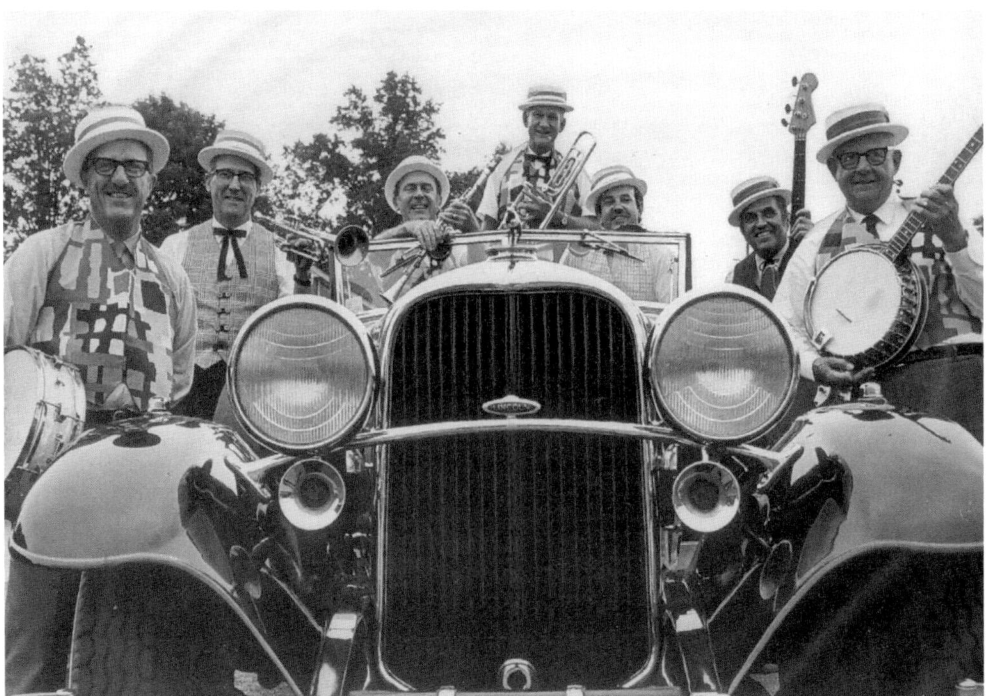

Muriel Hardy

As community life editor for the Berea *News*, later the *News Sun,* between 1950 and 1980, Hardy wrote about Bereans' weddings, awards, and travels in her columns, "Social Scene" and "Around the Town." Her feature writing helped the newspaper win state and national awards, and her series about high school band tour scams won her a Pulitzer Prize nomination. *Sun News* executive editor, Linda Kinsey, called Muriel Hardy a role model for herself and for many others. Hardy was part of the support group for the Berea Summer Theatre, which is how she met her husband, Bruce. She turned her writing talent in a different direction when she became public relations director for the then-new hospital known as Southwest Community Hospital. Her efforts were instrumental in creating a positive image for Southwest.

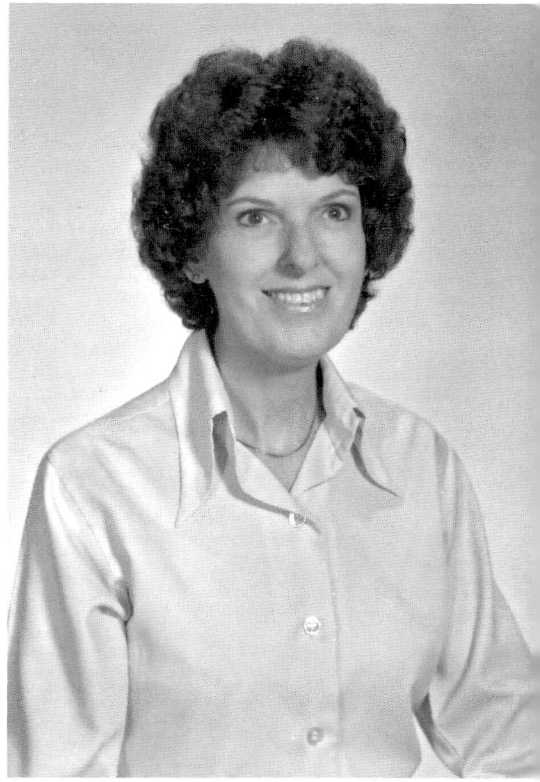

Dan Waugh

For 35 years, Waugh's column "Nature Rambles" appeared in the *Sun* newspaper chain papers. Baldwin-Wallace College honored Waugh when it dedicated the Dan Waugh collection of nature books at Ritter Library in 1975. NBC television sent a crew to Waugh's home overlooking the Rocky River where they filmed "A Walk with the Rambler."

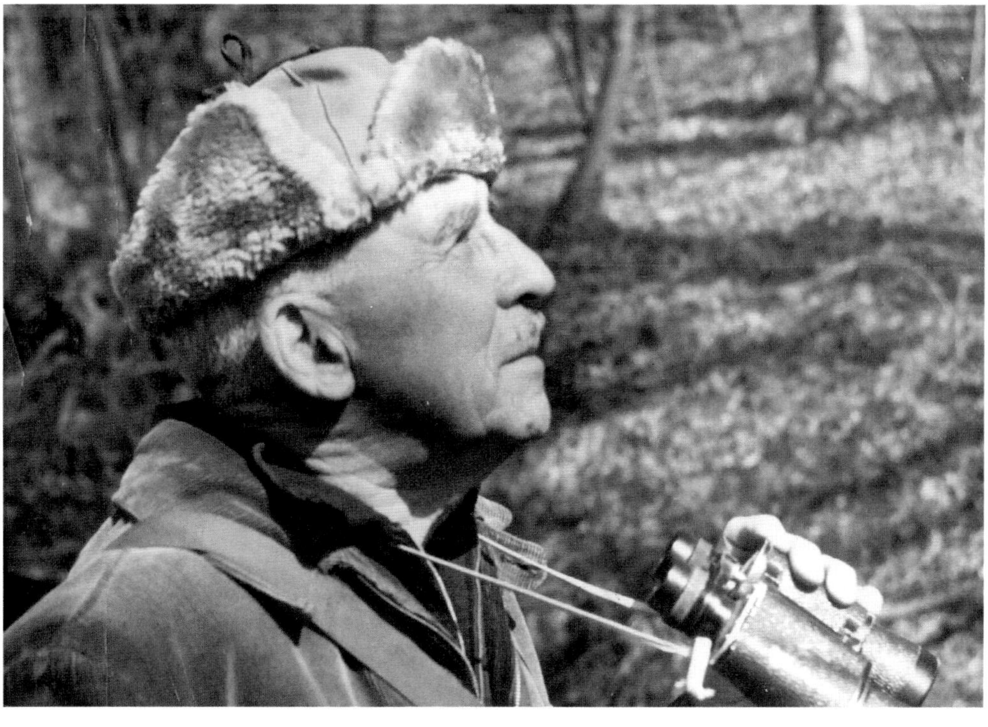

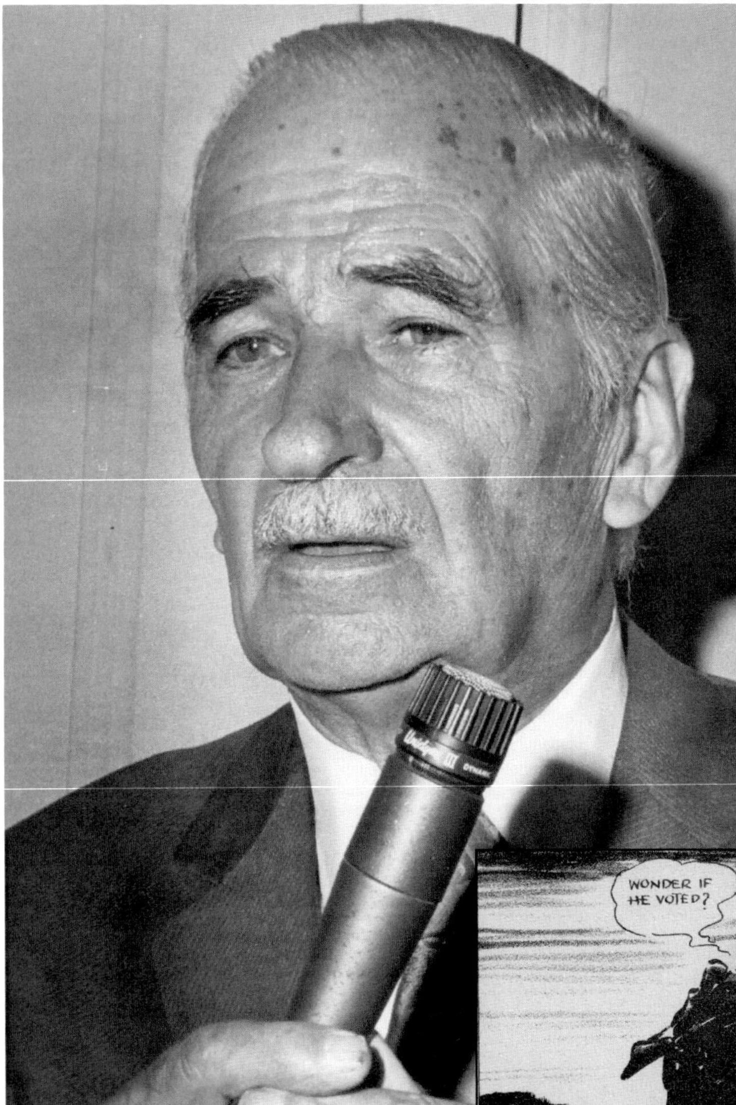

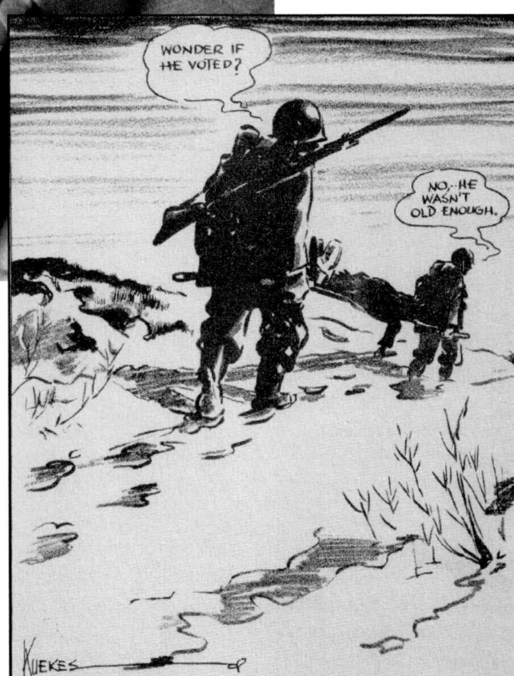

Edward Kuekes
To several generations, Kuekes' 1953 Pulitzer Prize–winning cartoon might need some explaining. Entitled "Aftermath," two soldiers carry the body of their buddy from the battlefield. One soldier wonders if their buddy voted. The other replies, "No, he wasn't old enough." Kuekes, editorial cartoonist for the Cleveland *Plain Dealer,* was inspired by his son's service at age 20 in World War II and by the movement to lower the voting age to 18. That did not happen until 1971. In the meantime, Kuekes' cartoon was reprinted many times.

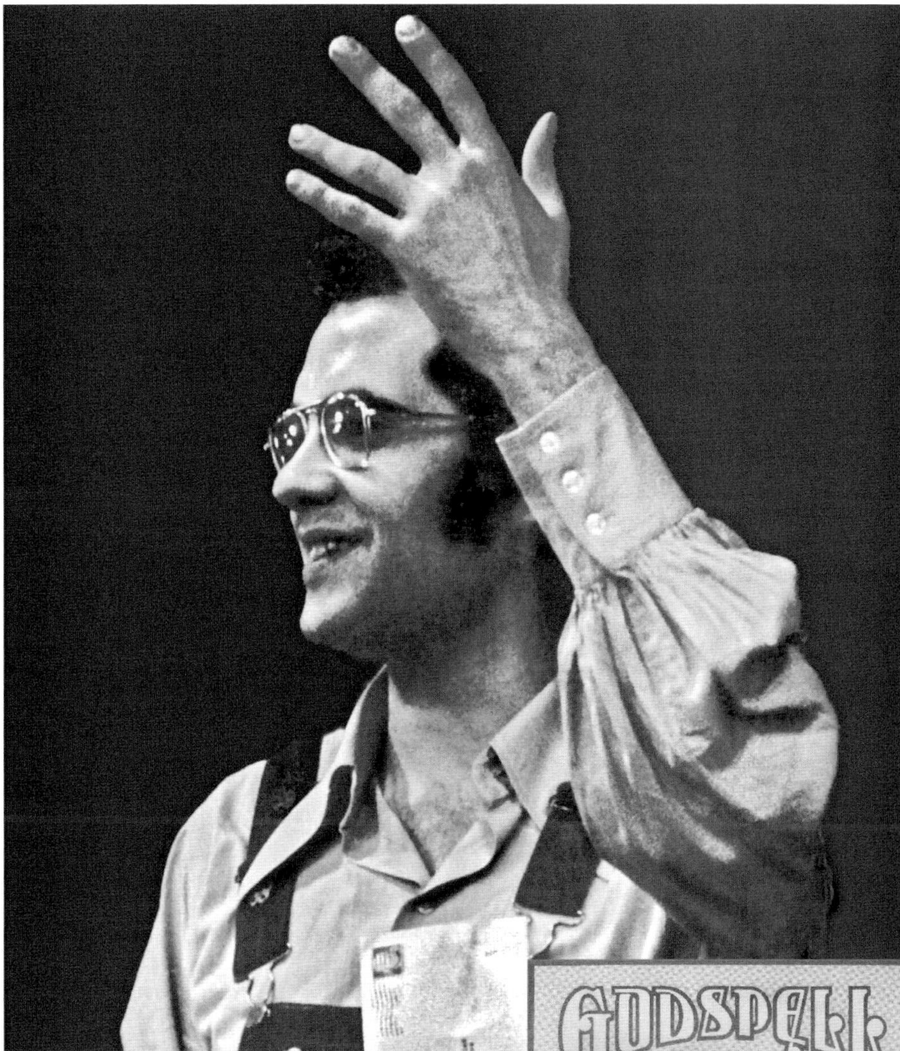

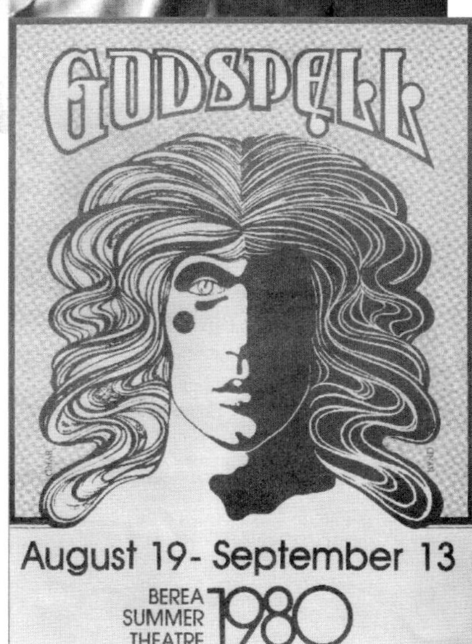

John-Michael Tebelak

Never mind that the play had its beginning as a master's thesis. Tebelak's ambitious undertaking to turn the Gospel of St. Matthew into a contemporary musical is theater history. With words and music by Stephen Schwartz, *Godspell* premiered at Cleveland's Great Lakes Theater Festival under Tebelak's direction in 1970. It went on to a long Broadway run and to theaters around the world. In 1980, he returned to his hometown where he visited his parents, John and Genevieve Tebelak, and directed *Godspell* for the Berea Summer Theatre. Tebelak died in 1985 at the age of 36. Cleveland *Plain Dealer* drama critic Peter Bellamy wrote, "*Godspell* guaranteed him (Tebelak) a spiritual legacy which will endure as long as Christianity and the theater."

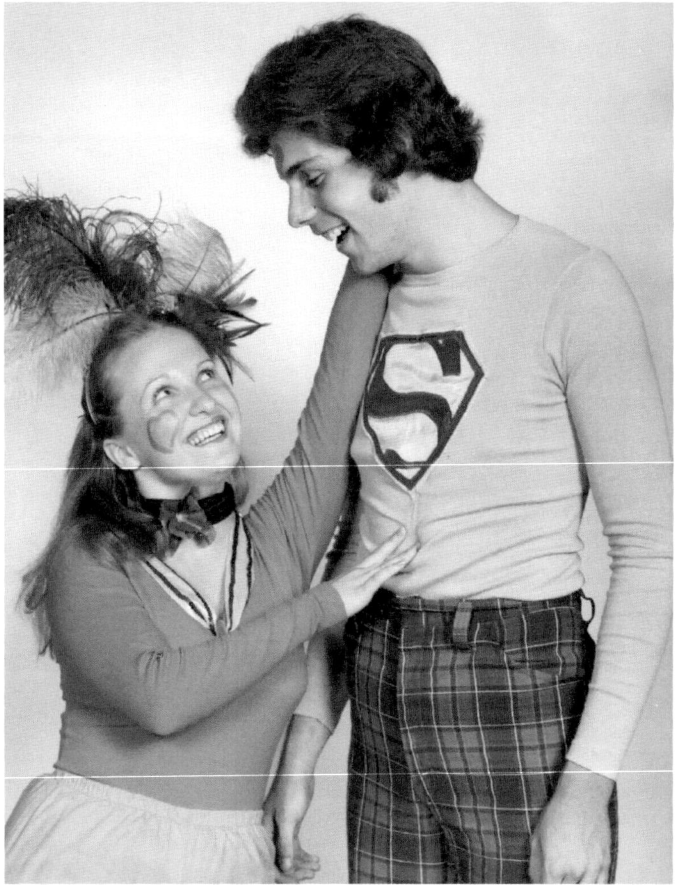

***Godspell* Cast, 1980**

When John-Michael Tebelak returned to the Berea Summer Theatre in 1980 to direct *Godspell*, he worked with these actors: Cathie Brenkus (left) played Mary Magdalene, and Christopher Smith portrayed Jesus.

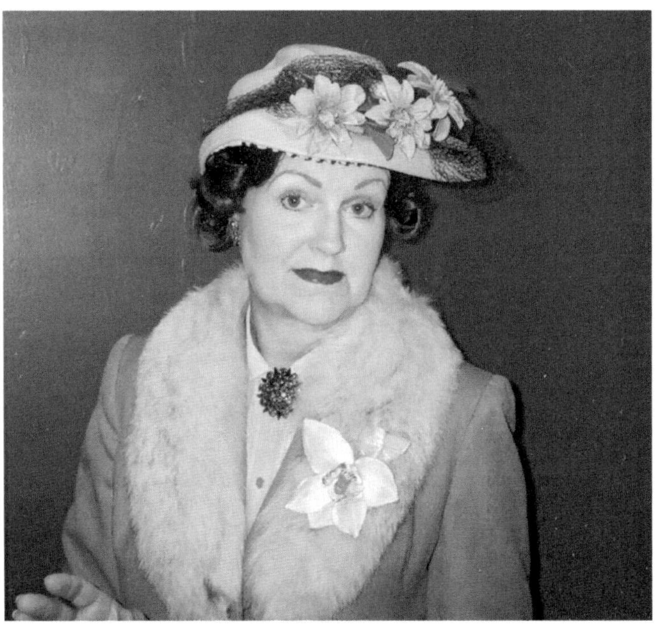

Carol Starre-Kmiecik

Baldwin-Wallace theater major Carol Starre-Kmiecik travels the state entertaining hundreds of audiences each year with her *Famous American Women* one-person performances. She was asked to portray Cleveland's legendary news personage, Dorothy Fuldheim, for Cleveland's 1976 celebration of America's Bicentennial. Since then, Starre-Kmiecik has added Jacqueline Kennedy Onassis, Amelia Earhart, and the "unsinkable" Molly Brown, among others, to her repertoire. Starre-Kmiecik found she could combine her made-to-order acting career with her family responsibilities.

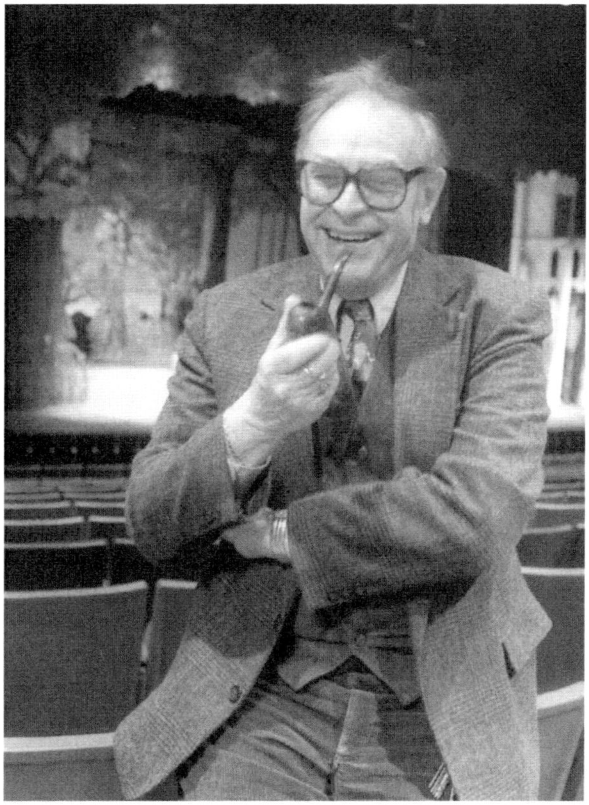

William A. Allman

"Colorful" and "gregarious" are words often used to describe Baldwin-Wallace drama professor William (Bill) Allman. But his serious devotion to the theater could never be disputed. In his tenure at the college and as managing director of the Berea Summer Theatre for 40 years, Allman directed more than 200 plays and musicals. He made regular trips to London and took his students to the Soviet Union to observe productions. Many of his students went on to graduate schools or careers in the theater. Well-respected in theater circles, he brought well-known figures to Berea to see and star in Berea Summer Theatre productions. Indirectly, Allman can take some credit for helping to restore the opulent theaters on Cleveland's Playhouse Square. In 1972, the Berea Summer Theatre, under his direction, produced *Jacques Brel Is Alive and Well and Living in Paris* in the Studio Theater at Baldwin-Wallace. A movement to restore the downtown Cleveland theaters had begun, and some of those visionaries, seeing Allman's production, were inspired to bring *Jacques Brel* as a cabaret theater performance to the State Theater lobby where it ran for two years. Five plays and three musicals had world premieres at the Berea Summer Theatre. Known for his wild ties and his ever-present pipe, Allman loved to interact a bit with patrons. After the final curtain, he would appear onstage, challenging the audience with his trademark line, "If you enjoyed the show", . . . And delighted playgoers would chime in, " . . . please tell your friends." Despite hue and cry from the community—indeed, all Cuyahoga County—the college discontinued funding the Berea Summer Theatre in the mid-1990s. Baldwin-Wallace College named its largest theater, site of the Berea Summer Theatre, the William A. Allman Theatre on July 8, 1998. Allman continued as professor emeritus of theater at Baldwin-Wallace for two years after the close of the Berea Summer Theatre. He helped found the Grindstone Players in 2002. He was scheduled to direct *Our Town* in the fall of 2005, but the final curtain fell for Allman when he died on July 28 of that year. The show did go on, as Allman would have hoped, with Ellen Rooney directing.

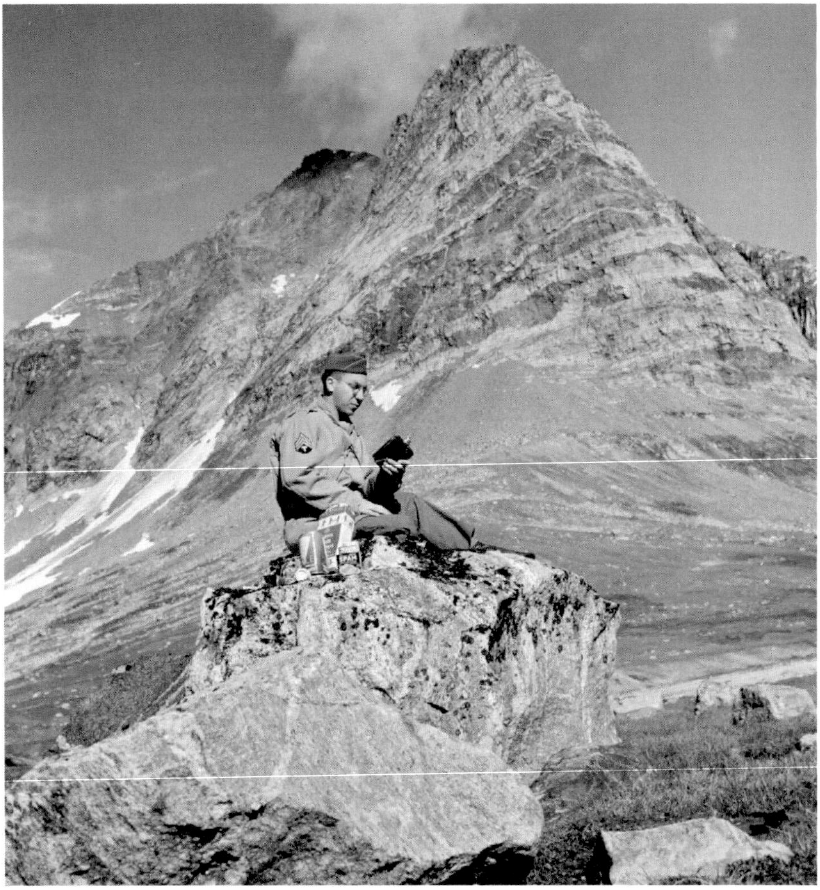

Henry Barr

Barr was an "alumnus" of the German Methodist Orphans Home (now the Berea Children's Home). He and his mother and two sisters came to the orphanage from Kentucky a year after Henry's birth. His mother was a Methodist deaconess and obtained a staff position at the orphanage. He lived there from 1918 to 1930. While Henry attended Berea High School and Baldwin-Wallace College, he worked for his friend, Otto Mahler, also an "alumnus" of the orphanage, at Mahler's popular confectionery on Front Street, Gray's Candy Kitchen. In 1943, Barr enlisted in the US Signal Corps and served three years as a photographer at the Air Force base in Greenland. Following the war, he married Margaret Caroline Aanons. He went into the photography business with James Gorman and later became successful in his own business, Ohio School Pictures and Royal Color, Inc., specializing in pictures of schoolchildren. The School Picture Industry honored Henry Barr with its Lifetime Achievement Award in 1987. He served on the Berea Board of Education for 20 years. This was a period of explosive growth in Berea during which 16 schools were built in an eight-year period. Barr's strong leadership and keen business judgment were recognized as vital to the progress made during those years. In 1970, he started Ohio Book Fairs to provide primary school children with suitable, age-appropriate reading matter at a reasonable price. For more than 40 years, he was the official photographer for the Cleveland Browns. Known to many as "Mr. Berea," Barr was involved in many facets of community life. He was president of Berea City Council and a charter member and president of the Berea Rotary Club. He always worked tirelessly as a trustee for the Berea Children's Home where he grew up. A treasury of Henry Barr photos of the community's people and places was left to the Berea Historical Society, a generous and valuable gift to researchers.

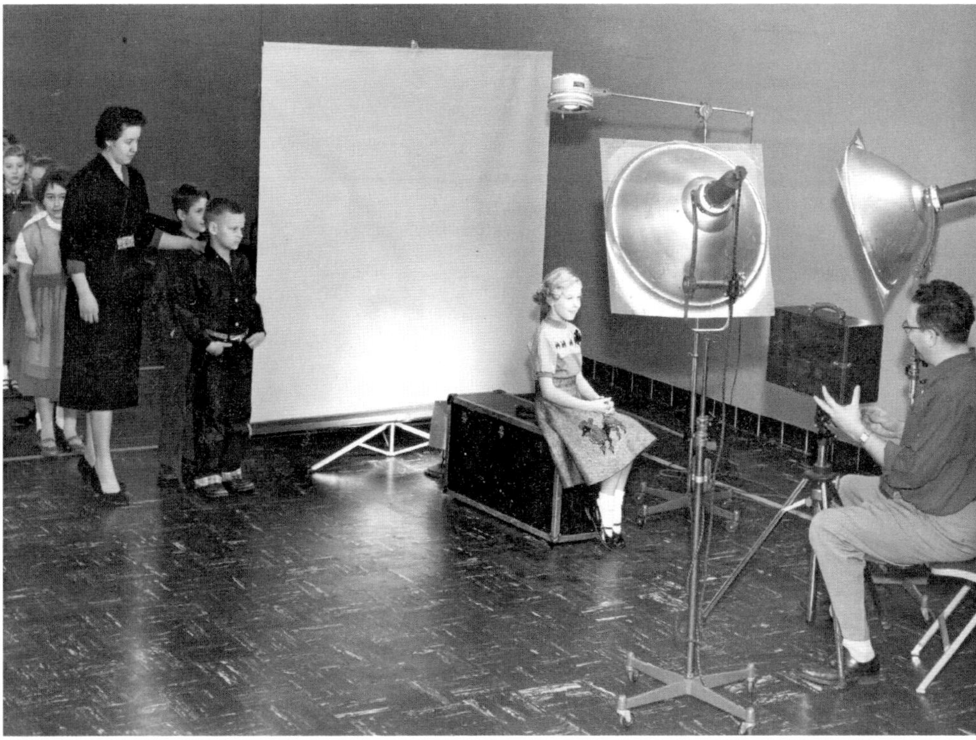

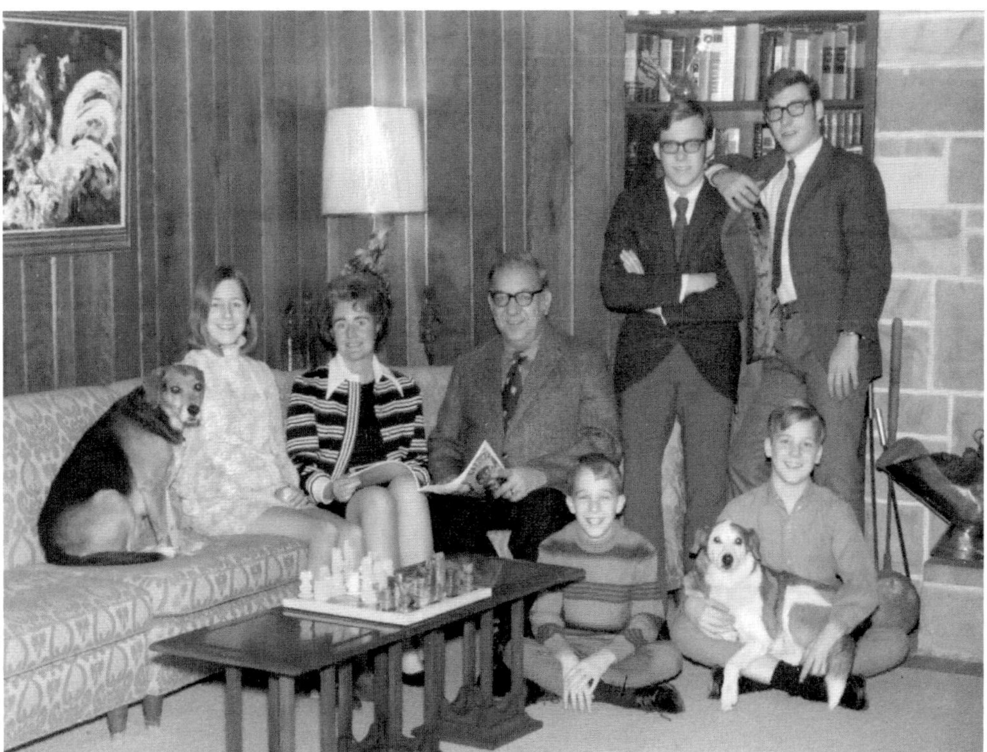

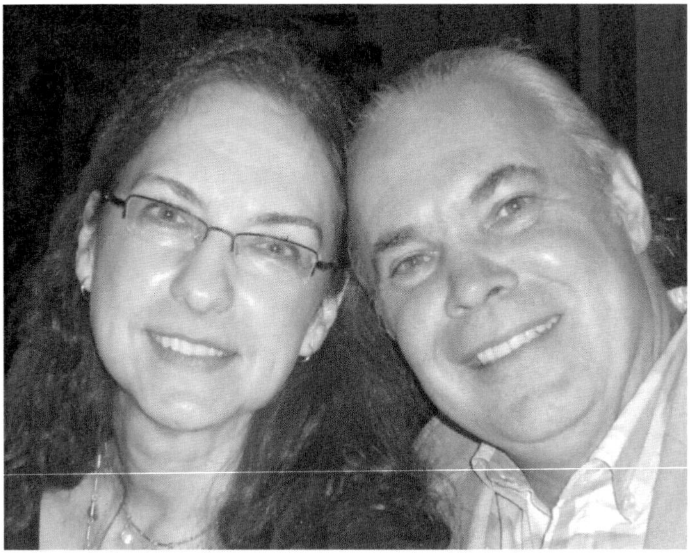

Kenneth and Donna McCarthy

In 1977, Ken and Donna McCarthy bought Gorman's Photo and Art on the Berea Triangle. McCarthy lent his artistic talents and his sense of community to spearhead the Grindstone Festival and the Berea Arts Fest. He designed logos for both annual events. After retiring from nearly 30 years in the retail world, Ken McCarthy now teaches art classes in a century-old schoolhouse. (Courtesy of Ken McCarthy.)

Hollywood Slim Band

Greg Lucic (Hollywood Slim) and his brother John grew up on Fairpark Drive in Berea. They started playing music together in 1974 and are still playing today. In this 1980 photo, all six members of the band were from Berea. (From left, Jeff Bergen, saxophone; Greg: "Hollywood Slim" Lucic, lead vocalist/harmonica; John Lucic, guitar and vocals; Jim "J.D." White, bass; Konrad Aukerman, trombone; and Jim Quigley, drums.) Today's version of The Hollywood Slim Band entertains Bereans frequently at the Eastland Inn and at the Coe Lake summer concerts in the park.

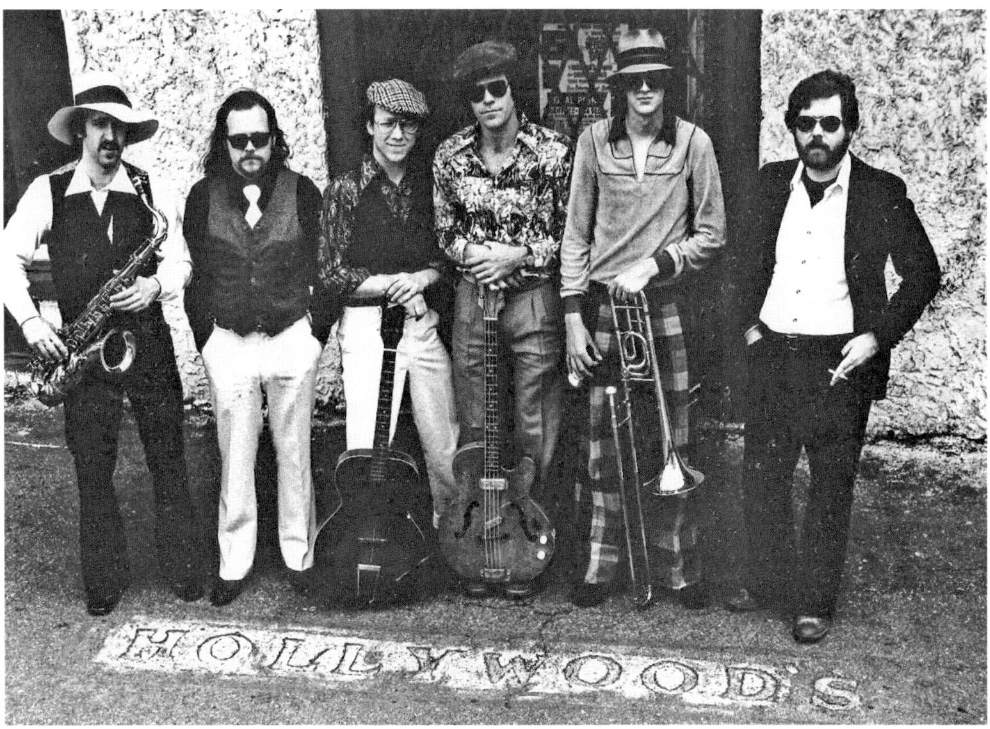

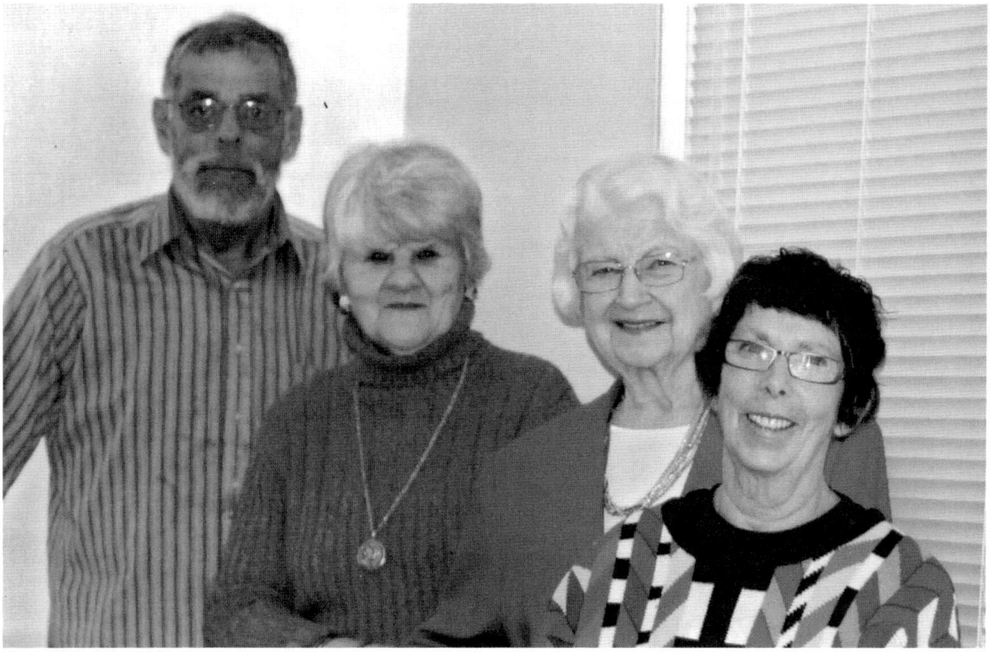

Grindstone Players. Legend in the Making

Berea Grindstone Players was founded by the "gritty gang of seven" in 1998. Bill Allman, Margaret Langer and Bruce Hardy spearheaded the project with (from left) Kent Overton, Shirley Moon, Jane Schneider, and Sue Overton. The group performs at St. Andrew's Presbyterian Church but hopes to find a permanent home in Berea. They are always searching for patrons and lovers of the arts to join the tradition and community of Berea theater.

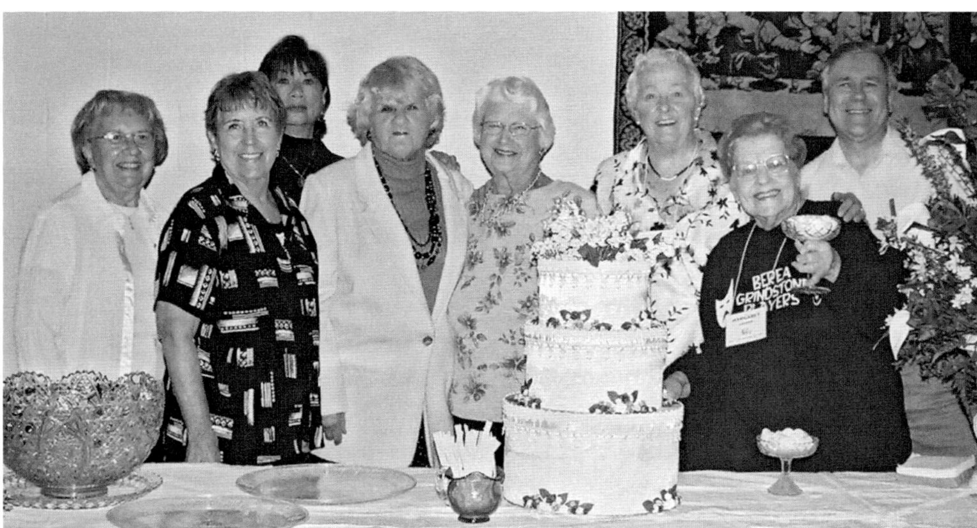

Grindstone Players

From left to right are the following: unidentified, unidentified, Rosemary Nunweiler, Shirley Moon, Jane Schneider, Georgia Bobinski, Margaret Langer, and Paul Runevitch.

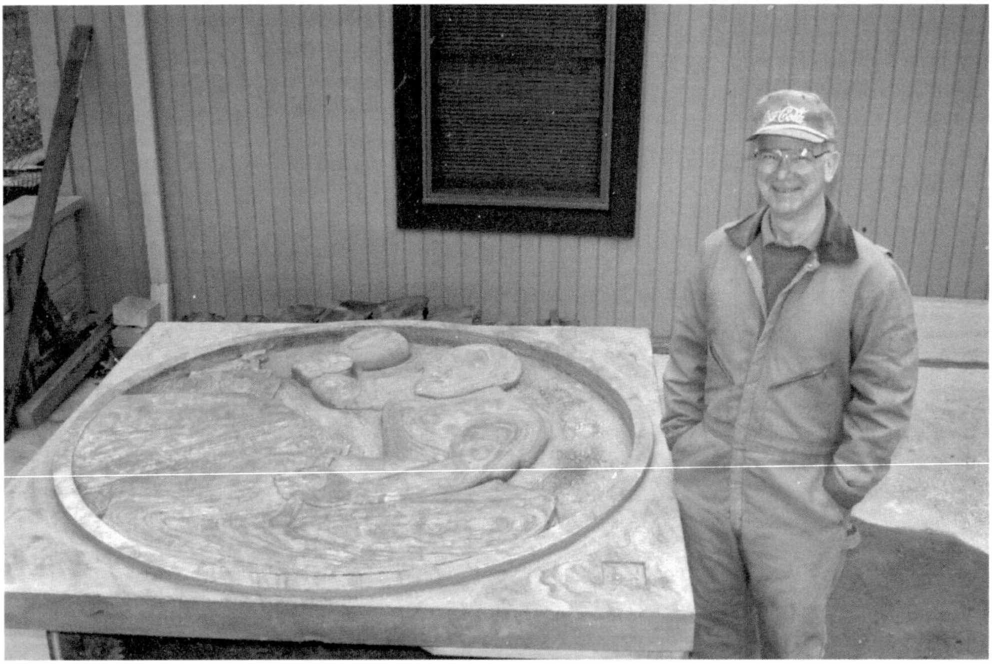

Thomas Harmon
His sculpture, presented as a lasting gift to the Berea Historical Society, depicts Berea's past in sandstone. Each image that Harmon created helps capture Berea's history as the sandstone capital of the world. The piece is now located in reference room of the Mahler Museum. In addition to sandstone, Harmon has been sculpting with marble and native American woods for more than 20 years.

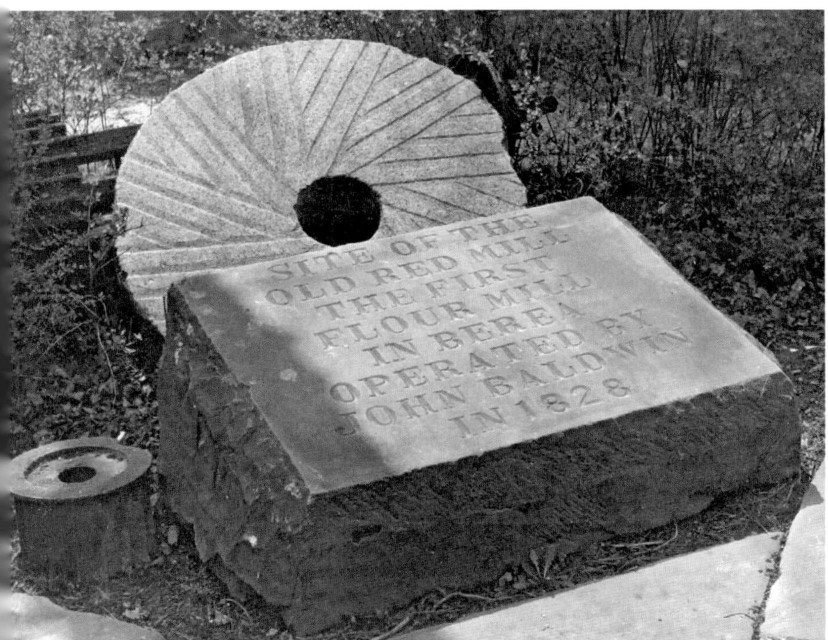

Grindstone Marker
The grindstone decorates the marker of the site of John Baldwin's mill, the first flour mill in Berea. The marker was once located on the college campus. Now, however, it is in the garden at the Berea Historical Society. Grindstones appear on many Berea lawns as ornamental sculptures.

CHAPTER EIGHT

Military

Many individuals included in this book have served in the military, beginning with veterans of the Spanish-American War. Several Bereans played leadership roles in the Civil War, including Capt. Edward Kennedy (see Chapter One), S.S. Brown, and Gershom Barber; all three of these were officers, then became mayors and community leaders upon the close of the war.

Berea's American Legion Post 91 named its post for Albert E. Baesel Jr. He was awarded a posthumous Congressional Medal of Honor for his valor in World War I. The return of his remains eight years later prompted one of the largest and most dignified parades in Berea's history.

Many men profiled from the last half of the 20th century could be marked with a flag in the index since so many appeared to be fine examples of what Tom Brokaw calls "The Greatest Generation." Names of World War II veterans are engraved on a monument on the Triangle near a statue of a Civil War soldier. Bereans line the streets for Memorial Day parades and services of respect for those who gave their lives. A nearby church erected a park-like memorial for Marine Cpl. Brad Squires, 1997 Berea High School graduate, who was killed by a roadside bomb in Iraq in 2005. US Navy personnel were a common sight around town during World War II. Baldwin-Wallace College had a V-12 unit stationed on the campus. The V-12 provided undergraduate education for selected applicants at major universities and small church-affiliated colleges. Successful trainees qualified for Navy midshipmen schools or Marine Corps Officer Candidate School, leading to commissions as Navy ensigns or Marine Corps second lieutenants. Many of these graduates had distinguished non-military careers on the national stage after the war, including Attorney General Robert F. Kennedy, Senator Daniel Patrick Moynihan, Jack Lemmon, actor, and Roger Williams, musician. The Navy personnel in the V-12 unit at Baldwin-Wallace were heroes to the city of Berea, especially one fateful day.

Berea was home to Capt. Charles A. Bassett II. A Berea High School graduate, Bassett was a NASA astronaut in the Gemini program. Like two of his classmates, Lieut. Cmdr. Roger B. Chaffee and Clifton C. Williams, USMC, Captain Bassett lost his life while serving in the space program.

A highly decorated veteran of three wars, Ret. Maj. Gen. Sylvester T. Del Corso's peacetime assignment was as Ohio's adjutant general. In that role, he commanded the Ohio National Guard at the time of the Kent State University shootings in 1970 that killed four students.

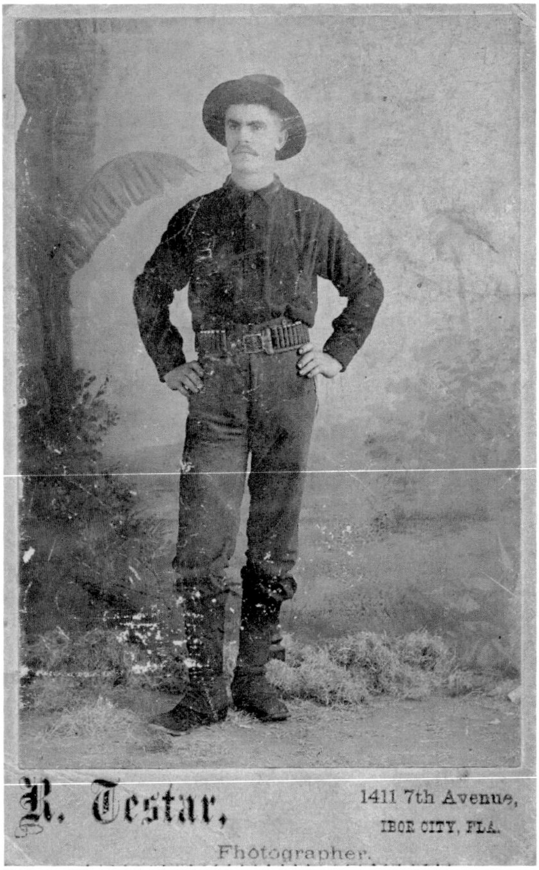

George Schmidt
A Spanish-American War veteran, George Schmidt evidently spent some time in Florida during his enlistment.

Bridge Street Armory around 1897
On horse, Charles Parker; on ground, from left, Fred Barendt ("Munch"), George Schmidt, and Ted Virginsky; standing on walk, from left, James Fowles and Fran Barendt. This was just before the Spanish-American War. (Lyle Chambers Collection.)

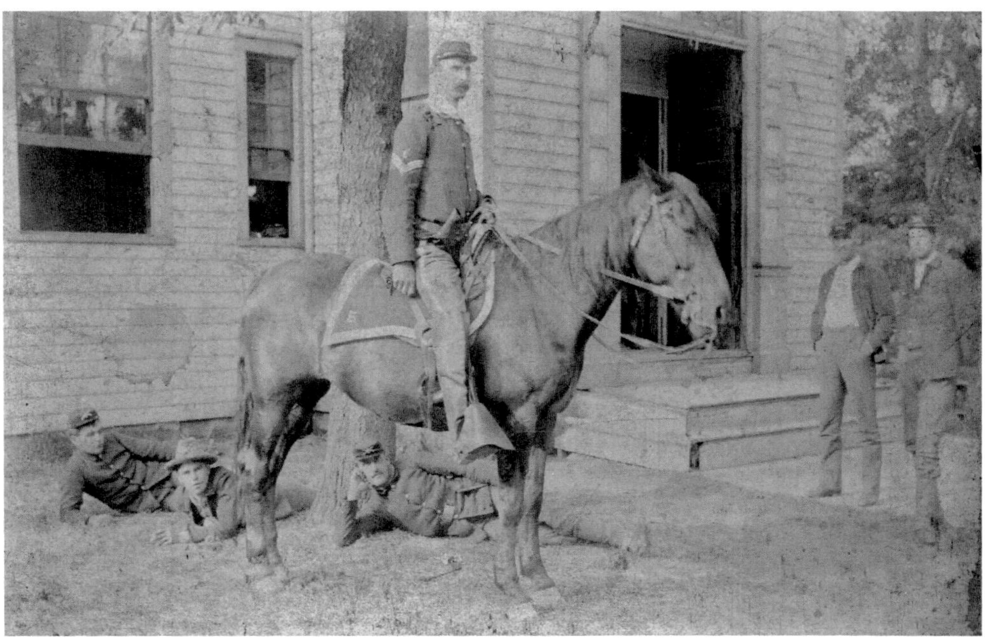

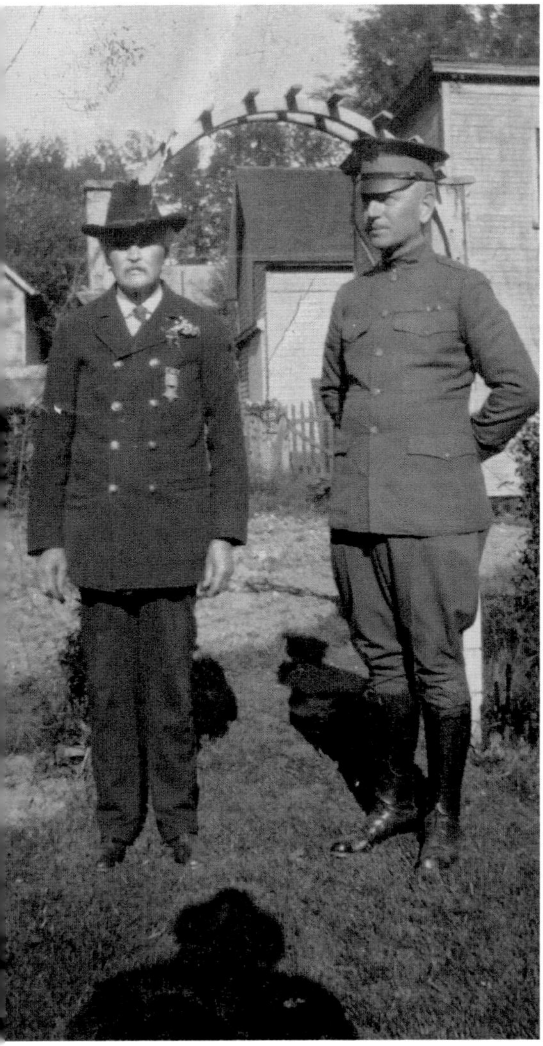

Thomas Marks and John Southam
Marks (left) is in the uniform of the Spanish-American War. He was the father of Berea historian Dorothy Marks McKelvey and also became commander of the American Legion Post 91. Southam, in World War I uniform, became a Berea mayor.

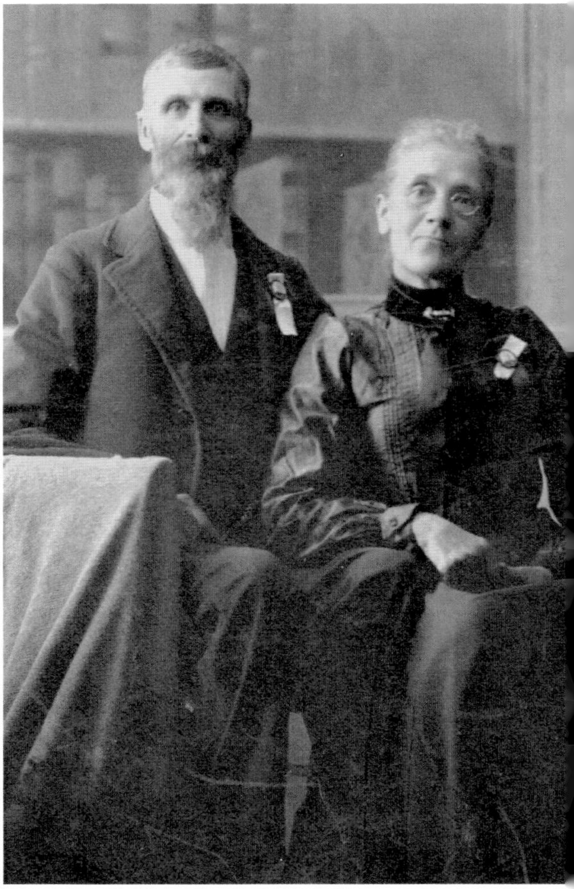

Henry J. Shapley
During the Civil War, Shapley served in Company M, 6th Ohio Volunteer Cavalry. After the war, he married Annie Ring and became a farmer in Columbia Township. In 1900, the Shapleys sold the farm to their daughter Pearl and her husband, Jesse Burnett, and retired to Berea. They lived at 176 Front Street. David Burnett, Berea Historical Society staff member, is a great-grandson of the Shapleys. (Courtesy of the Burnett family.)

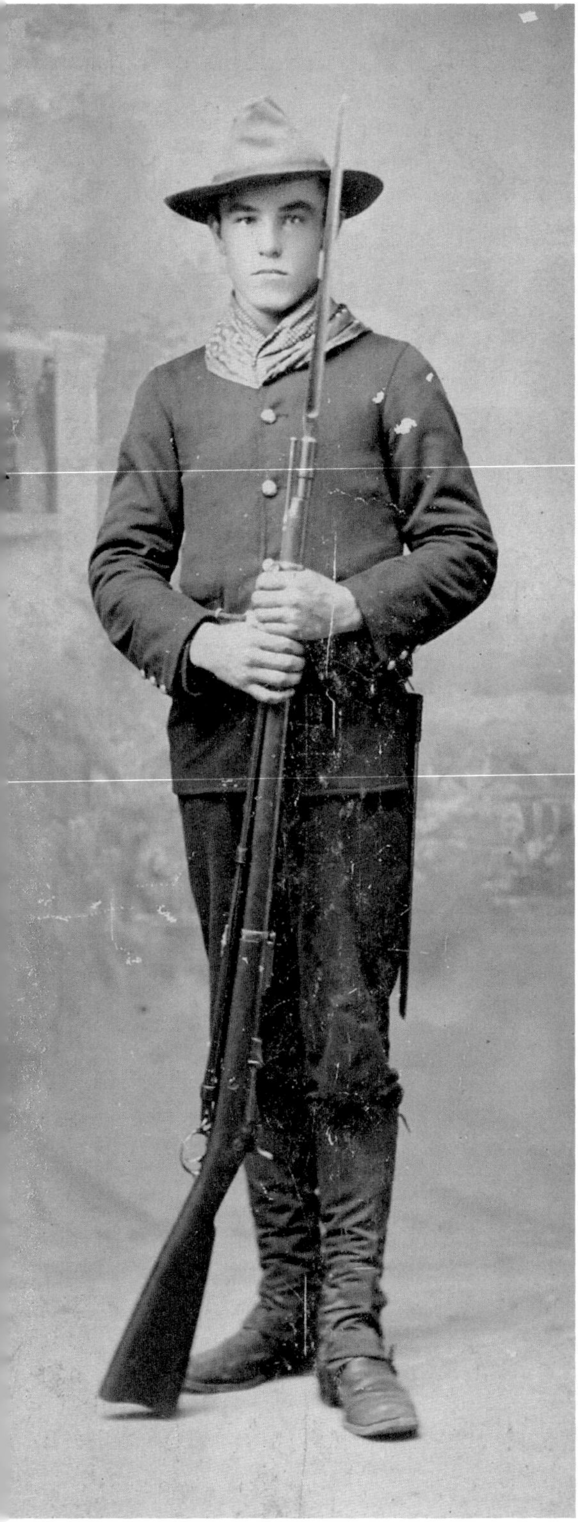

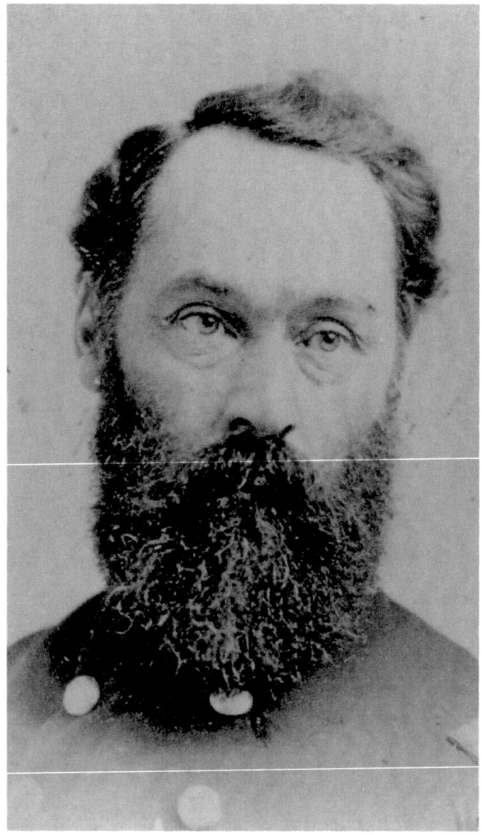

Gershom Barber
Known as Barber's Sharpshooters, the 6th Independent Company Sharpshooters was organized at Camp Cleveland, Ohio. Capt. Gershom M. Barber, as senior officer, commanded this company. The company mustered in December 30, 1862, and mustered out July 19, 1865.

George Schneider
A member of Company D, 5th OVI (Ohio Volunteer Infantry), Schneider was a veteran of the Spanish-American War. He was married to Susan Friedel. Schneider died in 1949.

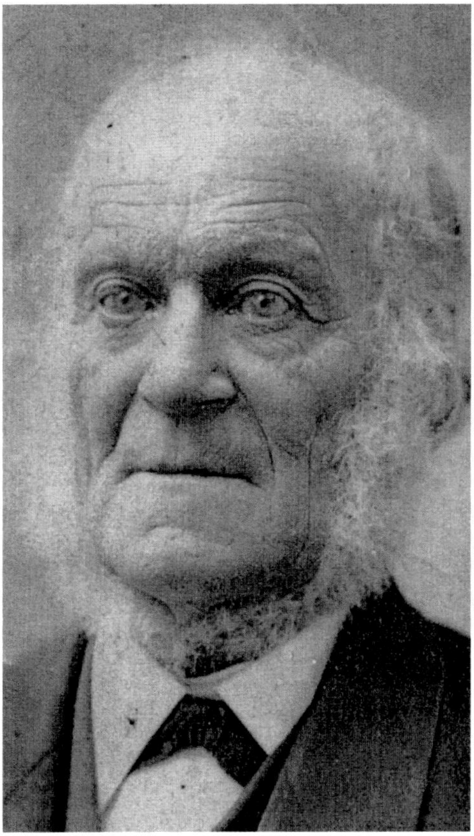

S.S. Brown
A Civil War veteran, Brown was a man of many trades and professions—watchmaker, blacksmith, lawyer, auctioneer, and newspaper publisher of the *Berea Grit*. He also called himself "a preacher of sorts." He was elected to three separate terms as mayor of Berea.

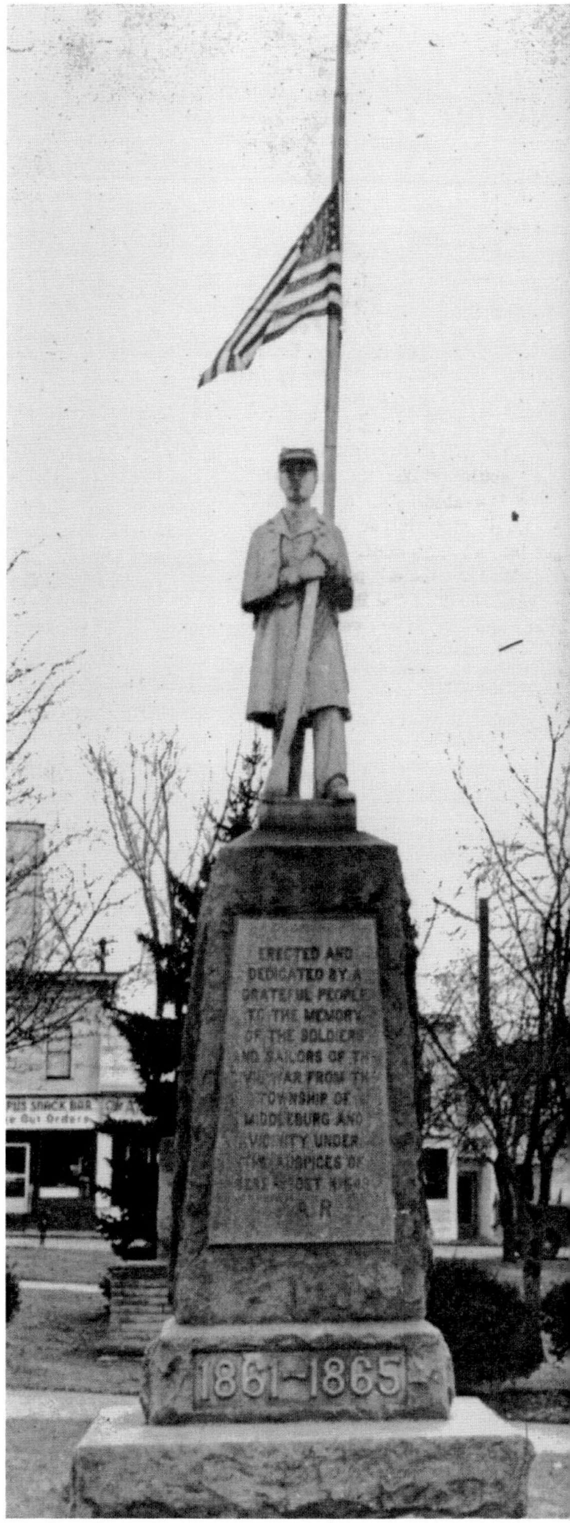

Civil War Monument
This monument graces the north end of the Triangle, which is the center of downtown Berea activity. It was dedicated September 10, 1917 and rededicated on Memorial Day, 1995. (Photograph by L. Walczak, Berea *News* file.)

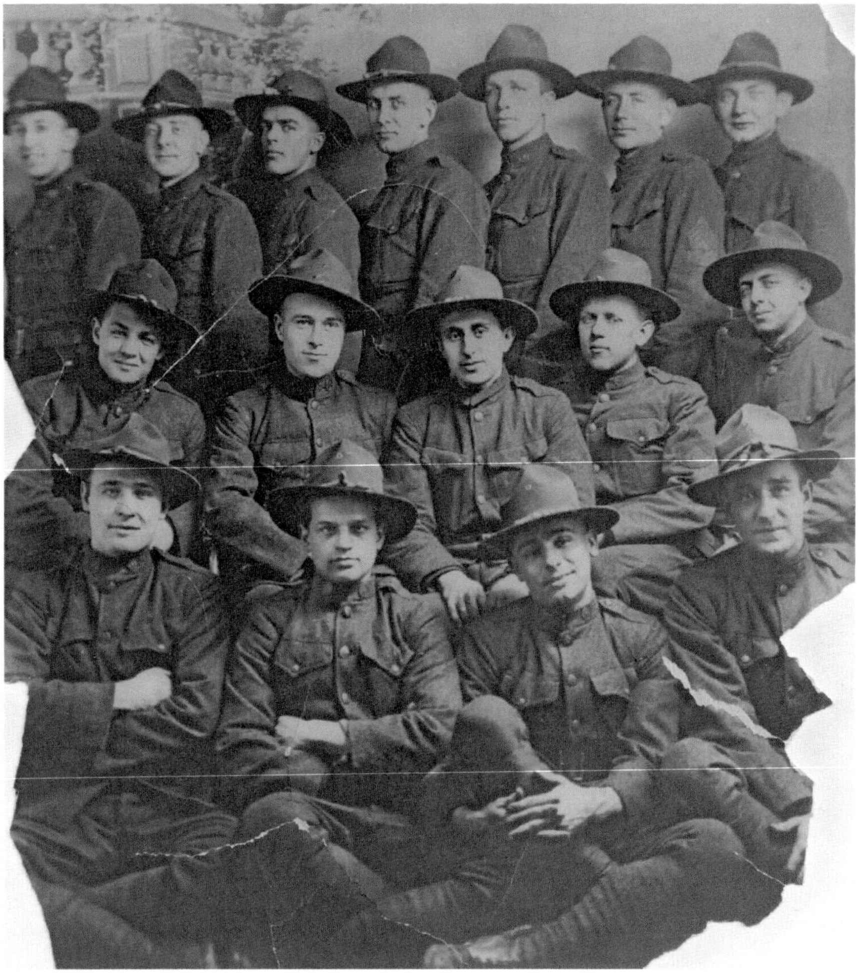

World War I Soldiers

The American Legion Post 91 in Berea proudly bears the name of Lt. Albert E. Baesel, posthumous Medal of Honor winner and one of the first Ohioans killed in World War I. These unidentified World War I soldiers from Berea may have served with Albert E. Baesel. His regiment, the Army's 148th Infantry, was the first to cross the Escault River during the Battle of the Argonne in France in 1918. The regiment was near Ivoiry when Cpl. Sterling Ryan was gravely wounded. Lieutenant Baesel pleaded to try a rescue in spite of heavy fire and deluge of gas. After gaining permission, "he (Baesel) worked his way forward and reaching the wounded man, placed him upon his shoulders and was instantly killed by enemy fire." Baesel's wife Lydia (Cole) accepted the Medal of Honor on December 23, 1922. Columnist Leigh Allan described Baesel in a Veterans' Day tribute in the Dayton *Daily News* in 1993. Baesel was an officer who was popular with his men. Pvt. Carl Schmidt wrote to Baesel's parents, "He led raiding parties into the enemy trenches and the men say he was fearless." The company dug a grave for Baesel with utensils from their mess kits and made a cross from tree branches tied together with bootlaces. The cross was no sooner finished than it was destroyed by German artillery fire. It was 1926 before French farmers, clearing shells from the old battlefield, found Baesel's body. It was shipped home and interred at Woodvale Cemetery, near his boyhood home. Lt. Albert Baesel's remains now rest beneath a granite marker erected in 1989 by American Legion Post 91. His parents lie on either side of him. Lt. Baesel's epitaph states simply, "He sought not glory but his country's good." He was 28.

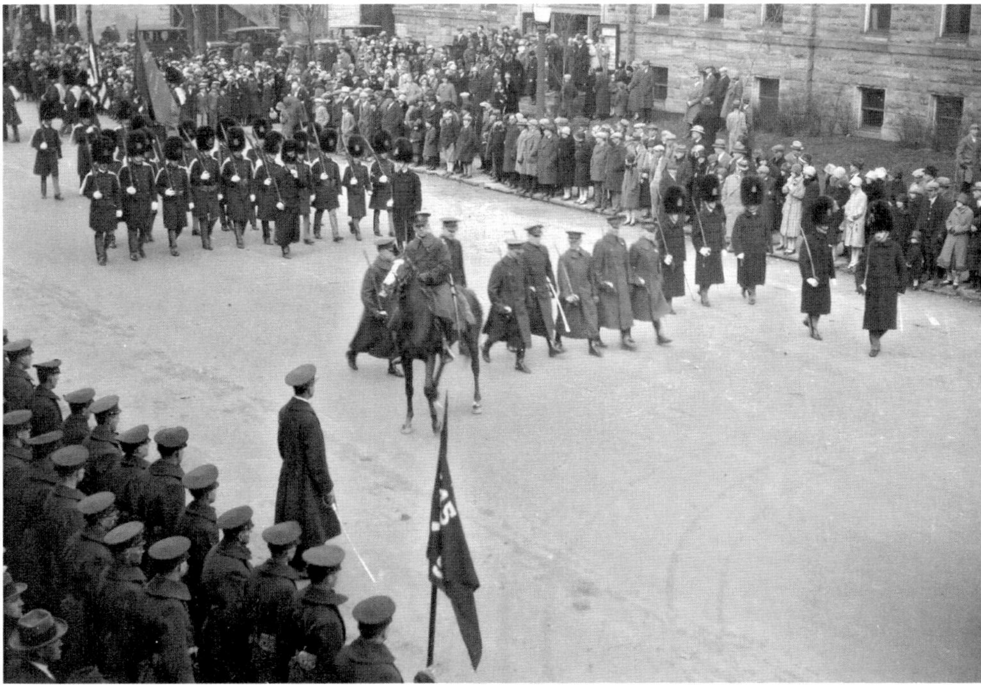

Lieutenant Baesel's Memorial Service

The funeral services for Lt. Albert E. Baesel on April 11, 1926, drew one of the largest crowds in Berea history. The town's population then was about 3,000. More than 10,000 people paid tribute to the Medal of Honor winner whose remains were found in France eight years after his death. Six hundred members of Baesel's original 145th Infantry Regiment marched in the procession. The Cleveland Grays, an elite military and social group to which Baesel belonged, the Grand Army of the Republic (GAR) veterans, Spanish-American War veterans, American Legion, and Veterans of Foreign Wars all marched in somber ranks. The procession began at the Baldwin-Wallace College Conservatory and ended at Woodvale Cemetery, Baesel's final resting place.

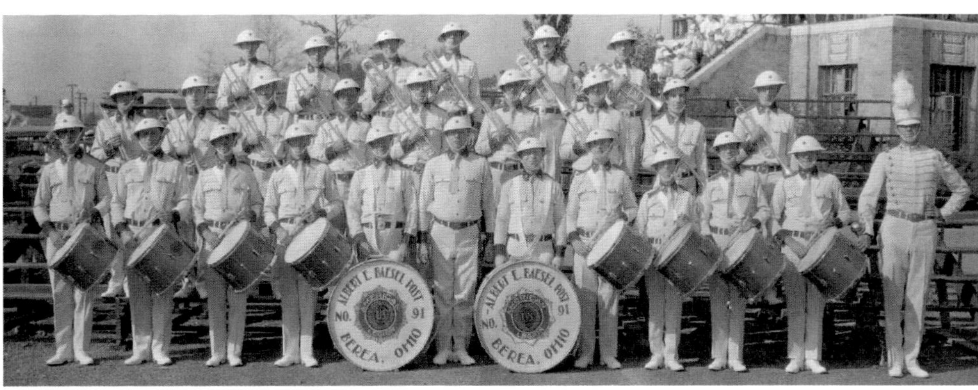

American Legion Marching Band

American Legion Post 91 at one time boasted a good-sized military band for a small community. The date of this photo is unknown, but it is possibly from the early 20th century when parades in small towns happened even more frequently than now, and high schools did not have large, well-equipped bands. (Courtesy of the Donald Rundle Collection.)

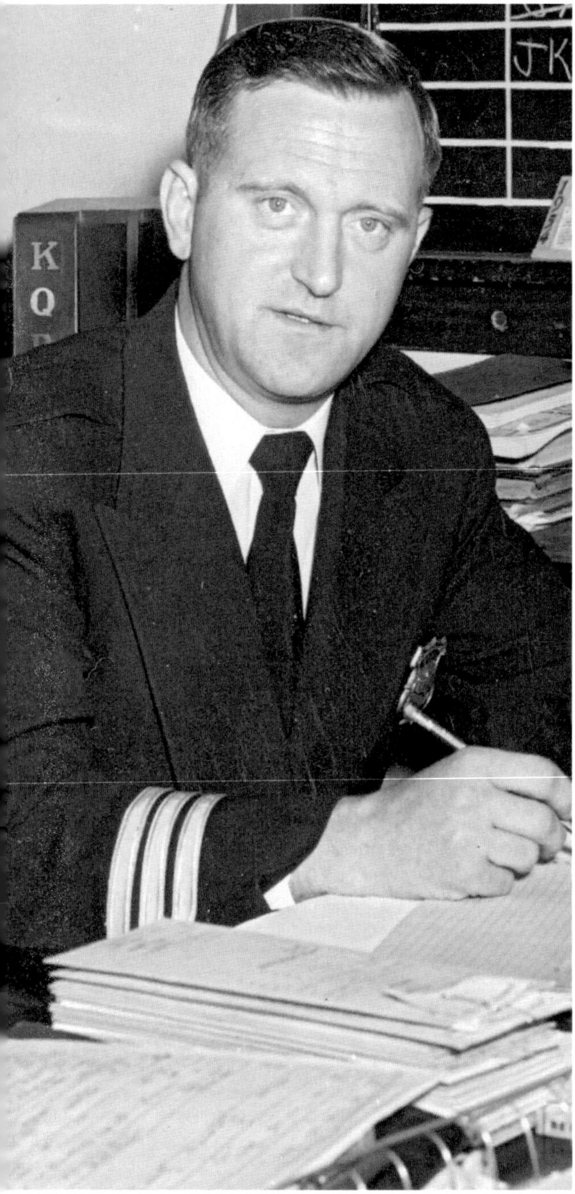

Augustine L. Yanke
No longer wearing a Navy uniform, Augustine ("Gus") Yanke assumed the role of chief of police of Berea when he returned home from the service after World War II.

Cpl. Richard Dettmer
Assigned to the Headquarters Battalion of the 5th Fighter Command in World War II, Corporal Dettmer manned communications that notified anti-aircraft artillery and all outposts of aircraft travels, US and enemy. His Air Corps unit participated in the invasion of the Philippines. In the late 1960s, Dettmer and his son Jim each put up $25 to buy a printing press. Thus, Berea Printing Company was born in their basement.

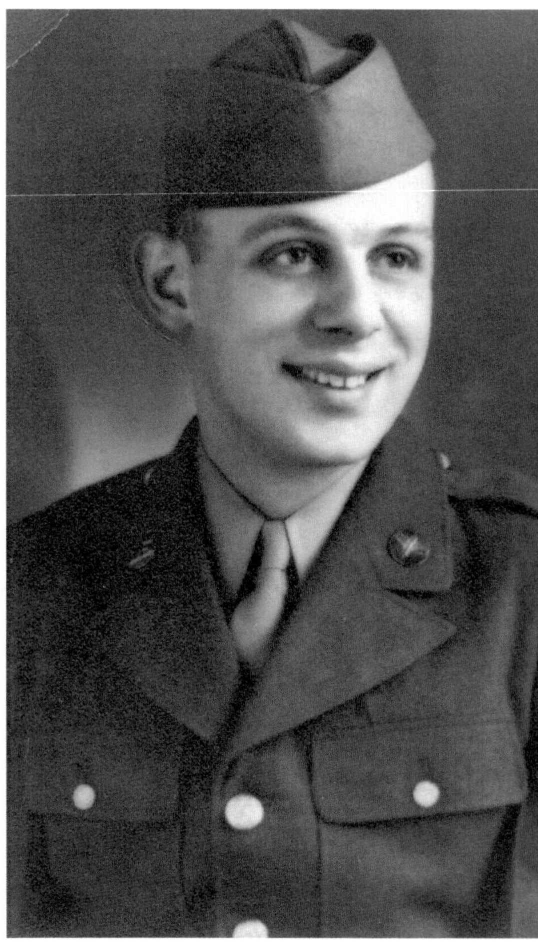

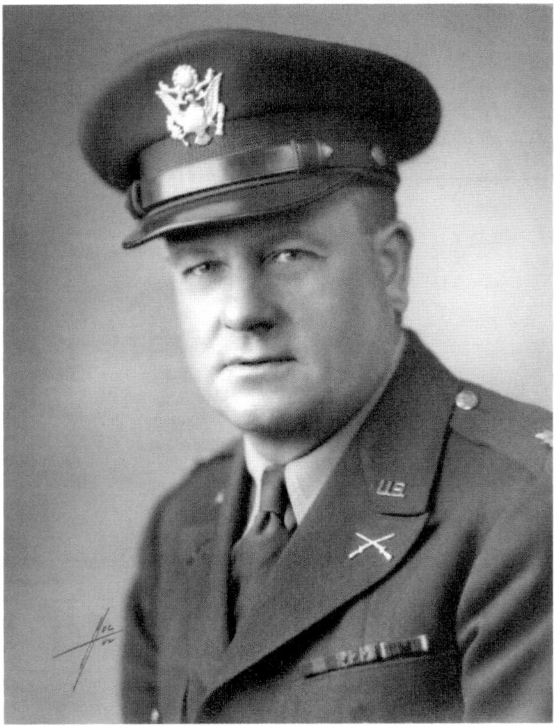

Maj. Gen. Sylvester T. Del Corso (ret.)
A decorated veteran of three wars, General Del Corso was Ohio's adjutant general and commander of the state militia in May 1970 when National Guardsmen fired upon anti-war demonstrators at Kent State University, killing four students. Del Corso originally believed a sniper was responsible for the first shot. Official investigations denied this, and Del Corso eventually accepted that conclusion.

Army Camp
During World War II, Del Corso served in Luzon, the Philippines. He was the officer who received the surrender of the Japanese at Luzon.

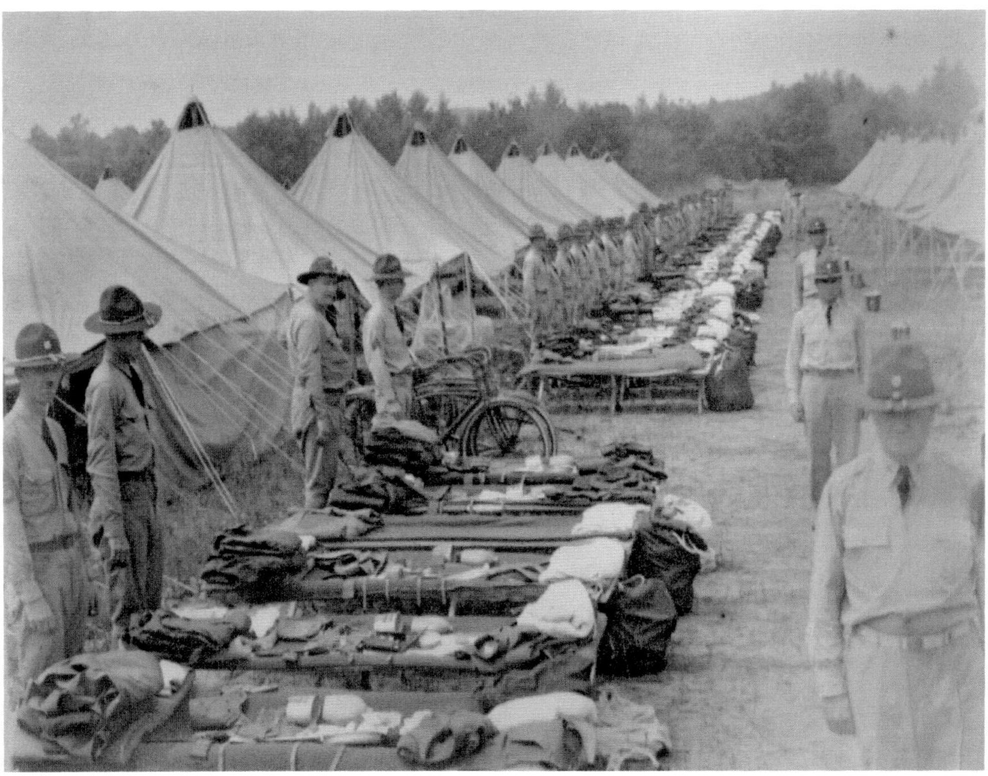

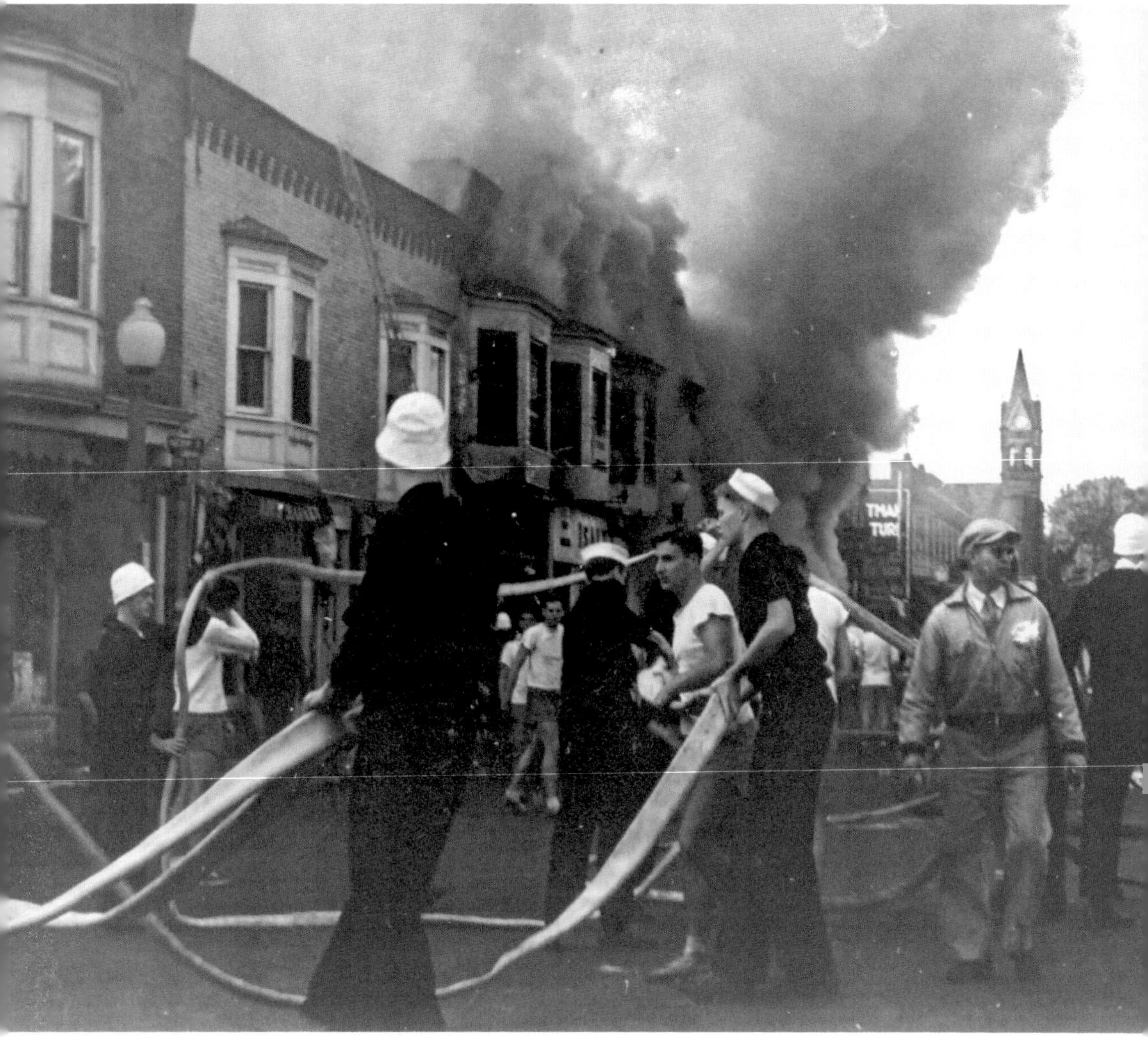

V-12 Students Aid Firemen

They were the heroes of the day—the V-12 students who answered the call for help from Berea's firemen in 1943. Without the students' willing assistance, the entire Triangle could have been destroyed. From 1943 to 1946, Baldwin-Wallace College housed a V-12 unit of US Navy personnel who were training to be officers if they completed the program successfully.

Cpl. Andrew Papp (RIGHT)

A Marine Corps veteran of the Vietnam War in 1965–1966, Corporal Papp was the husband of Mary Jane Papp. Once he lost his job when he displayed the POW-MIA flag on the building where he worked against his employer's wishes. He suffered from posttraumatic stress syndrome and died in April 2002 from lung cancer caused by exposure to Agent Orange. (Courtesy of Mary Jane Papp, Berea Historical Society Registrar.)

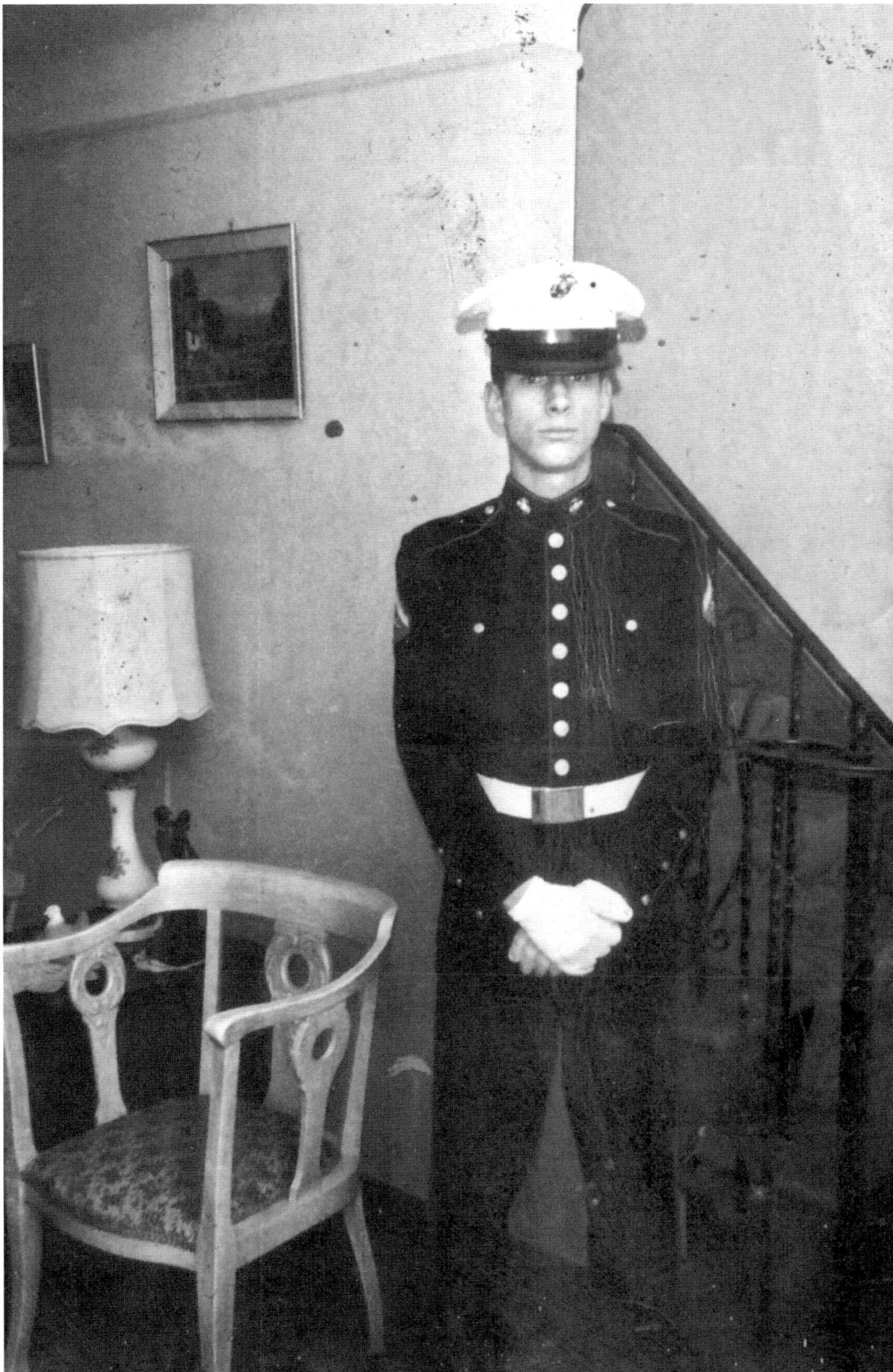

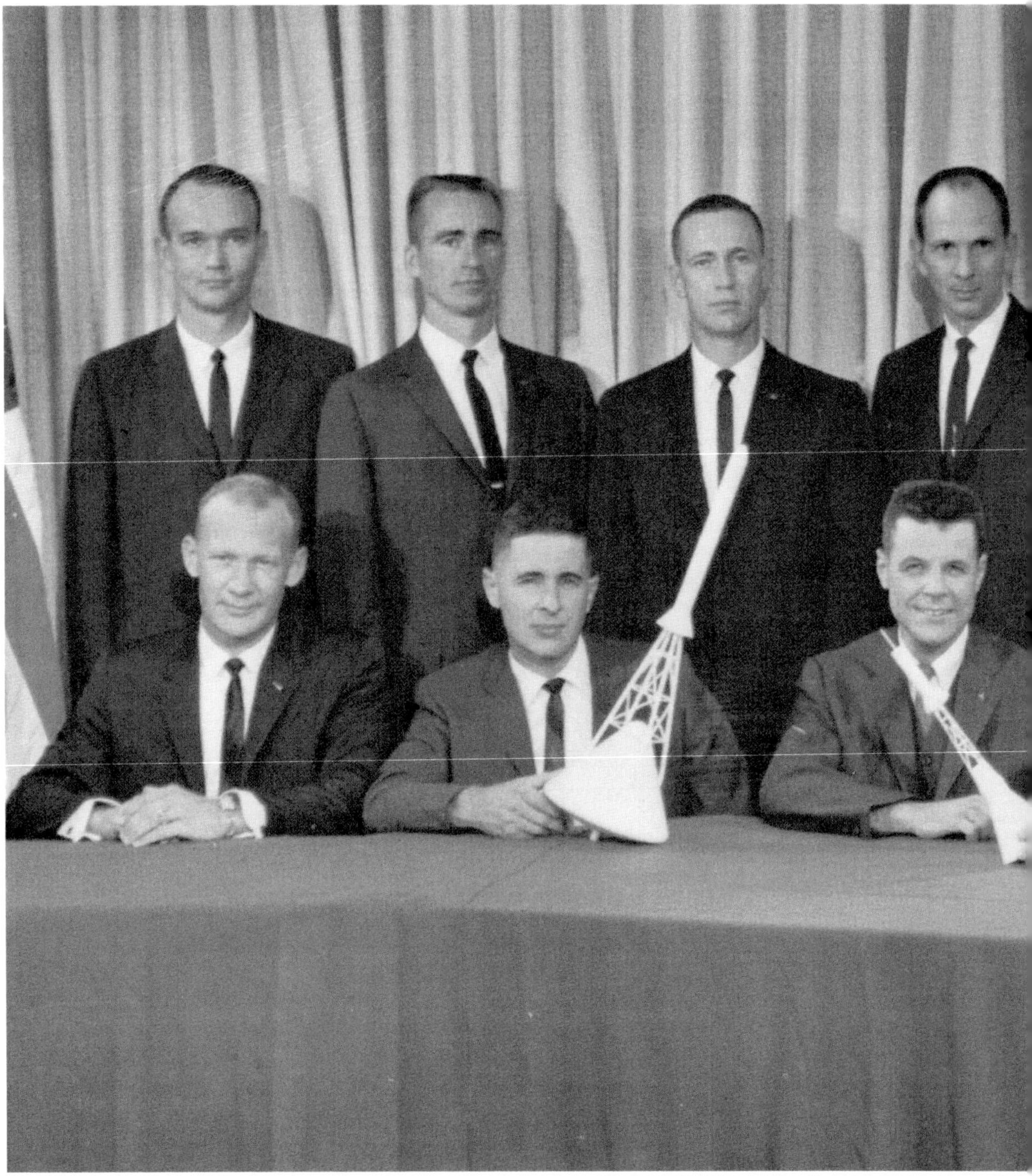

Astronauts

Berea native Charles A. Bassett II, Berea's astronaut, is pictured here with his Gemini class, the third class of astronauts to be commissioned. Bassett perished in 1966, along with his co-pilot, Eliot See. Their trainer jet hit a hangar near St. Louis while attempting to land in unfavorable weather conditions. Bassett was to have piloted the next Gemini mission. The astronauts are seated alphabetically. Front, from left, Edwin E. Aldrin Jr., William A. Anders, Charles A. Bassett II, Alan L. Bean, Eugene A. Cernan, and Roger B. Chaffee; Back, Michael Collins, R. Walter Cunningham, Donn F. Eisle, Theodore C. Freeman, Richard F. Gordon Jr., Russell L. Schweickart, David R. Scott, and Clifton C. Williams. Chaffee and Williams were also killed while in the space program. (Photograph by NASA, courtesy of Berea High School.)

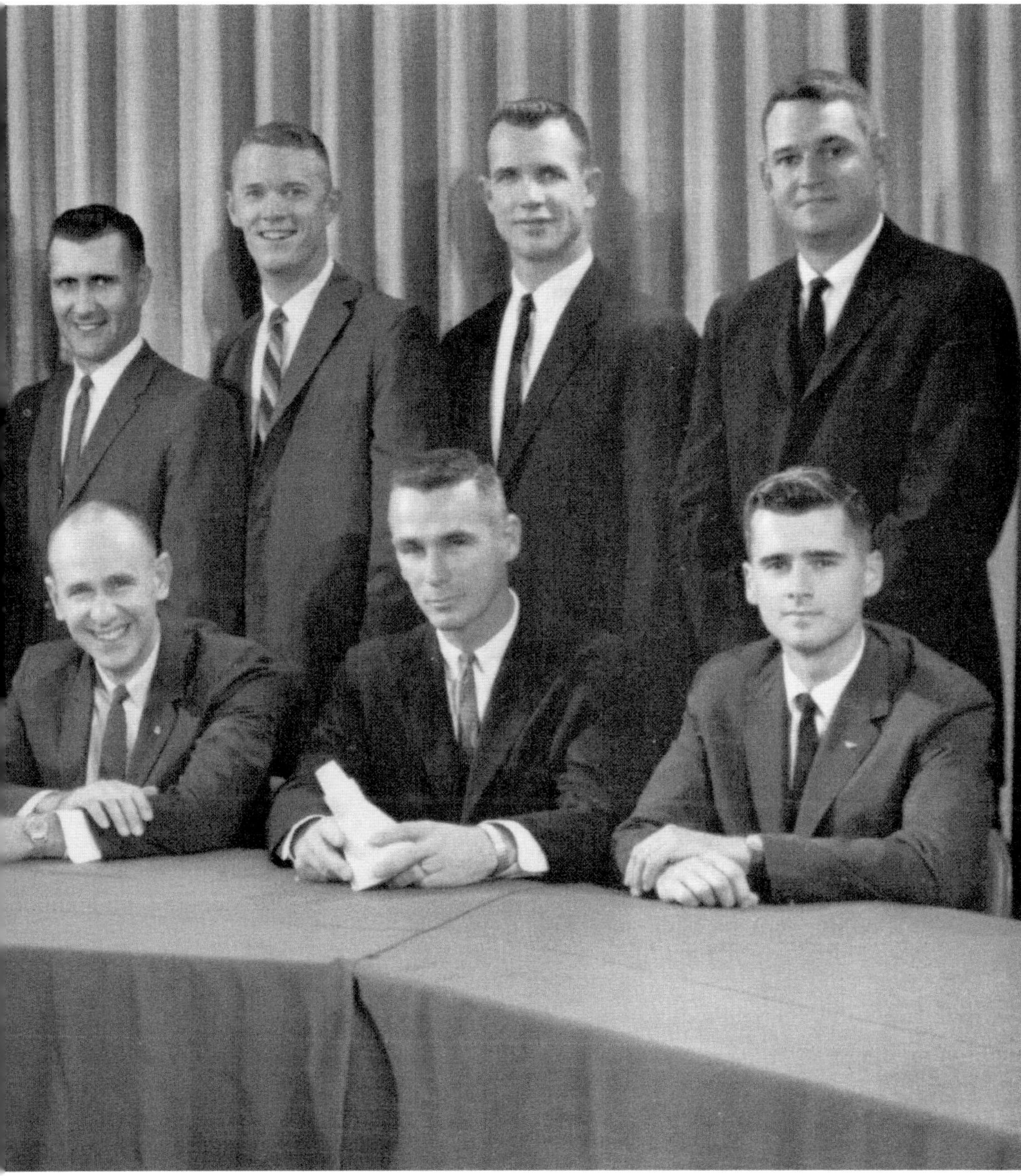

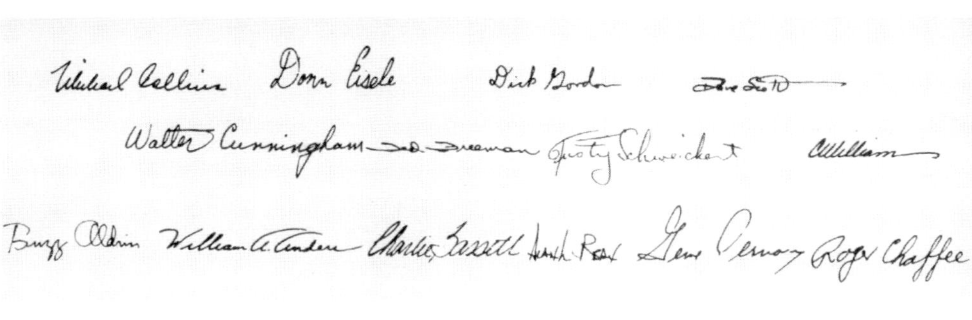
Michael Collins
Donn Eisele
Dick Gordon
Walter Cunningham
Rusty Schweickart
Buzz Aldrin
Charles Bassett
Gene Cernan
Roger Chaffee

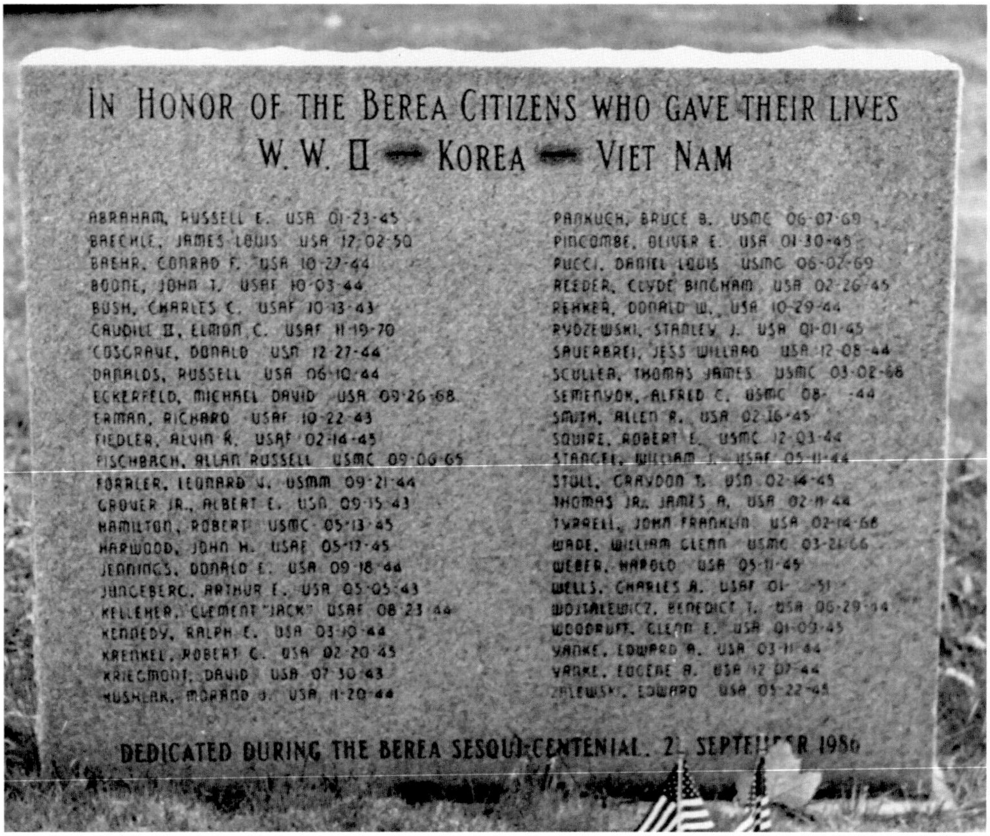

War Memorial

At the south end of the Triangle is this memorial to those citizens who gave their lives during World War II, Korea, and Vietnam. It was dedicated on the occasion of Berea's sesquicentennial in September 1936.

CHAPTER NINE

Sports

Names of two sports figures come to mind when Berea is mentioned—the Cleveland Browns' Lou The Toe" Groza and four-time Olympic gold medalist, Harrison Dillard. Also held in high esteem is the Tressel family. Baldwin-Wallace football coach and athletic director Lee Tressel coached the B-W Yellow Jackets for 23 seasons. He was named Ohio Coach of the Year four times and national Small College Coach of the Year in 1978. Two sons, Richard and James, became university football coaches, and a third, David, coaches and teaches swimming in Berea. Eloise, their mother, always filled the role as their greatest cheerleader.

The Cleveland Browns headquarters have been in Berea for many years. This is a boon to the city financially and socially. Players interact with the community, helping with food drives, collecting school supplies for needy children every August, and lending their presence to events that inspire young—and older—citizens. For the past several years, an event called Go Deep has attracted as many as 3,000 fans to an area church to hear inspirational talks from Browns' players about sportsmanship and their faith.

Berea offers the community's youth opportunities to participate in sports from an early age. The German Methodist Orphans Home (now the Berea Children's Home) emphasized sports for both young boys and girls early in the 20th century. Football and basketball have long been important in the high schools. Hundreds of other youth participate each year in swim teams, Little League, and soccer through the schools and the Berea Recreation Center. Summer evenings find residents flocking to Lou Groza Field, a city-developed ballpark, to watch softball leagues play. Some Olympians have come from Berea High School. One of these was L.B. Schaefer. Other talented and colorful sports personalities include athletic director Ray Watts, Touchdown Tommy Phillips, Myron ("Bree") Thornburg, and Arthur "Bud" Collins. Another Legend in the Making is Berean Dustin Kilgore, NCAA 2011 champion wrestler at Kent State University.

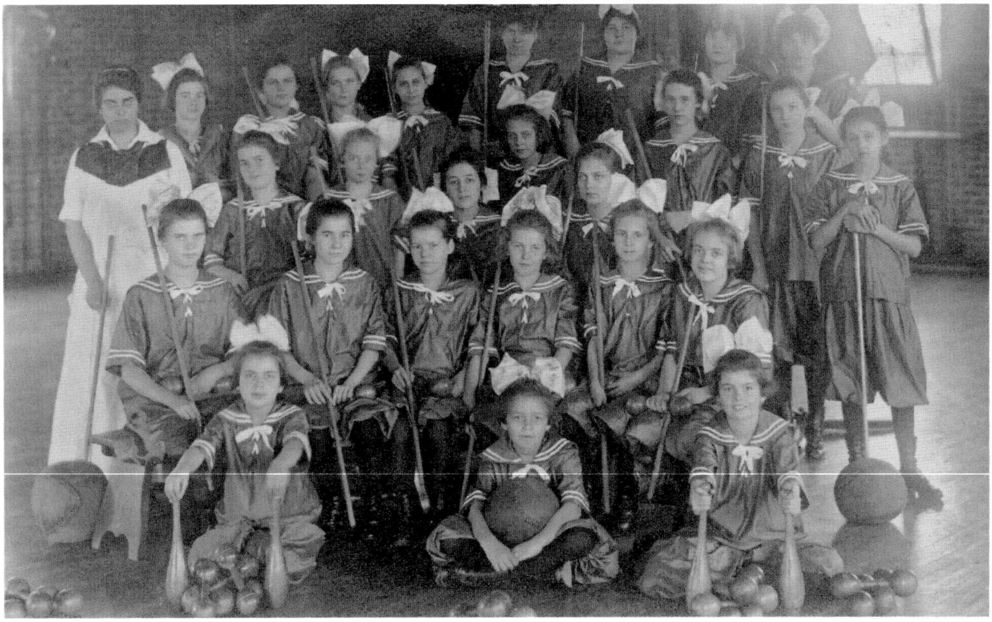

Girls' Sports at German Methodist Orphanage
Girls at the German Methodist Orphanage enjoyed sports long before girls in public schools were allowed to participate in them. Friendly competition and good sportsmanship were encouraged.

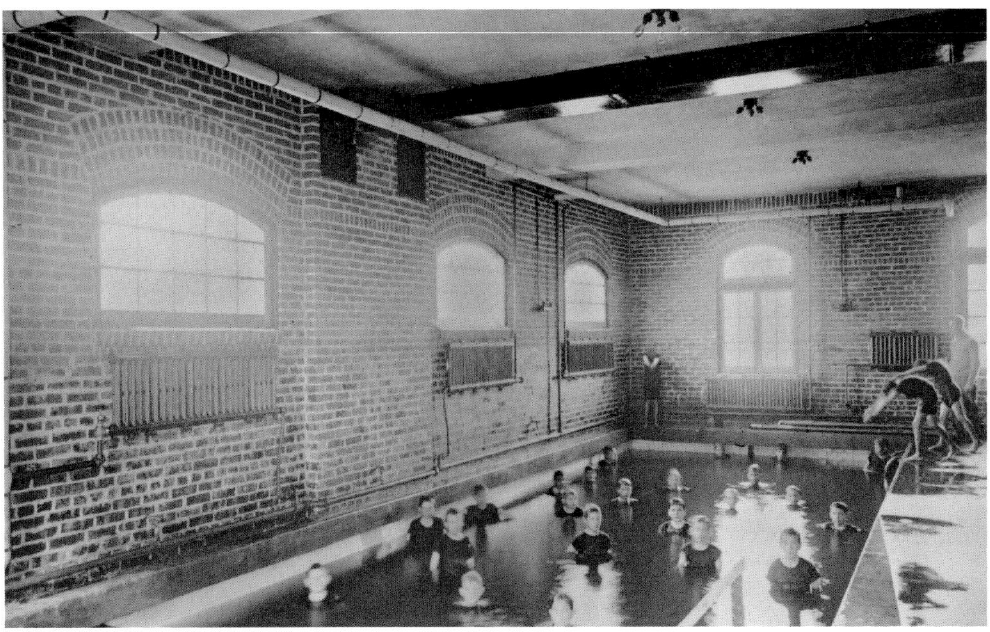

Swimming Pool at German Methodist Orphanage
When "Pappa" Kaletsch was superintendent of the German Methodist Orphanage in the early years of the 20th century, he determined that every child should learn to swim. Baldwin-Wallace and Berea High School students often used the orphanage pool. At that time, it was the only pool in the community.

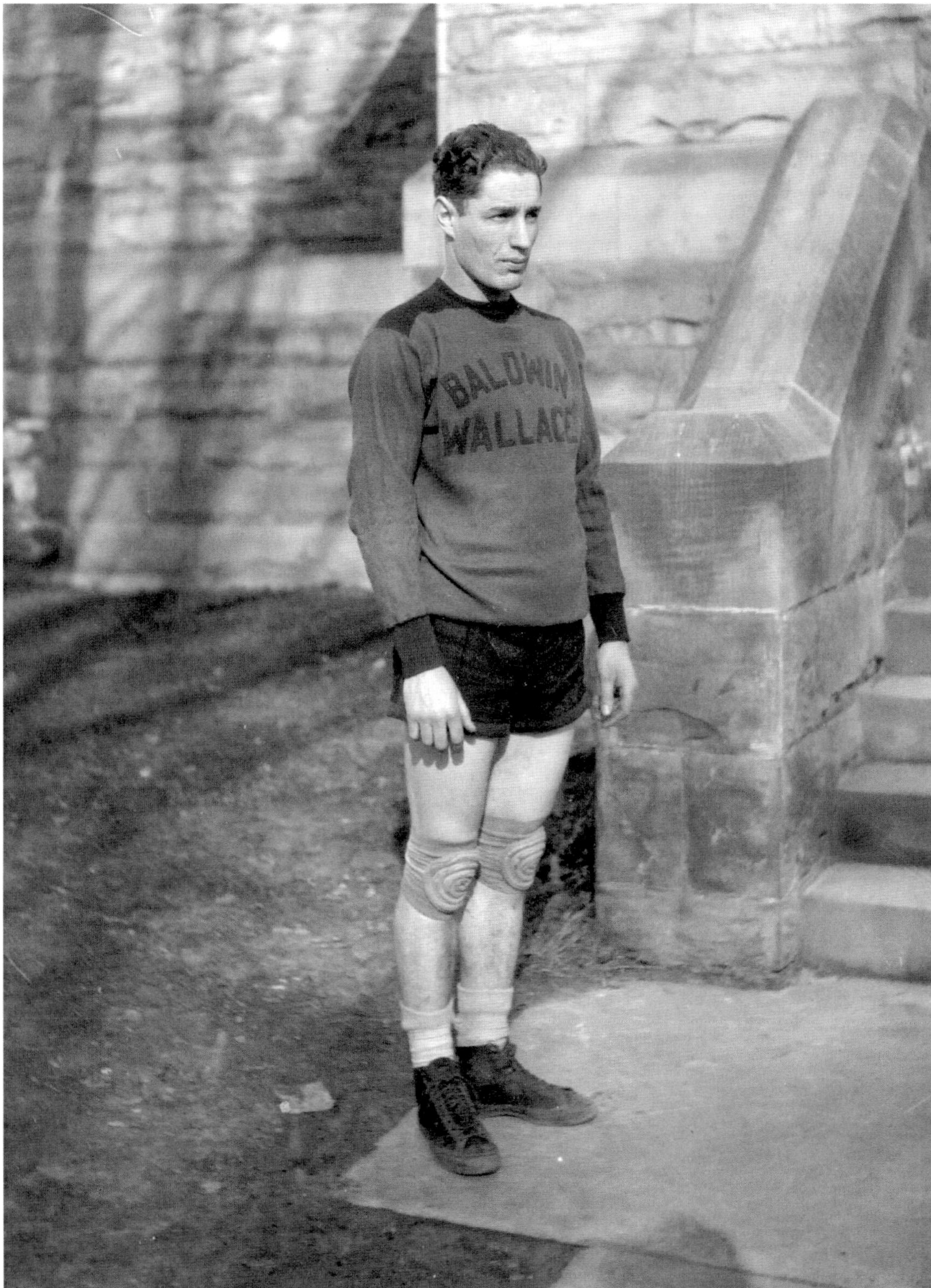

Otto Mahler as an Athlete
Mahler grew up in the German Methodist Orphanage and became a leading businessman and citizen of Berea. He excelled in both football and basketball.

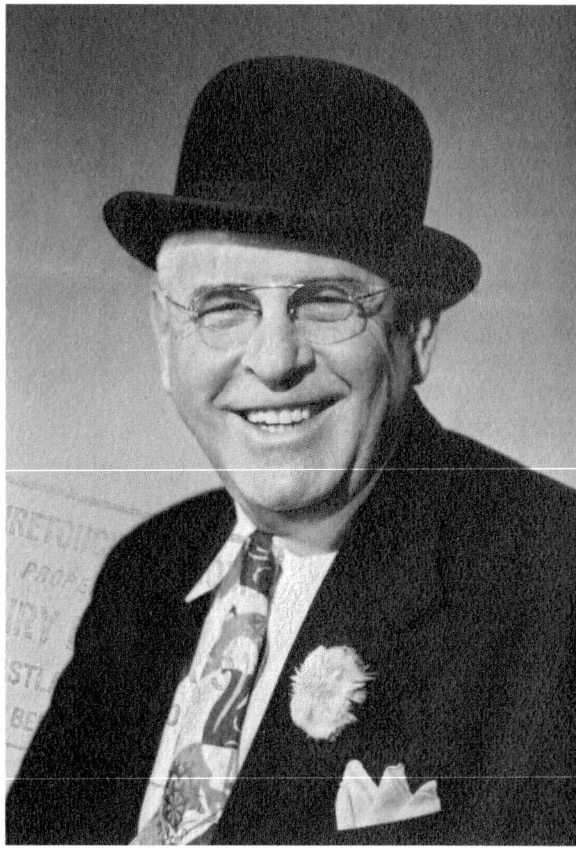

Myron ("Bree") Thornburg
His booming voice cheered on dozens of Berea and Baldwin-Wallace teams in every sport. Thornburg was an employee of the New York Central Railroad, but sports consumed his leisure time. Easily identified in the stands by his derby hat and megaphone, Thornburg earned the nickname "Bree" by the way his shouts echoed across the gridiron for Berea.

John Mucklo
After an outstanding career as a social studies teacher at Berea High School, Mucklo turned his talents to local government and served six years on Berea city council. Recreation was a lifelong interest for Mucklo; he founded the Berea Recreation Board in 1945 and was its director for 18 years. The Berea *News Sun* described him as a "beloved civic giant."

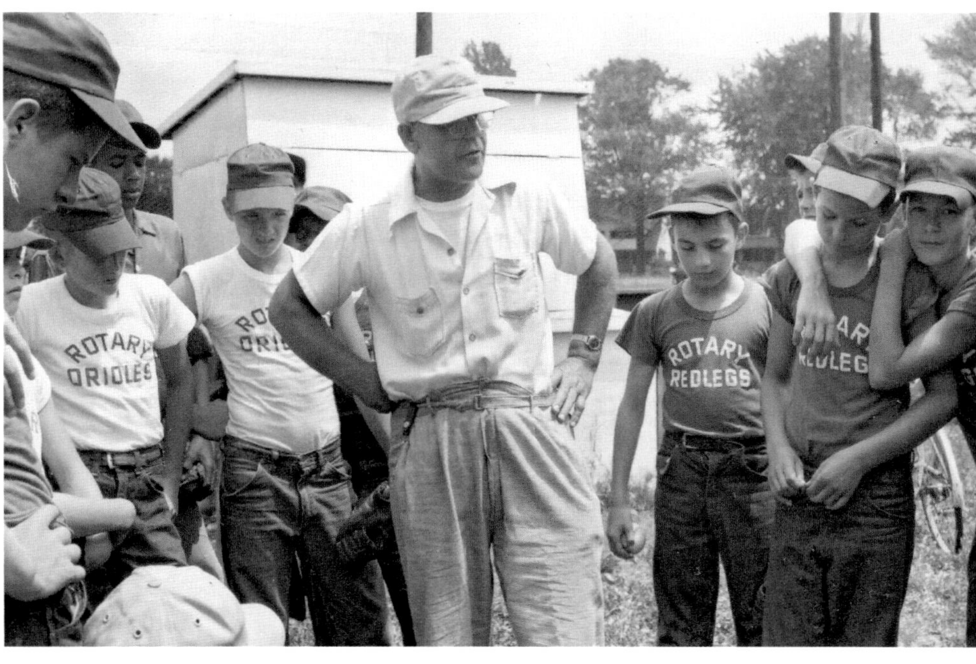

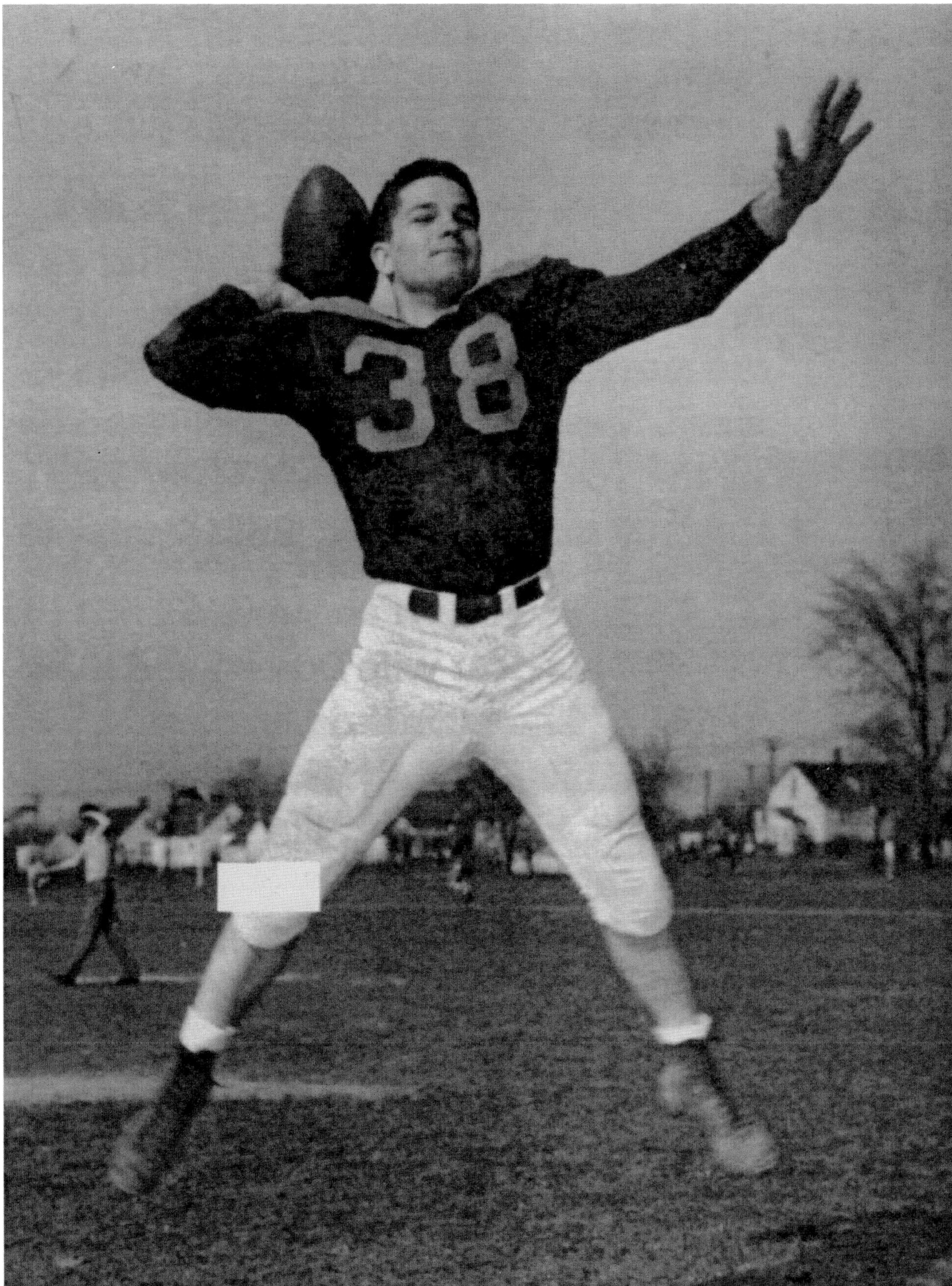

Touchdown Tommy

In the late 1930s and early '40s, "Touchdown Tommy" Phillips thrilled the crowds at Berea High football games. Coaches considered him the greatest passer in the game. A 1950 B-W graduate, he took advice from the great Cleveland Browns coach, Paul Brown: "Choose another career." He did and worked for the Forest City-Dillon Co.

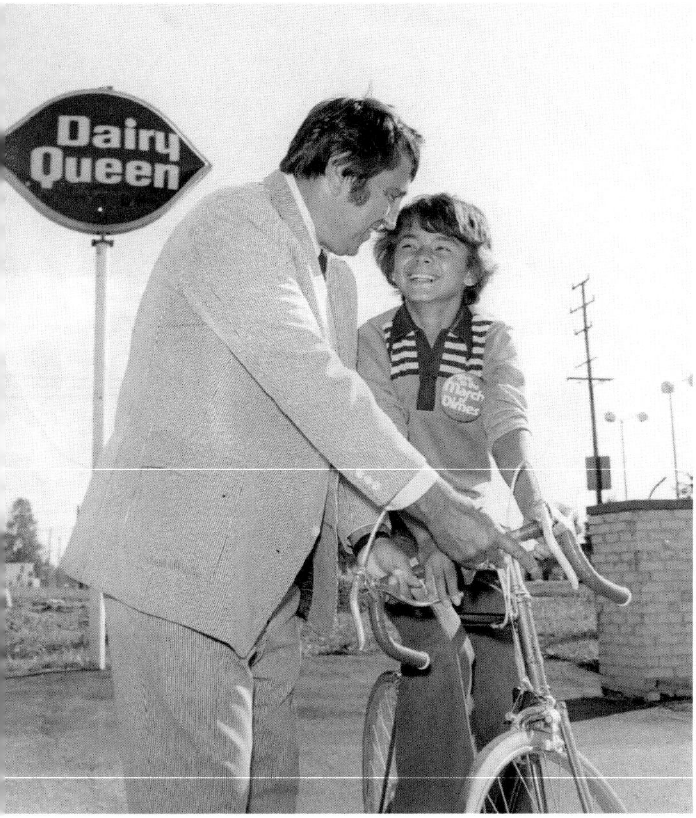

Lou Groza: Member of the Community

Unlike athletes who live in a city on a stop-gap basis, Groza chose to settle in Berea. He was a familiar figure around town—in eateries, at parades, or lending encouragement to Berea High and Baldwin-Wallace football teams—and to young competitors. Here he is advising a young boy (unknown) on competing in a benefit event. Groza was a valued asset to the city for his unwavering support of worthwhile causes.

Lou and Jackie

As co-marshals of the Grindstone Parade, Lou Groza and his wife Jackie ride in a 1960 Mercedes 290SL. Joan Kamper (at wheel) and her husband Rudi Kamper owned the car. Their son, Dolf, sometimes had to help his mother start the Mercedes, although he was too young to drive.

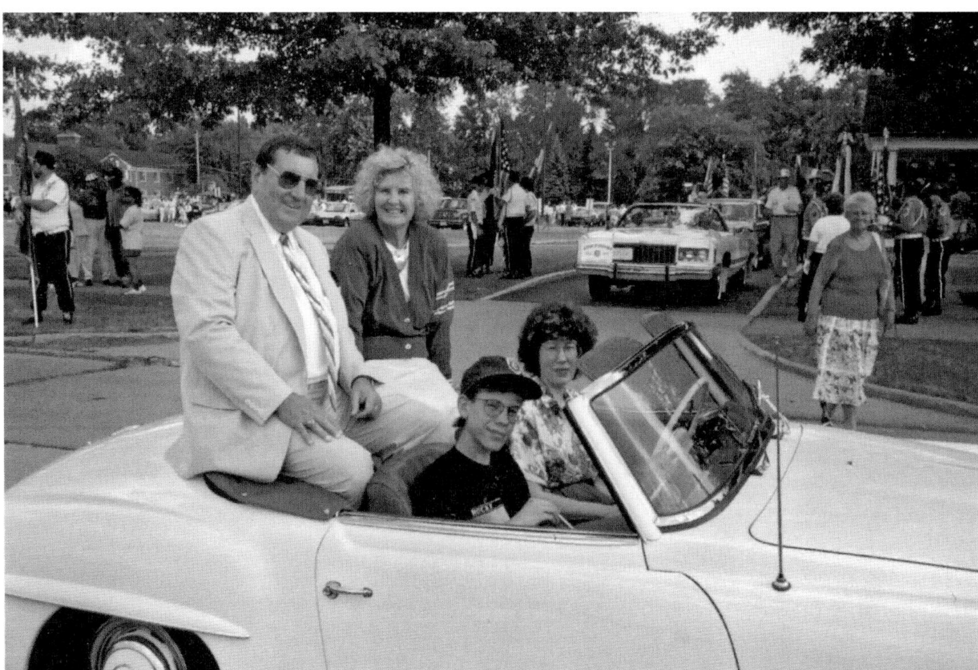

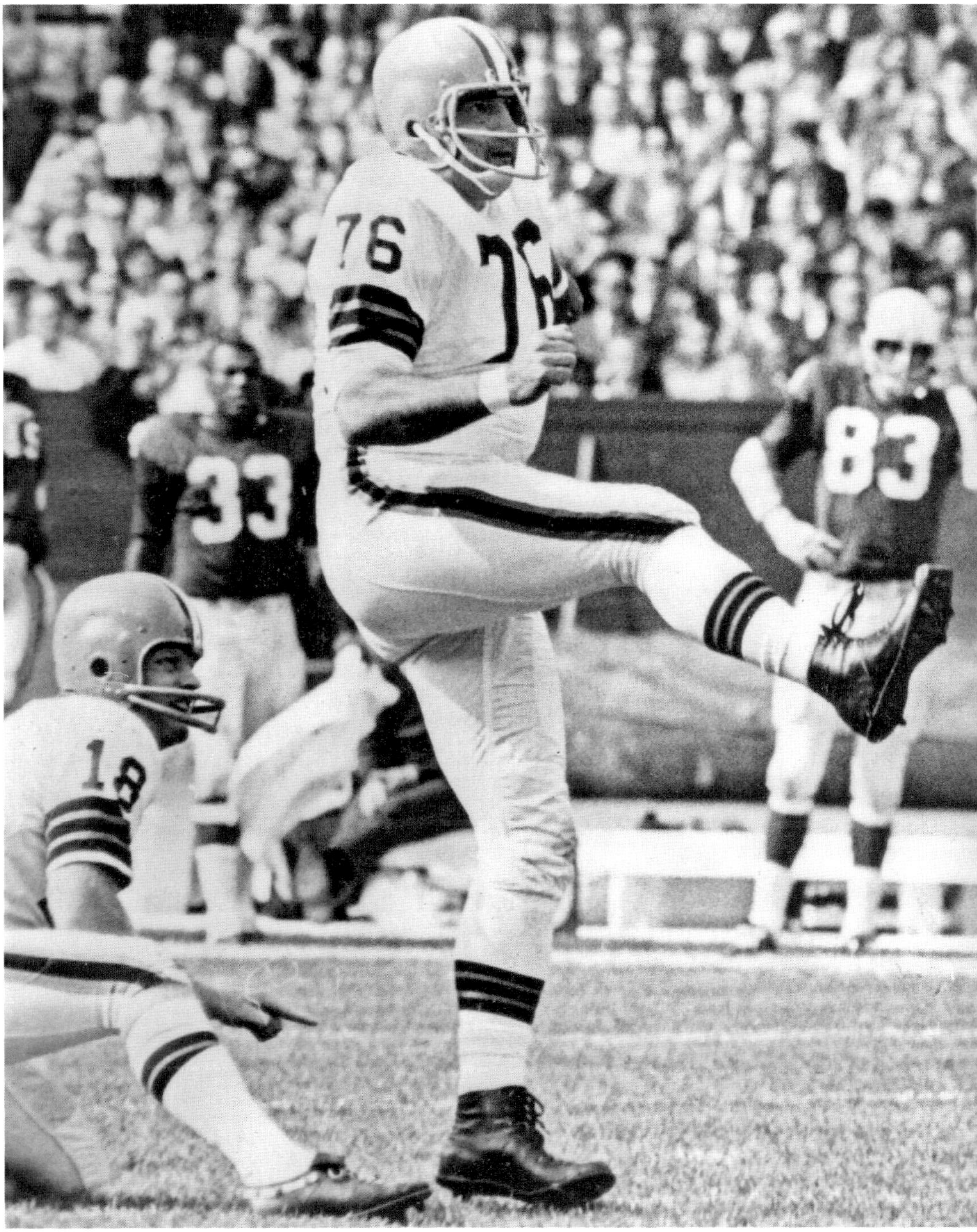

Lou ("The Toe")

In 1950, Lou ("The Toe") Groza kicked a field goal with 30 seconds remaining to defeat the Los Angeles Rams, 30–28, and win the NFL championship. *Sporting News* named him NFL Athlete of the Year in 1954. Known especially for his kicking ability, Groza also made his mark as a starting offensive tackle. In his 21-year playing history with the Cleveland Browns, Lou Groza scored 1,608 points. His 234 field goals and 641 extra points set NFL records at the time of his retirement to coaching status in 1968. He was the last remaining member of the original 1946 Cleveland Browns team. Although he had several business interests after he retired from the Browns, Groza and his family remained in Berea. He was married to the former Jackie Lou Robbins, and they had four children, Jeff, Jill, Jon, and Jud.

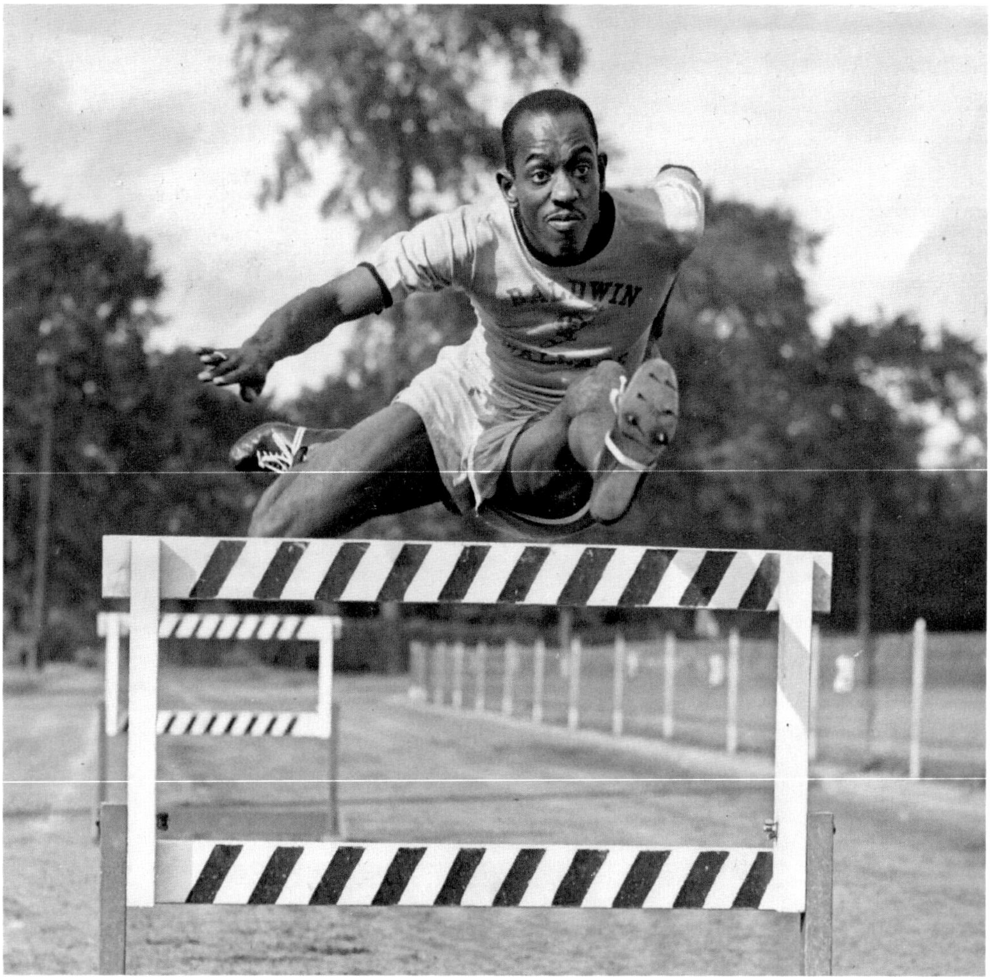

Harrison Dillard
A 1949 Baldwin-Wallace graduate, Dillard is a four-time Olympic gold medalist. In London in 1948, he finished first in the 100-meter dash, tying the record set by his idol, Jesse Owens. In 1952 in Helsinki, he won the gold in the 110-meter hurdles. Both years he was a member of the winning 4 x 100 relay team. Following graduation, Dillard worked nine years in public relations for the Cleveland Indians and several years as a sportscaster for old station WABQ in Cleveland. He retired after 27 years in various positions with the Cleveland Board of Education. When he was eight years old, Dillard had begun running makeshift hurdles over junked auto seats in Cleveland alleys. He graduated from East High School, as did Jesse Owens. Once when Owens was a visiting alumnus, he saw Dillard run and noticed his tattered shoes. He gave him a pair of his own. Both wore the same size, 8½. Dillard served nearly three years in the military in the early 1940s. One of his fondest memories was from his time in Frankfurt, Germany, at the GI Olympics. It was not the fact that he won four first-place medals, but rather that Gen. George S. Patton, who was in attendance, told sportswriters that Dillard was "the best damn athlete I've ever seen." Dillard said, "That's something I'll never forget." Dillard's teammate at Baldwin-Wallace College, Ted Theodore, claims Dillard would be a champion if he never won a medal because "he's a person of humility and compassion. Being his teammate left an indelible, positive influence on me." Nicknamed "Bones" for his tall, lanky frame, Dillard won the Sullivan Award, the "Oscar of Amateur Sports," as the nation's best amateur athlete in 1953.

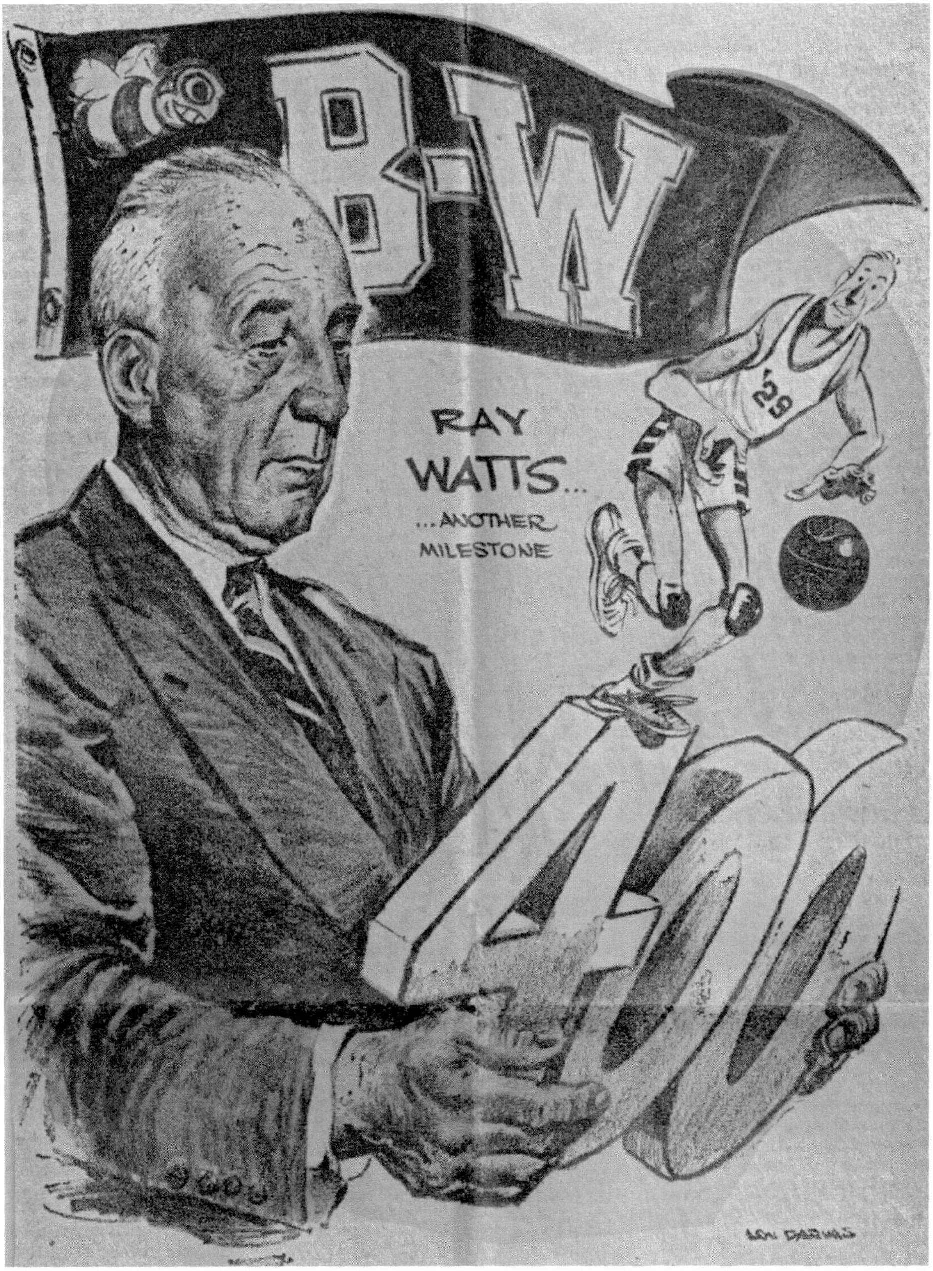

Ray Watts

The year was 1957, and those 400 games Ray Watts is celebrating span 22 seasons. The B-W Yellow Jackets won 232 games and lost 168 in Watts' colorful career. They finished .500 or better in 16 of the seasons. Watts would not have an opportunity to go for 500 wins because he would reach the college's compulsory retirement age of 65 in three years. A symbol of athletics at Baldwin-Wallace College, Ray Watts served as athletic director from 1928 until 1960. During that time, he also coached football for 21 years. He began his career in 1919 at age 24 as athletic director at Otterbein College, his alma mater. At that time, he was the youngest college athletic director in the state.

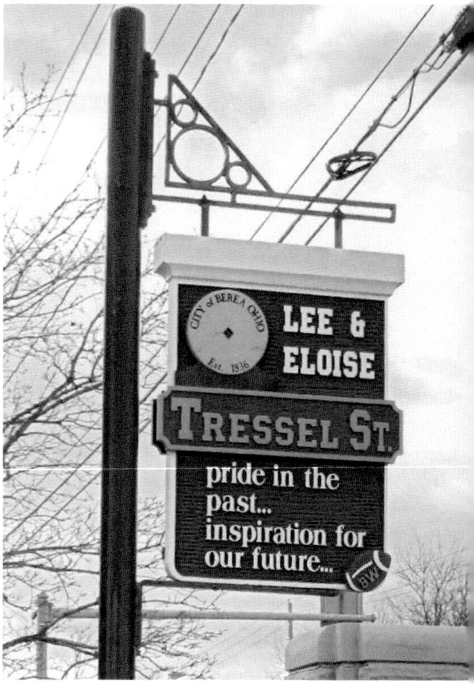

Tressel Sign

The sign says it all. Not just in sports but as good neighbors and friends, the Tressel family inspired excellence. This street sign is at the corner of Tressel Street and Bagley Road, opposite George Finnie Stadium. The Tressels' three sons all became coaches: Richard at Minnesota and Ohio State, James at Youngstown University and Ohio State, and David, who remains in Berea, keeping up the Tressel tradition. He taught in the Berea schools and coached swimming. (Photograph by Patricia Mote.)

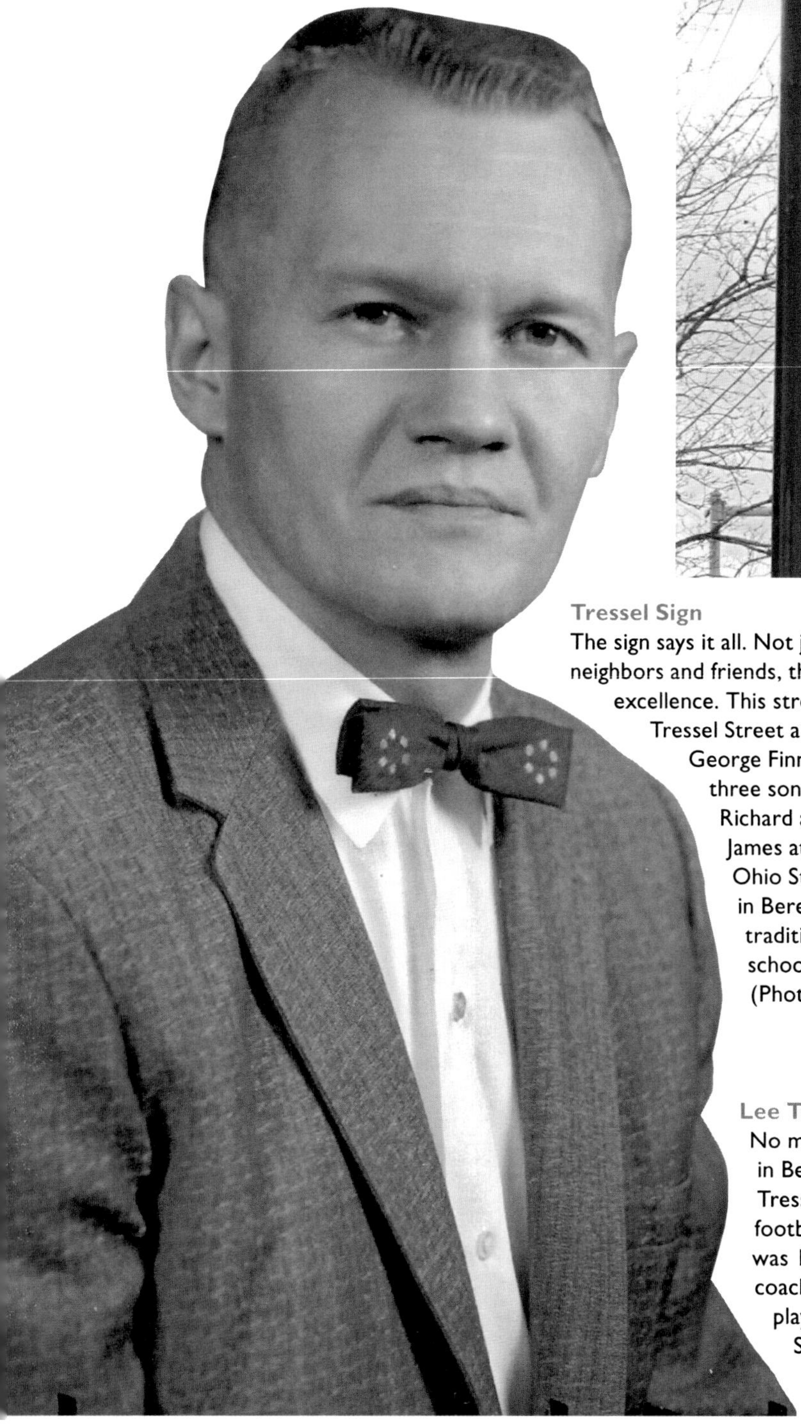

Lee Tressel

No more respected name exists in Berea than Tressel. Coach Lee Tressel's outstanding record as football coach at Baldwin-Wallace was 155-52-6 in his 23 years as coach of the Yellow Jackets. The playing field in George Finnie Stadium was named Tressel Field in 2008. Tressel died in 1981.

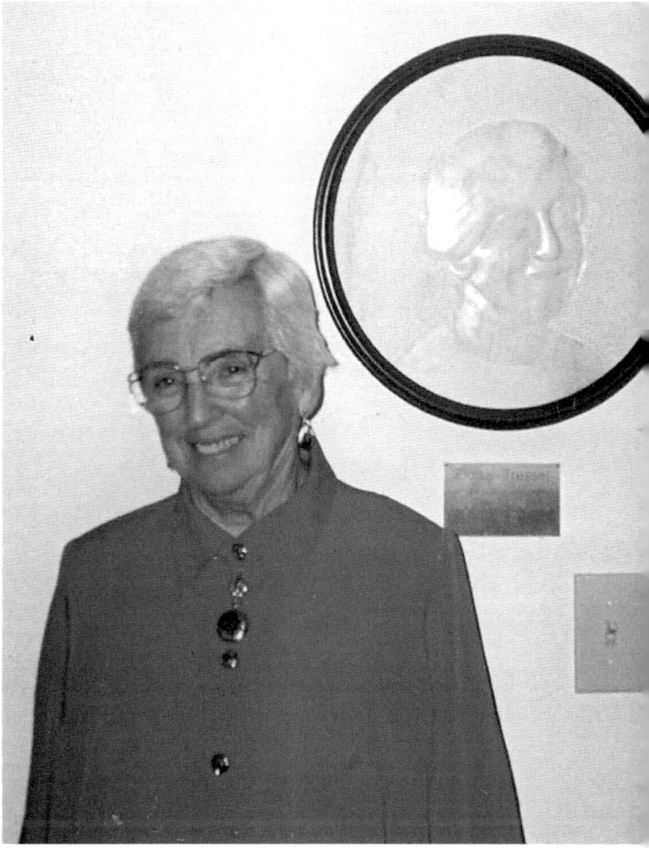

Eloise Tressel

The heart and soul of the Berea Historical Society, Eloise Tressel died in 2001. Yet her presence still seems to linger—in the research room, the meeting room, the Mahler Museum. Members often recall anecdotes describing Eloise's vitality and her ability to inspire everyone she met about history.

Eloise Tressel and the Victory Bell

Although she had a nursing degree when she and Lee moved to Berea, Eloise went back to college and earned a bachelor's degree from Baldwin-Wallace. She became the archivist for the B-W athletic department and one of its most enthusiastic (and loudest) supporters. Here she is ringing the Victory Bell. If you were ever on a committee with Eloise, you might have seen her sewing names on players' jackets during meetings.

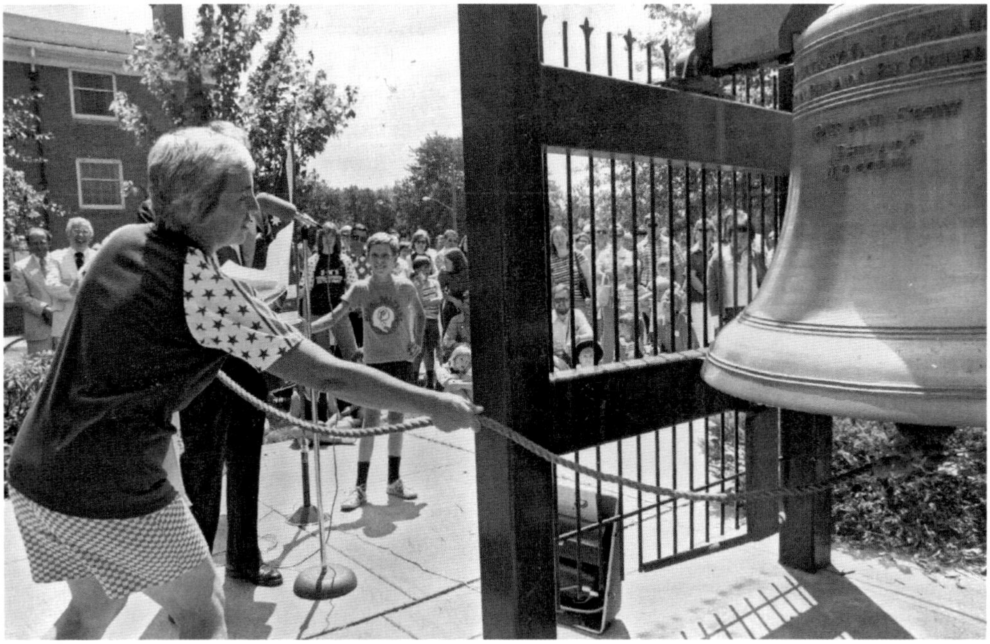

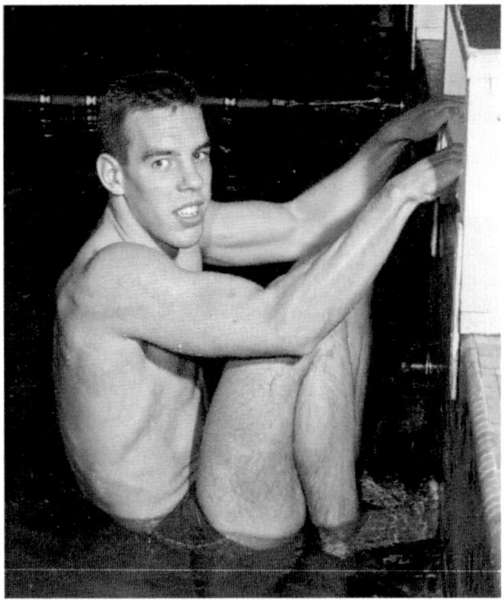

L.B. Schaefer

Berea High School champion swimmer L.B. Schaefer became national backstroke champion in the late 1950s. He later attended The Ohio State University. (Courtesy of The Ohio State University.)

Aquateens: Synchronized Swimmers

These Berea High School Aquateen members from the 1980s are first row (from left) Kim Schroeder, Stacy Miller, Sandy Stemitz, and Amy Andrews (from left) Liz Beyer and Sue Grabenhoff.

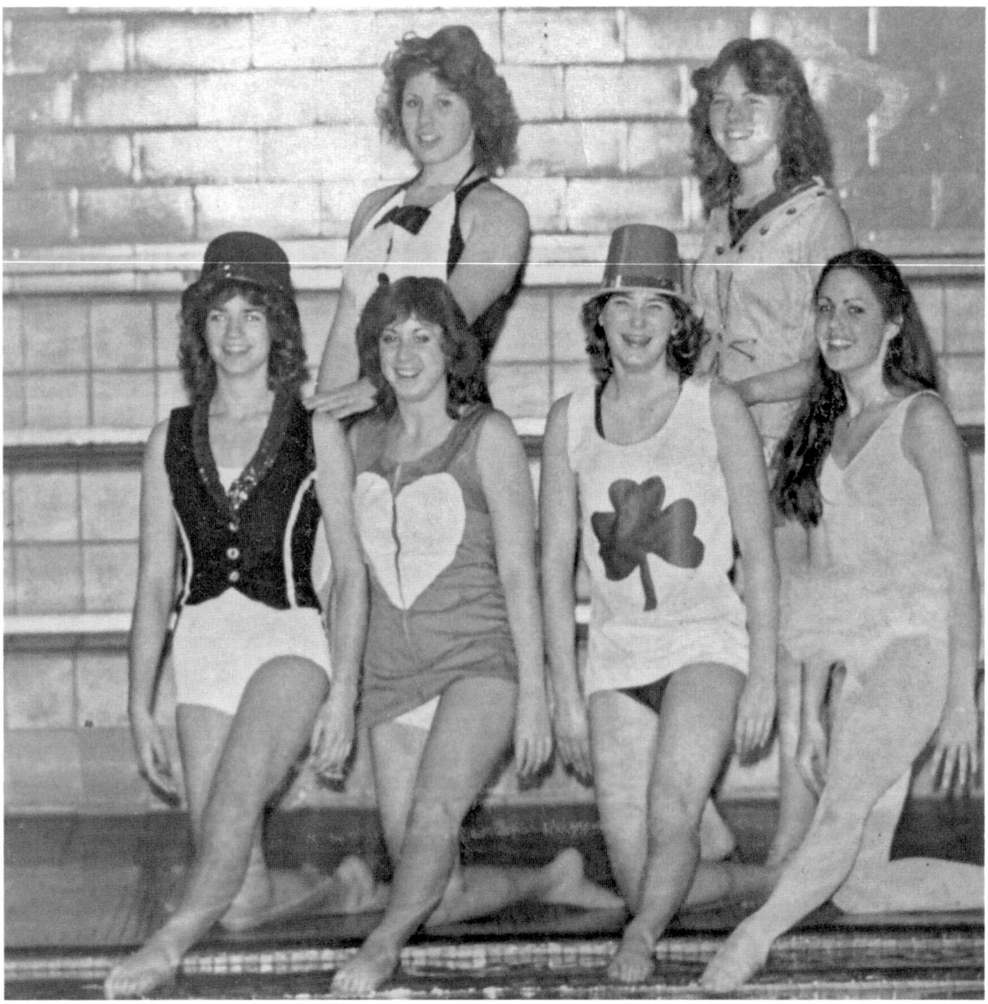

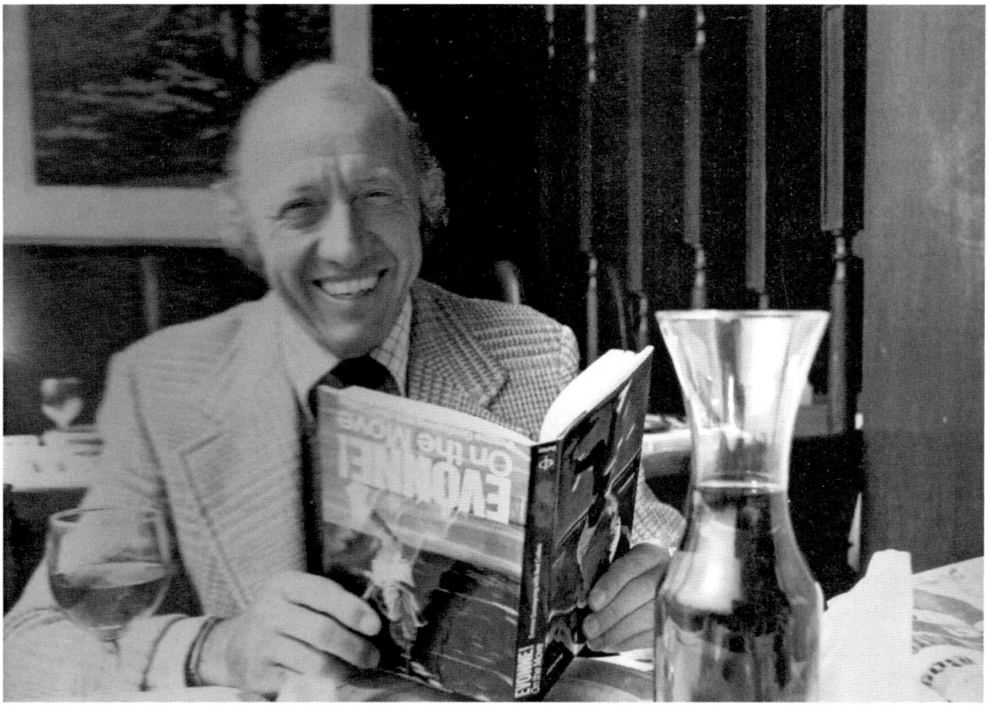

Arthur ("Bud") Collins

He said he rode Arthur Ashe's shirttails to network television. In 1968, Arthur ("Bud") Collins, covered Ashe's first important tennis title, the US Open. Collins, known for his colorful game commentaries and his outrageously loud pants, had a legendary career with NBC television and the Boston *Globe*. His start was as a teenaged sports editor of the Berea *Enterprise* for $5 a week, plus he had to empty the trash and make the coffee. "At that time the *Enterprise* had a circulation about the size of the Democratic Party in Crawford, Texas," Collins remarked.

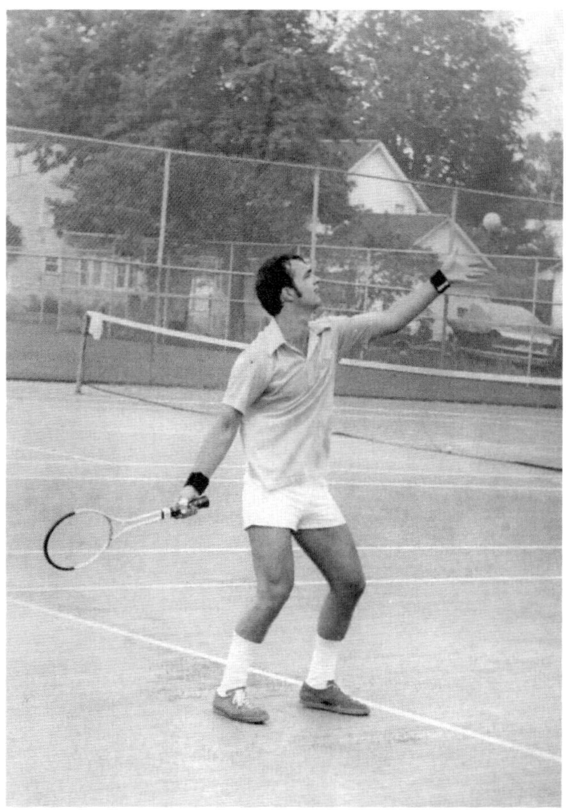

Tennis Player

When the old Central School was demolished, Baldwin-Wallace built new tennis courts and named them Collins Courts. Both Berea residents and college students use these courts. (Right) Art Manning practices his serve.

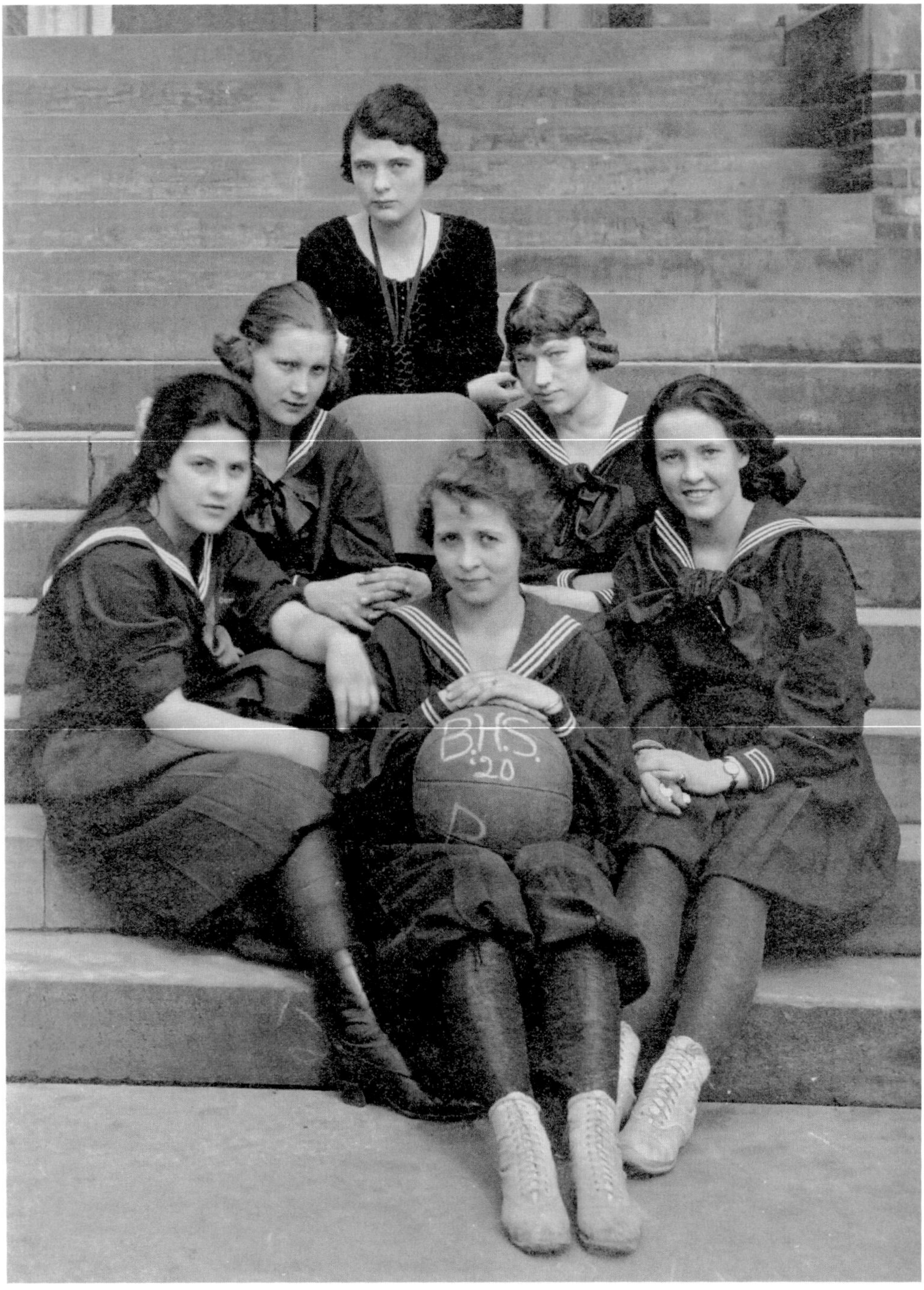

Girls Basketball

These girls could already play basketball for Berea High School in the same year women gained the right to vote. (Front, Lois Denver; second row, from left, Doris Williams and Helen Sheppard; third row, from left, Lucille Baese and Della Knight; top, Mildred Rice, coach.)

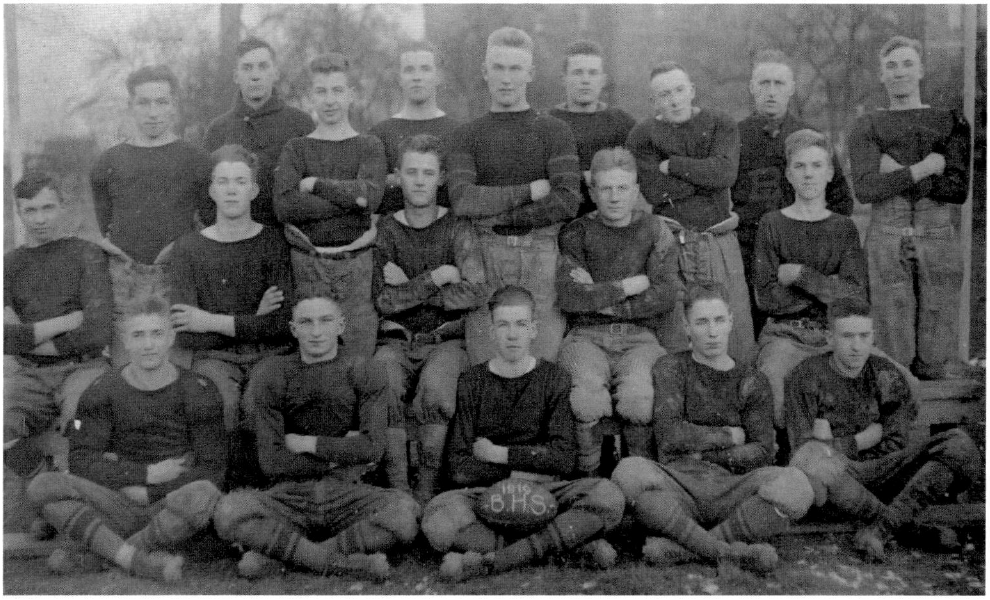

Boys Football

The 1919 Berea High School football team doesn't appear ready to receive any passes! Holding the football (front center) is Ron Tubesing. Otto Mahler is at his left. Others are not identified. This first Berea High team of the 1900s won all eight of its games.

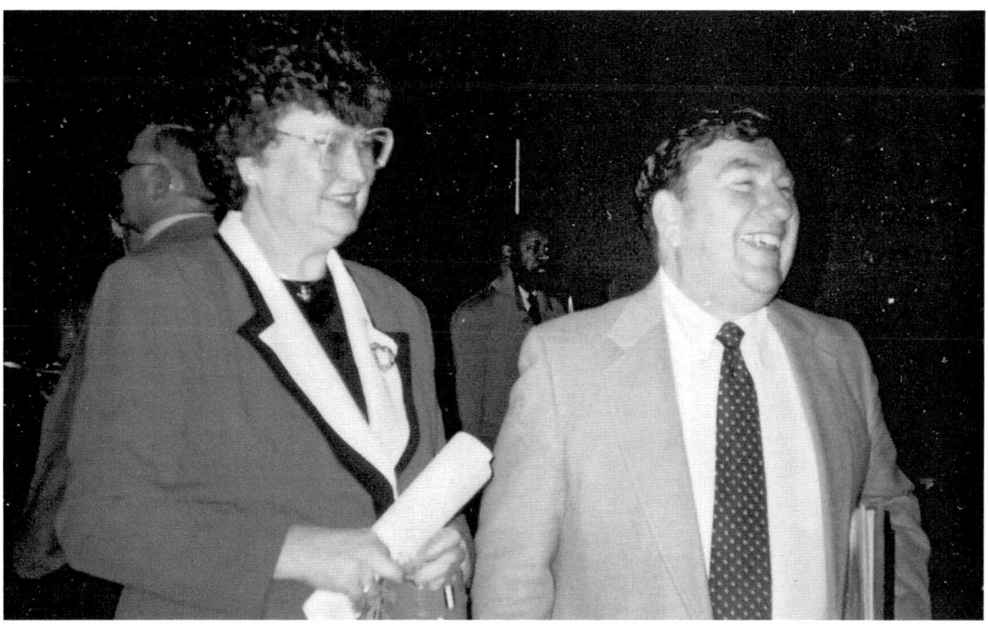

Thomas Madzy

Hailed as "the perfect model of a high school football coach" by Cleveland Browns' Hall of Famer Lou Groza, Madzy was head coach at Berea High School from 1967 to 1993. He led the Braves to eight league championships, qualifying for state playoffs five times. Colleagues agree that Coach Madzy took more interest in the success of others than his own. He is pictured here with his wife Sandy.

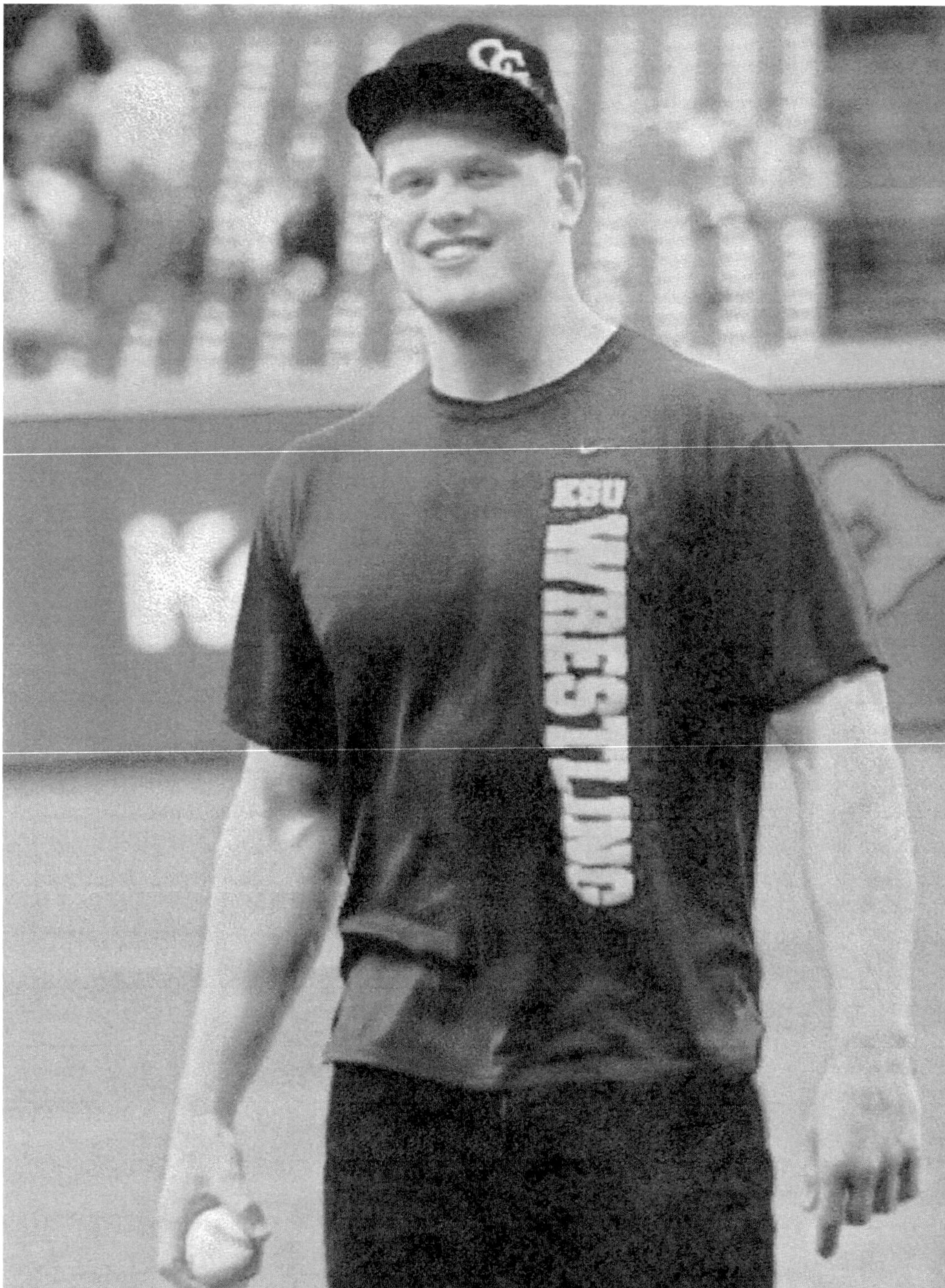

Dustin Kilgore, Legend in the Making

As an honor for being a winning wrestler, Dustin Kilgore threw out the first pitch at the Cleveland Indians/Chicago White Sox game on September 21, 2011. A Berea High School graduate and Kent State University junior, Kilgore took five straight matches to give KSU its first NCAA championship wrestling title. During the summer, he toured Europe with Team USA.

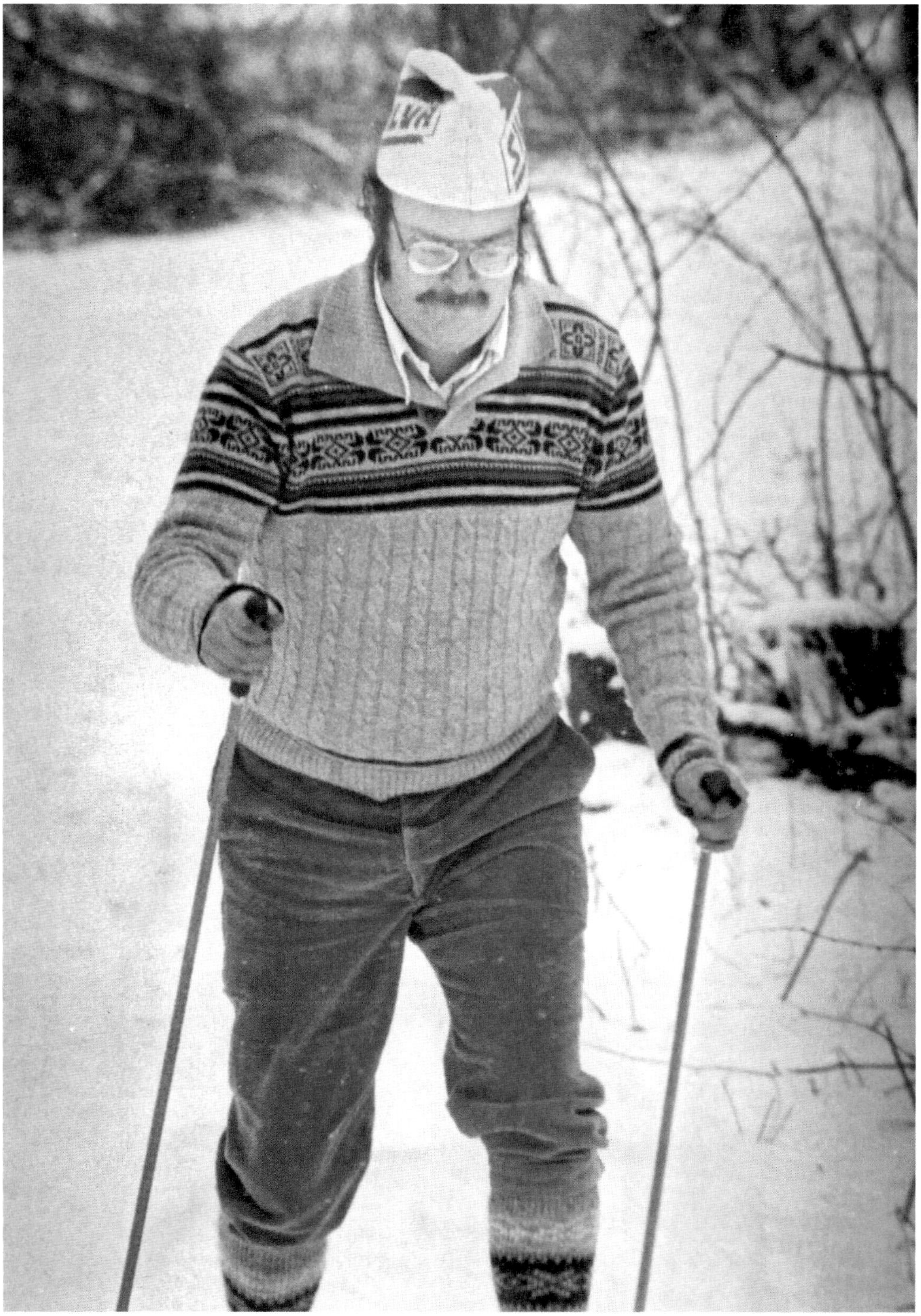

Cross-Country Skiing
The nearby Cleveland Metroparks offer opportunities for students and Berea citizens alike to enjoy cross-country skiing as well as ice fishing. Baldwin-Wallace student Tom Van Gunten tries out his skis.

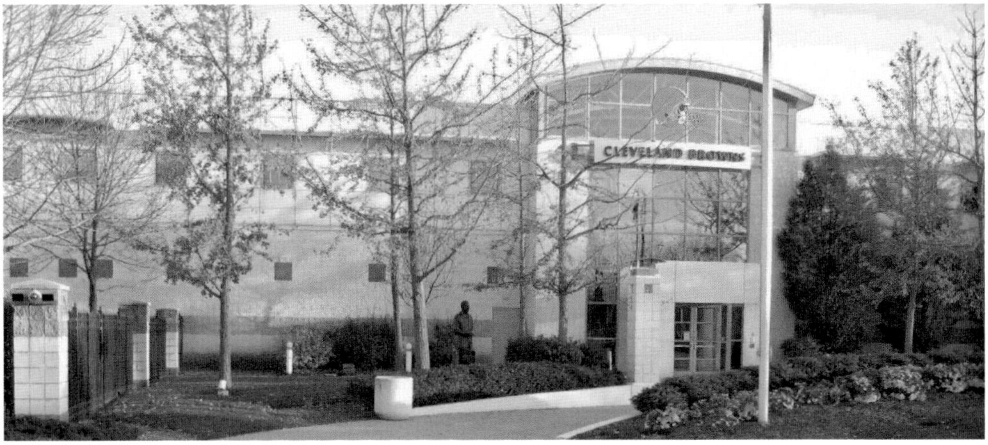

Cleveland Browns
Some Bereans nickname this edifice "The Taj Mahal." Located on Lou Groza Boulevard at the north end of town, the Browns' headquarters and practice facility attracts huge crowds of onlookers to the community during the late summer. The facility also is used for occasional galas, such as the Rotary Club's annual banquet and silent auction. (Photograph by Patricia Mote.)

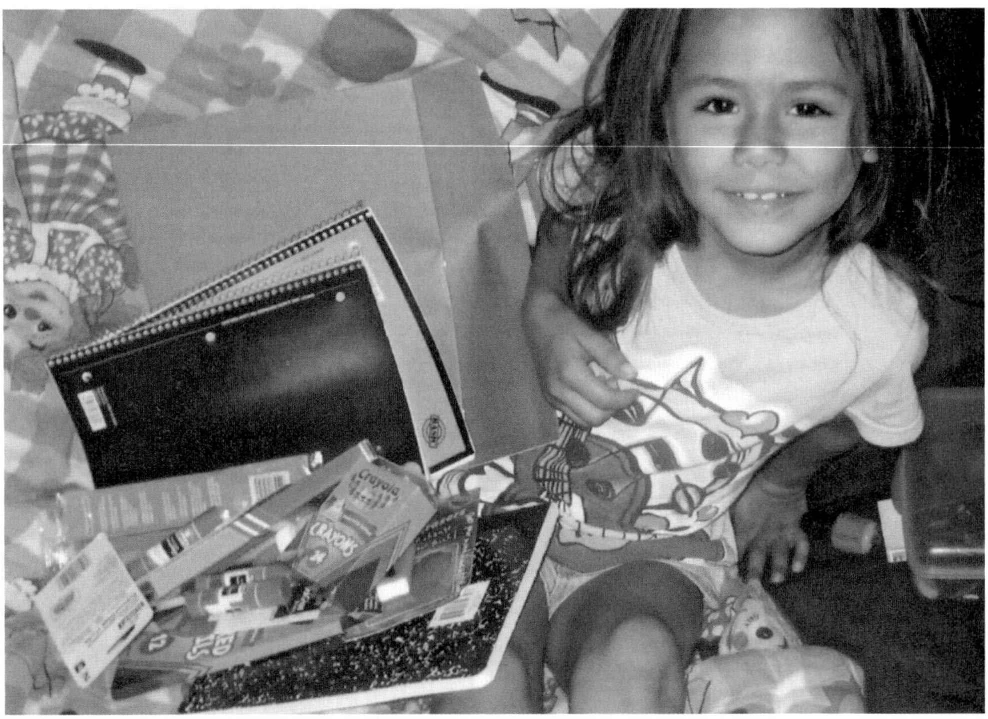

Girl with School Supplies
Cleveland Browns players have big feet! That means the shoeboxes they fill every August have lots of school supplies for children who need them. Working with the local charity Church Street Ministries, Browns players look forward to making children happy each year. Pictured here is an unidentified child receiving school supplies. (Courtesy of Church Street Ministries.)

APPENDIX

Grindstone Award Winners

The Grindstone Award is presented yearly by the Berea Chamber of Commerce to a citizen judged Outstanding Berea Citizen of the Year.

2011	Elaine and Larry Myers
2010	Edward C. White, MD
2009	Rev. Leroy McCreary
2008	Judith A. Stull
2007	John and Kathy Chapman
2006	Bill Tibbits
2005	Jack Kafer
2004	Award cycle revised
2003	Patsy Slater
2002	Harry Allen Tadych
2001	Barbara Peris Draves
2000	George and Carol Kanaan
1999	Rudolf D. Kamper
1998	Barbara Sherwood
1997	Robert Robinson
1996	Thomas Madzy
1995	Frances Millward
1994	Marie Douglas
1993	Kenneth McCarthy
1992	William Beyer
1991	Howard and Gladys Wyles
1990	Lou Groza
1989	Mary Hart
1988	C. Bruce Hardy
1987	Caroline Lageman
1986	Russell J. Hill
1985	Donald E. Williams
1984	Berneice Smith
1983	Eloise Tressel
1982	Joan Goering
1981	William A. Allman
1980	Doris James
1980	Lee Tressel (*Special Grindstone Award.*)
1979	Bernard V. Kelly
1978	Robert Purdy
1977	Muriel Hardy
1976	Henry M. Barr
1975	Glenn and Jean Snow
1974	Dorothy McKelvey
1973	Loni Flagner
1972	Dr. A. B. Bonds Jr.
1971	Ruth Taylor
1970	Arthur Gohlke
1969	Rudolph Ursprung
1968	Herbert Shalkhauser
1967	Otto Mahler

INDEX

Consistent with our mission to preserve history on a local level, this book was printed in South Carolina on American-made paper and manufactured entirely in the United States. Products carrying the accredited Forest Stewardship Council (FSC) label are printed on 100 percent FSC-certified paper.

MADE IN THE USA